# The Dynamic of Welfare

# The Dynamic of Welfare
## The Welfare State and the Life Cycle

edited by

*Jane Falkingham*
and
*John Hills*

**PRENTICE HALL**
**HARVESTER WHEATSHEAF**

New York London Toronto Sydney Tokyo Singapore
Madrid Mexico City Munich

First published 1995 by
Prentice Hall/Harvester Wheatsheaf
Campus 400, Maylands Avenue
Hemel Hempstead
Hertfordshire, HP2 7EZ
A division of
Simon & Schuster International Group

Printed and bound in Great Britain by
T. J. Press (Padstow) Ltd

Library of Congress Cataloging in Publication Data

Available from the publisher

British Library Cataloguing in Publication Data

A catalogue record for this book is available from
the British Library

ISBN 0-13-342841-9

1 2 3 4 5   99  98  97  96  95

# Contents

# List of Tables

# List of Figures

# Preface

This book was written, and the analysis on which it was based carried out, with funding for which we are most grateful from the Economic and Social Research Council under programme grant X206 32 2001. The project formed part of the Welfare State Programme within the Suntory-Toyota International Centre for Economics and Related Disciplines at the London School of Economics (LSE). All of the authors were either members or associates of the LSE Welfare State Programme at the time of writing. Maria Evandrou is currently Lecturer in Epidemiology and Public Health at University College London Medical School, Ann Harding is Professor of Economics and Director of the National Centre for Social and Economic Modelling at the University of Canberra, Carli Lessof is a Senior Research Officer with the Department of Social Security, and Carol Propper is Reader in Economics at the University of Bristol. The other members of the team are all based at the LSE.

The greatest debt which we owe as a team is to Ann Harding, on whose equivalent for Australia (see Harding, 1993) much of the original structure of the microsimulation model, LIFEMOD, discussed in Chapter 4 and used in subsequent chapters, was based. Not only did access to her model greatly help with the major computing exercise involved, but also discussions with her about the challenges raised by life cycle redistribution issues were a great source of inspiration and encouragement to us throughout the project.

We are also indebted to David Winter who designed and estimated the crucial 'earnings module' which lies at the heart of LIFEMOD. Without his input this book would not have been possible.

Outside the immediate team working on the project we have received help, advice and comments from a wide range of people to whom we are

xiii

very grateful, including Tony Atkinson, Bob Bennett, Peter Burrows, Frank Cowell, Stephen Edward, Karen Gardiner, Ruth Hancock, Rob Hart, Denise Marchent, Luba Mumford, Ceema Namazie, Nick Stern, Holly Sutherland, David Thomson, Nicola Tynan, Jonathan Wadsworth and Brian Warren, as well as staff and officials at the Department of Social Security and National Association of Pension Funds.

Some of the statistical relationships on which the simulation model, LIFEMOD, used in the book are based were derived from analysis of microdata from the Family Expenditure Survey and General Household Survey. Material from the surveys was made available through the Economic and Social Research Council Data Archive, the Central Statistical Office, and Office of Population Censuses and Surveys, and used by permission of the Controller of HMSO. None of these bears any responsibility for the analysis or interpretation of these data reported here.

The issues presented in several of the chapters were first presented at the Welfare State Programme's seminar series at the LSE and our work has greatly benefited from those discussions. An early version of the material in Chapter 3 was presented at the 1992 annual meeting of the British Association for the Advancement of Science in Southampton, and we are grateful for comments from participants in that and in seminars at the Institute for Fiscal Studies, Swansea University of Wales and University of Sussex. Chapters 5, 6, 7 and 11 contain expanded versions of material originally presented at the conference on 'Social Security 50 Years after Beveridge' held at the University of York in September 1992. The authors are grateful to the organisers of and participants in that conference for their advice and support. Chapter 8 builds upon work presented at a conference on 'Paying for Learning' to launch the research of the London School of Economics' 'Investigating Skills' project sponsored by BP Oil and the support of BP Oil for this work is gratefully acknowledged. Richard Upward provided efficient research assistance for Chapter 10, which was also supported by the ESRC under research grant R00231635, and which was made possible by study leave granted to Carol Propper by the University of Bristol.

Finally, we are particularly grateful to Jane Dickson, who produced the camera-ready copy for publication single-handed and who coped with exemplary efficiency and patience with all of the administrative problems entailed by a multi-authored book.

Jane Falkingham
John Hills

# Introduction

## Jane Falkingham and John Hills

The origins of this book lie in a growing awareness that much previous analysis – including our own – of the effects of the welfare state has been essentially static. It is all too common, for instance, for the distributional effects of welfare policies to be analysed as if all that matters is a cross-sectional view of its effects on, say, people who are rich or poor in a particular year. But this is a very partial view. In this book we argue that we need to look at the welfare state from a new angle, not just from a single snapshot, but looking at its effects across complete lifetimes. Amongst other points we conclude that:

- Income smoothing *over* the life cycle has been a main function of the welfare state, if not its major function.
- Moreover, income volatility and demographic changes of the late twentieth and early twenty-first centuries will make this task even more important than it was in the decades following the Second World War.
- Nevertheless, we have to re-examine the role which the state can or should play in this task, looking service by service at its current roles.

We are certainly not the first to take an interest in this area. Recent comparative studies have, for instance, paid attention to lifetime effects, but they have not been central to the analysis (Rainwater, Rein and Swartz, 1986; Jallade, 1988; Smeeding, O'Higgins and Rainwater, 1990). Rainwater *et al.* (1986) compare various forms of 'income packaging' received by different kinds of family groups, but without any explicit focus on lifetime redistribution as such. The separate country-by-country chapters in Jallade's (1988) book do include sections on lifetime redistribution, but it does not feature in the international overview. In

1

Britain, O'Higgins, Bradshaw and Walker (1988) explicitly look at income distribution over the life cycle using broad categories by family type from the Family Expenditure Survey.

But it is the recent growth of studies using microsimulation techniques to synthesise a wide variety of different life histories which offers the most illumination in this area. We summarise this development in Chapter 4, and then present results from our own model, LIFEMOD – the first of its kind developed for Britain – in subsequent chapters. In interpreting these results, readers need to be aware of their limitations: conclusions drawn from a variety (albeit a large one) of *hypothetical* life histories constructed using various 'steady state' assumptions do not necessarily represent what will actually happen to any individual; still less do they give predictions for what will happen to the whole population in the future. None the less, they do give invaluable insights into a crucial dimension of the way in which the welfare state operates. Just as an architect's cross-sectional plan of a building tells one little without also having a picture of the elevation, so one needs the life cycle dimension to make sense of what the welfare state does – and how one should think of policy towards it.

## Organisation of the book

While this book has been a collective enterprise and we have all benefited from each other's comments and ideas, the individual chapters are the responsibilities of their authors, rather than necessarily representing a collective view of the particular topic. What we have tried to do is to present a variety of perspectives on a central set of questions: if one thinks about it from the point of view of the life cycle, or looks at cumulative effects over completed lifetimes, how is our understanding of welfare services (taken in the broad, European sense) and of policies towards them affected?

In the first three chapters we approach the subject from different angles. First, in Chapter 1, Howard Glennerster provides an overview of why the life cycle is an issue – indeed a central issue – for social policy, and traces how concerns over the effects of the welfare state across the life cycle have developed over the last two centuries. These concerns have been at the practical level as social policies have evolved in response to crucial life cycle changes: with lengthening periods of time spent in childhood and education, and in old age and retirement (the whole idea of 'retirement' being a relatively new one for the majority). They have also been theoretical, as authors from Adam Smith and Marx onwards have grappled with the variation of living standards over the life cycle. In particular, Rowntree's (1902) conceptualisation of 'five alternating periods of want and plenty' has remained part of our understanding for nearly a century, and had a profound influence on Beveridge's (1942) proposals for the reform of 'social insurance and allied services'. More recently, theoretical interest in the area waned, but, Glennerster argues, life cycle issues are gaining added salience as life patterns become more varied and fragmented in the late twentieth century.

Stating that distribution over the life cycle is an important issue is not, however, the same as showing that state intervention is needed in order to change it. In Chapter 2, Julian Le Grand explores the theoretical reasons *why* the state should be engaged in activities where what is achieved is redistribution between different periods of the *same* individual's life cycle, rather than redistribution between *different* individuals when viewed from the perspective of complete lifetimes. He runs through the economic reasons why the market, left to itself, might 'fail' in achieving a satisfactory pattern of living standards over the life cycle. While finding force in some of them, he concludes by finding more substance in the problems raised by the short-sightedness or myopia of individuals operating in today's markets, and in the philosophical literature which discusses whether as a society we should visit the full consequences of such short-sightedness on our future selves.

In Chapter 3, John Hills carries out a more empirical exercise. Given that the welfare state in Britain has been financed on a 'Pay As You Go' basis, with those currently of working age largely paying for welfare benefits and services for the young and old, there may have been substantial effective transfers between different generations. Some age cohorts may be 'welfare generations', getting more out of the system over their lives than they put in; others may be 'born to pay', for whom the reverse is true. To investigate this question requires an exercise in 'generational accounting' (Kotlikoff, 1992). This is provided by looking at how the benefits from state education, health services and social security have been distributed between five year age cohorts. Crucially, one also has to look at which generations have paid the bills for welfare services from taxation, and to project receipts and payments into the future to look, under a variety of assumptions, at what may have happened by the ends of the lives of currently middle-aged and younger cohorts.

While Chapter 3 looks at variation between different cohorts taken as a whole, the rest of the book is concerned with variation within a single cohort as it ages, abstracting from the effects of other changes in the economic and social policy environments over time. In Chapter 4, Jane Falkingham, Ann Harding and Carli Lessof describe the way in which the computer-based simulation model, LIFEMOD, was constructed in order to allow this. They describe what the model is and the complex procedures required to construct it; the ways in which results can be derived from it; and the limitations to the inferences which can be drawn. In essence, the model generates the results of a complete longitudinal study of the incomes and use of welfare services of a single synthetic cohort of 4,000 individuals, whose life histories are built up according to the demographic, social and economic relationships in Britain in the mid-1980s, on the assumption that such relationships remain in a 'steady state' for complete lifetimes.

It is only by constructing such a model that one can isolate the lifetime effects of particular welfare and taxation systems (see Fullerton and Rogers, 1993, for an analogous exercise for the US tax system). Not only are there no long term longitudinal datasets containing this kind of information on complete life histories, but even if there were, they would represent the accrued effects of a whole series of evolving systems, rather than allow analysis of the structure of the current system.

In the next three chapters we present LIFEMOD results for three aspects of the operation of the welfare state looked at as a whole. In Chapter 5 we look at the variation of incomes and welfare services by age, that is over the life cycle. The chapter describes how original incomes from earnings and other market sources move with age for different groups of the population, and how these are affected by receipts from social security, direct tax payments and public health and education services. The chapter explores the extent to which the welfare state as it was constructed in the mid-1980s 'smooths out' life cycle incomes, and looks at the impact of reforms to the tax and benefit systems which had been introduced by 1991.

Chapter 6 investigates the distribution of lifetime totals of income, benefits and taxes. It compares the distribution of total lifetime income generated by LIFEMOD with the distribution one would see looking at a cross-section of incomes in a single year. This sheds light on the extent to which inequalities in cross-sectional surveys result from life cycle factors, rather than reflecting inequalities between individuals when looked at from the perspective of complete lifetimes. The chapter then examines the differences between the lifetime redistributional effects of the welfare state, looking at the differences between lifetime income groups and between men and women, as well as examining the characteristics of those who are 'lifetime rich' or 'lifetime poor'.

Chapter 7 builds on these results to analyse a more specific question: to what extent is the lifetime effect of the welfare state one of redistribution across the life cycle of the same individual ('intrapersonal redistribution'), and to what extent is it redistribution between different people ('interpersonal redistribution')? To the extent that, looking from the grave-side, it does redistribute between individuals, to what extent does this reflect its 'insurance' effects, with some individuals actually affected by the contingencies covered, while others are not?

The final four chapters look individually at four of the areas of life cycle redistribution where key policy concerns are raised. They use results from LIFEMOD, and elsewhere, to analyse the area and to investigate the effects of selected policy reforms.

In Chapter 8, Howard Glennerster, Jane Falkingham and Nick Barr use LIFEMOD to investigate financing options for higher education, a problem which can only properly be examined using techniques which allow the modelling of lifetime incomes. They discuss the policy problem raised by the difficulties of individuals financing their own higher education, and the equity problems raised by systems which provide state subsidies to a group which is actually in general rich in lifetime terms. In their analysis they discuss a series of options including: the current UK student loan system; a graduate tax; an 'income contingent' loan system; and 'user-charges' on the employers of graduates.

In Chapter 9, Maria Evandrou and Jane Falkingham explore the gendered nature of the distribution of lifetime income. Experience of an episode of lone parenthood is identified as a key predictor of low lifetime income in earlier chapters. However, the impact of lone parenthood on lifetime income patterns is not unique, but varies according to the type of lone parenthood, its duration and the stage of the life cycle at which it occurs. They examine the dynamics of lone parenthood, identifying where in the lifecourse the major stresses for lone mothers occur. They appraise the role of the family, the labour market and the social security system in protecting living standards.

In Chapter 10, Carol Propper examines the lifetime distribution of health needs and use of health services, carrying out a lifetime analogy of a cross-sectional study of health care and its financing. She explores results from the 'health module' of LIFEMOD in greater detail than in earlier chapters, and uses results from LIFEMOD to simulate a policy change in which something close to the current Dutch health care system was introduced in Britain, with the richest 30 per cent of individuals expected to take out private health insurance, receiving a tax credit in substitute for NHS services.

Finally, in Chapter 11 Jane Falkingham and Paul Johnson examine the structure of state pensions in Britain. They explore the shortcomings of the current system and discuss the various proposals for reform which have been made recently. They then present the results of an examination, using LIFEMOD, of their own proposal for a 'Unified Funded Pension Scheme' which would replace both state and occupational pensions in their current forms, with the intention both of improving pensions in retirement for those with low lifetime earnings, and of giving clearer, and more robust, systems of redistribution between individuals and generations.

As the chapters of this book make clear, the life cycle perspective on the welfare state is a crucial one. We hope that, if nothing else, this book will stimulate further debate on this aspect of its operation.

**Chapter One** *Selected MDC's*

H55
H22
H23

# The Life Cycle: Public or Private Concern?

## Howard Glennerster

### 1. Seven Ages?

Philosophers and poets had the idea of a 'life cycle' long before social scientists ever came upon it. Cicero presented a moving account of life's changing patterns, the pleasures of old age and the depth of his grief at the death of his grown-up son. Shakespeare's view of old age was less positive. His seven ages of man, from the 'mewling and puking' babe to the old person, 'sans teeth, sans eyes, sans taste, sans everything' (*As You Like it*, Act II Sc. 2) have been impressed on generations of school children. Yet, the pains and pleasures of youth and age and the financial fluctuations that accompanied them, were private concerns or of charitable and local interest. Life for most people was short, even if it was not brutish. There was no extended life cycle.

From the work of the Cambridge population group and other recent social historians we now know a great deal more about the lives of ordinary people in the years before and after industrialisation (Thompson, 1990).

At the beginning of the eighteenth century the median age of death for men was no more than about 30 years. It was only a little more for women. Three-quarters of the population were dead by the time they were 65. Britain, at the time of industrialisation, was an extraordinarily young society, just as developing countries are today. In 1826 two in every five people were aged under 15. Dependency was a problem of youth not age.

Industrialisation and the social changes of the nineteenth century, however, made the life cycle a social phenomenon, a public as well as a private issue.

## 2.    A Social Phenomenon

Several features of emergent modern life contributed to this change and have become increasingly important in the late twentieth century. The most obvious and widely discussed was the growing expectation of life. By 1891 the median age of death for men had reached nearly 60 and for women 70. This created considerable difficulties for all the institutions that had previously not had to cope with an elderly population. The sick clubs and mutual benefit organisations that had been able to support short periods of sickness amongst members could not cope with the increasing number of long term unemployable elderly who were a drain on their finances. More and more wives were outliving their husbands and were financially unsupported. Families had never, on any significant scale, housed or been responsible for their elderly relatives. Perhaps only about 5 per cent of the population in the late eighteenth and early nineteenth centuries lived with relatives and most of these were children living with aunts or uncles. Even as late as the 1930s grandparental sharing in the household was very uncommon (Gordon, 1988). Housing conditions were extremely crowded and spare financial resources were negligible. Families were not in a position to care for their parents (for a summary of this evidence see Anderson, 1990). The voluntary hospitals were financially overburdened with the rising numbers of elderly people they knew would stay for long periods and not give them any income (Abel-Smith, 1964). The elderly were transferred as quickly as possible to public poor law or, later, local authority hospitals.

Childhood was also lengthening as the state imposed limits on the ages at which children could work. In the nineteenth century many children were taken from their parents who could not afford to support them. They were absorbed into the households of those who employed them or kept as apprentices or taught the trade with employers. As the rewards to enhanced human capital grew and the period of education needed to gain it lengthened, so too did the difficulty of financing education, especially for families who had no capital or access to borrowing.

As the level of skills demanded by the labour market grew, so the periods of training and preparation grew. In a competitive and increasingly mobile labour market it was not in the interests of any one employer to pay for the training of his employees who would be enticed away by another employer (Becker, 1964). Young apprentices were paid very little, effectively financing their own training or relying on their families to do so. As technical change quickened, individuals' skills wasted faster, their marginal product declined earlier and without further training working lives shortened, a process that was expedited by pension arrangements and high levels of unemployment. Between 1851 and 1891 80 to 90 per cent of the male population over the age of 65 were in paid employment. In the 1920s pensions at 65 for men helped to enhance the incentive to retire as did the rules of occupational pension schemes. High levels of unemployment in the 1980s and the shake out in manufacturing industry during that period particularly affected men over the age of 55. By the 1980s only 10 per cent of the male population over 65 had any earned income.

In short, the major demographic and economic changes of the nineteenth and twentieth centuries moved the fluctuations in individuals' lifetime incomes and lifetime basic needs further and further apart. This is not to imply that the state or the family or the private capital market have any necessary superiority in their capacity to bridge the gap between these two divergent cycles.

## 3.    Social Scientists Discover the Life Cycle

The early social scientists did not address the notion of the life cycle directly, if at all. A good early example is Adam Smith (1776) who came close to discussing the issue in his famous chapter on 'The wages of labour' in *The Wealth of Nations* but never quite focused on the issue.

He argued that, overall, the market wage for the poorest labourers would not support large families and the interaction of the supply and demand for labour would have the beneficial effect of bringing the population into balance, unlike Malthus' scenario. Since this discipline would only affect the lower classes it had a doubly beneficial effect:

> ... in civilized society it is only among the inferior ranks of people that the scantiness of subsistence can set limits to the further multiplication of the species; and it can do so in no other way than by destroying a greater part of the children which their fruitful marriages produce (p. 182).

But at what level would the equilibrium wage come to be set? In Smith's view wages had to be set at a minimum level sufficient to maintain not merely the worker but his family. Since half the child population died before adulthood that meant a wage sufficient to support four children and a wife. It meant employers paying the labourer twice his own minimum living wage, just as slave owners had realised they must pay their slaves twice their own living standard if they were to reproduce (p. 171). Just why any employer should pay more than the worker's marginal product when it was not in his immediate self-interest to sustain the next generation of workers, is difficult to see. Smith himself left this problem unaddressed.

The nineteenth century political economists' solution to the difficulties the life cycle posed the working family was self-restraint, self-help and thrift. To be sure, the more prosperous working class did develop a great variety of self-help organisations and large numbers took out life assurance from door to door salesmen of the new insurance companies. Rowntree (1902) reports that in York at the turn of the century no less than 75 insurance salesmen were employed full-time to collect premiums from the working classes of the town, collecting about 8d (3.3p) a week from each family out of moderate incomes of £1 a week or less. These sums mainly covered funeral expenses for the family, including the children, that parents knew were only too likely to be needed. However, political economists' ignorance of working class incomes and life styles was profound. Moral advice took the place of analysis and understanding.

Even Marx, who did not share these views about working class incomes or the virtues of supply and demand solutions in the labour market, failed to grasp the significance of the life cycle for the working class family. His chapter on 'The Working Day' in *Capital* (Vol. 1, 1867) remains one of the most powerful accounts ever written of the hours and conditions of work suffered by men, women and young children in Victorian Britain. The individual capitalist, he argued, had every incentive to work his employees for the maximum number of hours and to employ wives and children in the same way. It was of no concern to the capitalist employer that the long term health of the population would decline or that children did not survive. It might be to the long term benefit of the class or the economy to treat labour better but no one employer in a competitive situation could survive if he took such things into account:

> Capital therefore takes no account of the health and the length of life of the worker, unless society forces it to do so (p. 381).

Hence, he argued, Britain had evolved Factory Acts, opposed by the employing class, but helpful to the long term survival of capitalism. These Acts limited hours of work, especially for women and children, and limited the ages at which children's employment could begin. This helped children survive, and enforced education raised the quality of the labour force. But the Education Acts steadily extended the years of dependency. Even though these Acts were imperfectly enforced the financial burdens of family life grew as a result.

Marx saw the positive consequences of this legislation for the working class too and argued that they had won the gains for themselves.

> For 'protection' against the serpent of their agonies, the workers have to put their heads together and, as a class, compel the passing of a law, an all-powerful social barrier by which they can be prevented from selling themselves and their families into slavery and death by voluntary contract with capital (p. 416).

Yet he did not dwell on the difficulty it caused families in stretching their incomes over the longer period of dependency that resulted. He essentially ignored the problem of family need. Marx's analysis took labour time or content as the proper unit of value and therefore took no more account of the family circumstances of the worker than Adam Smith had. Nor was he concerned with old age.

As the century progressed other social scientists began to show more interest in the financial circumstances of families. Charles Booth (1892), through his own research on the poor, had come to see the importance of old age as the main reason for pauperdom, especially for women. It was this which led him to suggest a state old age pension as a solution preferable to the Poor Law. Here, he was essentially differentiating the life cycle from other causes of poverty that required a separate solution.

It was Rowntree (1902) who, in Britain, first fully conceptualised the issue in terms of a life cycle of needs. As Murphy (1987) points out, Russian sociologists had developed a very similar analysis at about the same time but in the social policy tradition it is the Rowntree version that predominates. His famous exposition of the life cycle comes at the end of his analysis of the immediate causes of poverty amongst the families he studied in York. It was, he observed, families with children who systematically fell below his harshly drawn poverty line. He calculated what difference it would make if universal old age pensions had been introduced as Booth had argued for, and a policy much in debate at the time. He claimed that 28 per cent of the population of York were living in poverty but that pensions sufficient to relieve poverty among the elderly would only reduce that figure by 1 per cent. This showed that the bulk of poverty arose when children were dependent on the earnings of the father and mother which took no account of family needs. He concluded:

> The life of a labourer is marked by five alternating periods of want and comparative plenty. During early childhood, unless his father is a skilled worker, he will probably be in poverty; this will last until he or some of his brothers or sisters, begin to earn money and thus augment their father's wage sufficiently to raise the family above the poverty line. There then follows a period during which he is earning money and living under his parents' roof; ... this is his chance to save some money and pay for furnishing a cottage, this period of prosperity may continue after marriage until he has two or three children when poverty will overtake him. This period of poverty will last perhaps for ten years *ie.* until the first child is fourteen years old and begins to earn wages... The man enjoys another period of prosperity only to sink back again into poverty when his children have married and left him, and he himself is too old to work for his income has never permitted his saving enough for him and his wife to live on for a very short time (pp. 170–1).

Figure 1.1 shows what was to become Rowntree's seminal diagram charting a family's typical income stream through life, high initially, falling with children, stabilising and then declining sharply in old age. Mapped onto this was the life cycle of need, the income required to

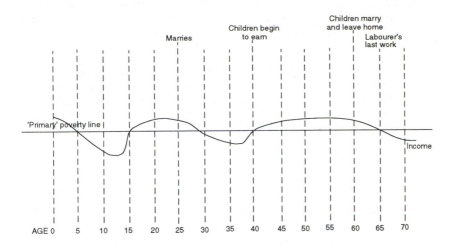

**Source:** Rowntree (1902, p. 170)

**Figure 1.1** Rowntree's Cycles of Want and Plenty

survive as a family. It graphically showed the gap between income and the needs of families in the child rearing years, especially for the poorest.

Rowntree's solution was a minimum wage, advocated in a book published at the end of the First World War, *The Human Needs of Labour* (1918). 'The war has torn the scales from our eyes.' But where should a minimum wage be pitched? Much of the analysis in that book is concerned to work out how big was the typical family at whom a minimum wage could be targeted. How many children did families have, for what periods? Rowntree then worked out how many children would be inadequately catered for if the minimum wage were set at different levels. If it were set on the assumption that the wage be set high enough to meet the needs of a two child family, even so, a third of all children would live in poverty for fifteen years or more and four-fifths would be in poverty for one year of their lives. They would be in families that consisted of more than two children at any one time.

At the other extreme, if the minimum wage were set at a level that met the needs of a family of six it would all but eliminate long-term poverty. This would, however, involve setting far too high a minimum wage, one that would cause widespread unemployment.

He compromised on three children as the norm for setting a minimum wage. On his own calculations this meant leaving a fifth of all children in poverty for fifteen years of their lives. He tried to meet the criticism that wages at this level could not be afforded by industry by listing ways in which general productivity levels could be raised. These difficulties clearly worried him, and in the final chapter, summarising his conclusions, he accepted that it would be a long time before minimum wages could be raised even to the level three children would suggest and there was no prospect of raising them beyond that. He concluded:

> The only remaining solution – and I admit that it is fraught with many difficulties – is to fix minimum wages sufficient to secure physical efficiency for, say, three dependent children and for the state to make a grant to the mother in such cases... This suggestion may appear revolutionary, but it is nothing new. Such a principle is already admitted in the case of Income Tax, where a substantial abatement is made for every child.

Titmuss was to make the same point forty years later (Titmuss, 1958).

The idea of a family allowance as a more general solution to child poverty was launched in 1918 with the creation of the Family Endowment Association.

It was Eleanor Rathbone (1917, 1924) who took the argument further. During the First World War she had become interested in the improved lot of women whose husbands were away fighting. They received allowances proportional to the size of their family. In an article in the *Economic Journal* (Rathbone, 1917) she pointed out that after the War women's economic position would be likely to worsen as these allowances were withdrawn and as they were once again excluded from the work force by trade union activity. She was not impressed with the solution of a minimum wage. Any attempt to match the cycle of varied family needs to a single minimum wage figure was doomed to failure. Not only would any feasible minimum wage under-provide for the needs of the large family, but it would push wages higher than was necessary for workers with no or few children and would raise labour costs and endanger jobs. The only way to meet the burdens of this part of the life cycle was to carry the costs of children collectively through a system of child allowances modelled on those of the armed services (Rathbone, 1924).

As worries about the birth rate grew she was able to add a nationalistic string to her bow and argue that families must be paid to keep the race going during the years of financial stress they faced in child rearing. She was also increasingly able to point to schemes that related wages to family responsibilities in other European countries (Rathbone, 1941). For an account of her contrasting approaches to the cause of economic independence for women see Dyhouse (1989).

Despite Rathbone's work what was to prove decisive in the wartime debates was the recognition within the Treasury that if the social security scheme was to give cash support to unemployed workers' families in a way that reflected the number of children in the family, many unemployed people would be better off financially out of work rather than in work (Macnicol, 1980). The only way to prevent that perverse incentive, the Cabinet came to see, was to give all families support during the period of child bearing.

The life cycle was now firmly established as a key political issue not only in connection with old age but with the burdens of child rearing too.

By the time Beveridge came to write his report in 1942, then, the idea that social policy could be viewed as a kind of counter-life-cyclical device was all but in place. In a way it ran parallel to Keynes' *economic* counter-cyclical policy. Presented in this way Beveridge could emphasise that his report was not an attempt to take money from the rich and give it to the poor but a way of smoothing out the average person's income from periods of comparative plenty to periods of want. He was greatly helped in this interpretation by Rowntree's new study of poverty in York (Rowntree, 1941). The main reasons for poverty, Rowntree argued, had changed from low wages in 1901 to unemployment and old age in 1939. Together with large families they made up over two-thirds of the causes of poverty.

Such factors were amenable to counter cyclical measures both of the Keynesian and the life cycle kind and *hence* need not disturb the rich. Just how important to Beveridge was this insight we can see from his notes on reading Rowntree's book (Evans and Glennerster, 1993). He notes to himself:[1]

Poverty could be abolished by redistribution within the working classes.

He elaborated on the theme in the eventual report (Beveridge, 1942):

The argument in this section can be summed up briefly. Abolition of want cannot be brought about merely by increasing production, without seeing to [the] correct distribution of the product; but distribution does not mean what it has often been taken to mean in the past – distribution between the different agents in production between land, capital, management and labour. Better distribution of purchasing power is required among wage earners themselves, as between times of earning and not earning and between times of heavy family responsibilities and of light or no family responsibilities (para. 449).

Writing just after his report was published (Beveridge, 1943) he puts the point even more clearly:

Social surveys in a number of principal towns in Britain showed that want was due either to interruption or loss of earning power or to large families. The Plan for Social Security is a plan for dealing with these two causes of want, by a double redistribution of income – between times of earning and not earning (by social insurance) and between times of large and small family responsibilities (by family allowances) (p. 60).

---

1    BP VIII 28 SIS (42) 3.

This view underpins his stress on everyone paying the same contribution and receiving the same benefit. His 'plan' could be paid for out of the same basic contributions from everyone. This was, as the Treasury was quick to point out, 'a fraud' (Evans and Glennerster, 1993) since contributions would pay for only a small proportion of the cost, but it was an important selling point. Moreover, his 'particular assumptions' that he wrote into the report – that Government would secure full employment, introduce a national health service and family allowances – met the other costly elements in the life cycle out of taxation. Proposals to create a system of free secondary education and support for students were under active discussion at this point too. The Government's education green paper was in circulation.

It is no accident, then, that this combination of Second World War social policies came to be presented as a system of security from 'cradle to grave'. To a very large extent what emerged in the legislation of the 1940s was a system that was designed to smooth net income and needs through the lifetime of the ordinary family. It was not primarily an attempt to redistribute income from rich to poor, though this might result as a by-product.

## 4.    The Life Cycle Forgotten

For a decade or more after the Second World War interest in the life cycle declined. The comprehensive range of services that emerged in the 1940s was seen to have solved the problem. The birth rate rose. Naturally social scientists turned their attention to other matters. Economists, in so far as they showed any interest in distributional questions at all, were concerned that the income distribution between the rich and the poor had narrowed too much as a result of the new welfare state and the taxation needed to finance it (Paish, 1957; Lydall, 1959). Social policy experts began to focus on the inequalities between rich and poor and on unequal access to services like education. Barbara Wootton's book *The Social Foundation of Wages Policy* (1954) was concerned to analyse the reasons for unequal wages and other incomes. Titmuss (1961) contested the economists' claims that incomes had equalised by pointing to the flawed basis of the Inland Revenue statistics. Sociologists did not give up their interest in the life cycle but they emphasised its continuities, the socialising role of the family, the importance of links between the generations, links that had been close in the East End of London and were then being broken by housing development (for example, Young and Wilmott, 1957). Educational sociologists (Floud, Halsey and Martin, 1956) were concerned with continuity of a different kind. They demonstrated the importance of parental class and education on children's own educational achievements.

Equality of opportunity between working class children and others, between ethnic minorities, between girls and boys at school and college, between men and women in the work place, became the new concerns. The welfare state in the late 1960s and 1970s came to be criticised for not redressing such inequalities and above all for not reducing the gap between rich and poor (Bosanquet and Townsend, 1972; Le Grand, 1982). Major new data sources were exploited, notably the Family Expenditure Survey, which enabled the regular analysis of income distribution. The Central Statistical Office (CSO) began to produce annual surveys of the value of benefits received by households in different income groups and the level of taxes paid by them. This data source naturally tended to concentrate attention on questions of redistribution between rich and poor. It would be not too much of an exaggeration to say that intellectual interest of social scientists and social policy concerns in the decades from 1950 to 1980 came to be dominated with issues of vertical redistribution.

## 5.      New Interest in the Life Cycle

More recently, interest in aspects of the life cycle have begun to revive, not least, perhaps, because the life cycle in the late twentieth century is changing in important ways and looks very different from that which Rowntree sketched. Also, it came to be realised that intervention by the state over the life cycle could itself affect the life cycle, encouraging early retirement, for example, or single parenthood, thus adding to the problems of life cycle dependency.

Thirdly, state intervention could have deleterious economic consequences, reducing saving for retirement, for example, and hence investment and economic growth.

Fourthly, the new school of public choice economists, and others, began to analyse the electoral implications of life cycle finance through taxation. They argued that one generation of voters had an incentive to vote themselves high pensions at the cost of the next. This bred fiscal irresponsibility.

Fifthly, private market means of redistributing income through the individual's life cycle, economists argued, had become more accessible to more people. Insurance schemes were growing in sophistication helping families pay for their children's education, financing pensions and services in old age.

Was the state needed any more to smooth life's contingencies? Where should the balance of public and private responsibility lie?

## 6.     A New Life Cycle?

The late twentieth century life pattern differs by social group and by gender but certain features and trends are common.

### The length of schooling

The length of time required to attain qualifications that bring an adequate income is growing. In the United States between 1975 and 1990 the earnings of high school drop-outs fell in real terms from about a quarter of average earnings to less than a fifth. The earnings of those who had not been to college also fell. Only college graduates' incomes rose in real terms in that period (US Government, 1992). Similar but less dramatic trends can be seen in the UK (Bennett, Glennerster and Nevison, 1992c).

In the 1950s very few children in the UK stayed at school beyond the age of 15. Only just over 5 per cent of the age group went to university. The increasing personal gains to be made from staying on at school into full-time education compared to part-time training or apprenticeships, have increased the demand for higher education. The UK Government is proposing to expand places in universities to cover 30 per cent of the age group. Who should pay? Who should be responsible for enabling individuals to invest now in a larger future income stream?

In the late 1950s and early 1960s a whole new branch of economics developed that explained individuals' decisions to stay on at school or go to college. Decisions to forego earnings and pay tuition fees were rational in a lifetime context. Enhanced future earnings streams could be expressed as rates of return on the costs of education. It was found that earnings of more highly educated people were lower in youth but did rise faster over a lifetime even after controlling for ability (Becker, 1964).

This, of course had implications for studies of income distribution. If people were deliberately reducing their income at one point in their lives in order to increase it at another stage of their lives, it made no sense to label them poor. What mattered was their lifetime income. If people chose leisure now for work later or worked long hours now to retire earlier, differences in income were a matter of choice, not enforced inequality or poverty. As Alan Blinder (1974) pointed out:

> Some portion of observed inequality in annual incomes is surely attributable to life cycle influences that wash out when the unit of time is taken to be the lifetime.

He produced figures that suggested that 30 per cent of the inequality in US incomes measured by the Gini coefficient was the result of life cycle influences (see Chapter 5 for our own findings on this).

The policy response of UK governments in the 1960s was to accept that the task of meeting the investment risks and costs of education should be met by the whole community. University education should be free to undergraduates, at least, and the costs of living at college, too, should be borne on a parental means-tested basis. While sustainable for 5 per cent of a population, is it for 30 per cent? We discuss this in Chapter 8.

## Middle life

In the 1970s and 1980s sociologists' interest in the life cycle began to revive too, for very different reasons, not least because of the work of feminist writers and a recognition of the social changes that were affecting most western countries. Old stereotypes of the normal life course no longer fitted the changing social world. The traditional family cycle model only fitted about half the population of Britain (Murphy, 1987). Rowntree's model, we recall, assumed a four child median family with two children dying, the wife not working and the family remaining together for life. In 1986 the British Sociological Association devoted a whole annual meeting to reassessing the life cycle (Bryman *et al.*, 1987). What emerged was that there is no such thing as 'a life cycle'. But there *are* life *cycles* that vary widely between social contexts, over time, between life styles.

Modern life cycles are not any less, and are probably more, variable and more vulnerable than the one Rowntree described:

- Preparation for entry to the labour market takes longer, so young people are dependent on their parents for longer.

- The labour market itself is becoming more uncertain, rewarding long service and high skills increasingly well but penalising the reverse increasingly harshly. The pattern of the United States suggests a future economy in which there will be more increasingly temporary, part-time and 'lousy jobs' (Burtless, 1990). As Hewitt (1993) points out for the United Kingdom:

  The full-time employee working a standard five day week is now a minority (p. 25).

  The age at which the average male worker is no longer employable has fallen steadily since the 1970s in the UK. Labour participation by males beyond the age of 55 is falling fast (Piachaud, 1987; Hills, 1993, Figure 25).

- Health care costs are rising relative to average earnings so that periods of sickness, assuming no free health care, become increasingly burdensome and potentially disastrous.

- Marriages are more fragile, patterns of partnering more complex. Legal, financial and employment fringe benefit arrangements have not kept pace with this complexity. Broken marriages leave women out of the growing benefits that accrue to long term employment in the favoured part of the labour market.

These trends have made the firm and the family less secure sources of support in times of distress.

On the other hand:

- Families are having fewer children and the period when families have young children has shortened.
- The opportunities for women's employment have grown.
- Women can acquire their own pension rights.
- Increasing owner occupation may increasingly enable households to move capital to income over a lifetime more readily.
- The range and sophistication of market instruments and insurance policies have grown.

Not everyone is in a worse position to cope with the life cycle. Some are undoubtedly better able to cope than previous generations. This is, in itself, a cause of growing inequality between social groups and between men and women.

**Later life**

The expectation of life has grown. In 1991 just over two million people in Great Britain were aged 80 or more. By the year 2026 the number will be over 3.5 million (OPCS, 1993b). It is by this age that disability and the need for long term care become particularly important. It is in the second decade of the next century that the numbers of people over the age of 65 begin to rise significantly in the UK and the United States – even before that in many European countries.

It was these facts that alerted politicians and economists to be concerned about the economic effects of ageing and who would pay (Rivlin and Weiner, 1988).

In the UK the improved pensions promised by the Labour Government in 1975 were scaled down by the Conservative Government in 1986. The community care reforms of 1993 were driven by the Government's concern at the rising cost to the social security budget of payments for long term care in private old people's homes. The consequences are also worrying families who will have to bear the cost, one way or another.

In short, the new life cycles of the twenty-first century will pose as much of a challenge as did those of the nineteenth century.

The next question then, is what agency is best fitted to meet that challenge?

## 7.    The Economic Costs of State Involvement in the Life Cycle

Money, economists argue, is the essential redistributive mechanism. Properly invested it holds its value. Part of individuals' savings behaviour is the result of their attempt to sustain their consumption in retirement, 'hump saving' as Harrod (1948) called it.

Individuals, the economists' model argues, make rational choices about distributing their income streams through life. During the early stages of life people borrow to buy houses or finance their children's education. They build up assets in pension schemes and in property or shares in middle age. These assets are run down in old age. This life cycle of saving and dissaving illustrated in Figure 1.2 redistributes an individual's income through life in a calculated and fore-thoughtful way. But, as Feldstein (1974) was to argue, if the state interfered, giving benefits in old age, it might merely replace savings that individuals would have otherwise made and it caused people to retire earlier. In many ways these arguments paralleled the attacks made on Keynesian counter-cyclical intervention by the state by the same author and his followers.

The impact of social security was not neutral, they argued: the reduced level of saving reduced investment and also growth. Real incomes were thus less than they would have been in the absence of *enforced* lifetime redistribution. This set of arguments began a furious

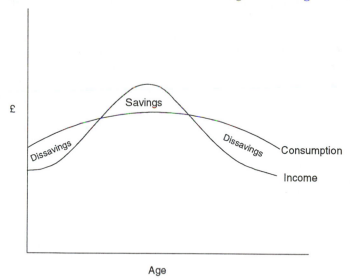

Source: Johnson and Falkingham (1992, Figure 4.7, p. 110)

**Figure 1.2**  Hypothetical Income and Consumption Profiles of a Life Cycle Saver

debate that has not yet been resolved (Aaron, 1982; Blinder, Gordon and Wise, 1982; Feldstein, 1985).

In the same way that individuals could use the market to redistribute through time so they could use the family to self insure against greater than average longevity (Kotlikoff and Spivak, 1981). Since the family is an efficient means of risk-sharing, it provides an incentive to keep families together. The greater the role social security or other government agencies play in retirement, or the greater other means of financial security, the greater the incentive for family instability. This was a theme taken up by Murray (1984). Support for single parents in the part of their life cycle when they had children actually encouraged, he suggested, single parenthood by reducing the costs single parents had to endure.

Life cycle redistribution by the state, these arguments go, therefore has negative or self-defeating results, as argued for Keynesian counter-cyclical measures.

Finally, economists and others have argued that so long as public pension schemes exist electorates will be induced to vote themselves high pensions and pass the costs on to future generations of electors. Thomson (1991) argues that this was true of those who voted themselves a welfare state in New Zealand between 1920 and 1945.

That is exactly what American politicians and voters have been happy to do in the period since 1935, Kotlikoff (1992) concludes. The form in which the national accounts and budgets are calculated makes this difficult to see but, he argues, social security and medicare legislation will land the future US taxpayer with 20 per cent higher tax bills. Similar claims were made during the debate in the UK on the State Earnings Related Pension Scheme in the mid 1980s. As a result, future benefits were substantially reduced. On the other hand attempts to reduce the tax burden in the United States in the 1980s were taken largely at the cost of young families. Old people's claims on the future national purse did not decline. As we have seen this was not the case in the UK.

On a more general level, therefore, Kotlikoff claims that we need 'generational accounting' so that we know 'who pays and when'.

> The idea of generational accounting is to summarize ... the net amount we are currently paying the government .. along with the net amount we are likely to pay government down the road (p. 26).

In Chapter 3 John Hills seeks to do just that, at least so far as the main components of 'the welfare state' are concerned.

In this book we look at social policy as a means of redistributing income through the life cycle. Why should the state be involved in this activity at all? Is the case stronger in some areas of risk than others? Have some generations voted themselves big handouts at the cost of others? Who pays when for what? What are the arguments for and against public means of achieving that redistribution?

**Chapter Two**

H55
D91

# The Market, the State and the Distribution of Life Cycle Income

## Julian Le Grand

The previous chapter discussed some of the historical reasons why the state has intervened in the life cycle distribution. This chapter addresses the same question but takes a rather different approach. It examines some of the theoretical reasons why markets might fail in the context of the distribution of income across the life cycle – intrapersonal distribution – and why, as a consequence, there may be a theoretical case for the State to intervene in that distribution. Put another way, it tries to answer the question: why do many countries have some kind of compulsory state social insurance system whose intention is, at least in part, to redistribute income across the life cycle?[1] Why cannot people be left to their own devices in making decisions as to how to distribute their own incomes throughout their lives? Why should the state involve itself in, for instance, individuals deciding on how much to save for retirement, or how much to insure themselves against the possibility of income loss due to unemployment? Are there reasons to suppose that in making the decisions in the relevant markets, without any state intervention, people will in some sense make the 'wrong' insurance or savings decisions? It is to these questions that this chapter is addressed.

The issues involved have been discussed in many contributions to the economics literature, and in what follows I summarise some of the principal arguments. I conclude that many of these offer accounts of market failure that are far from convincing. I go on to argue that a better case can be made by using some of the arguments in the recent philosophical literature, notably those derived from the work of Derek

---

1  Of course, redistribution of this kind is not the only reason why a state system of social insurance system might be desirable. Another important justification is to redistribute income *between* people, that is, interpersonal redistribution.

Parfit (1984). These have important insights that can be used to reinforce some of the more conventional economic justifications. The chapter concludes with some reflections as to whether the fact of market failure itself justifies state intervention – or whether the possibility of state failure needs also to be explored.

## 1.      The Market and the Distribution of Lifetime Income

A case can be made that state intervention in the redistribution of life cycle income is neither necessary nor desirable – this despite the fact that, as is demonstrated in subsequent chapters, in the absence of state intervention, individuals' incomes fluctuate widely throughout their lifetimes. These fluctuations are the consequence of a series of life events, such as marriage, the arrival of children, spells of unemployment or sickness, and eventual retirement: events that are all either predictable or, if not predictable, insurable. Hence if people do not like the income fluctuations the events induce, they are in a position to do something about it. To cover income reductions due to events that are predictable or largely so (marriage, children, retirement), they can save or borrow; for those that are due to unpredictable events (unemployment, sickness), they can insure. If they do neither of these things, we can presume that they prefer an income that fluctuates to one that is steadier; and, in that case, the state has no business intervening to 'correct' their decisions by itself engaging in intrapersonal redistribution.

One argument against this view may be disposed of immediately. This is the claim that state intervention of this kind is justified because there will be poor people with low lifetime incomes who as a consequence of their poverty cannot afford to save, or to take out the necessary insurance. However, the existence of such individuals does not make a case for state intervention in *intra*personal distribution; rather, it is an argument for the state engaging in *inter*personal redistribution. That is, the state should ensure that all individuals have an income at least sufficient so that they can engage in the normal activities in society, including accumulating savings or taking out insurance. If the problem is a low lifetime income, it seems appropriate to deal with that problem directly, instead of trying to address it by redistributing *within* that low lifetime income.

It is, of course, possible that, because of the political and other difficulties associated with redistributing income between people, the state may wish to use a system that is apparently concerned with intrapersonal redistribution to engage in some more-or-less clandestine interpersonal redistribution. However, that is simply an argument for using social policy apparently aimed at one end to achieve another. It does not itself justify the original end; in this case, it does not justify state intervention in intrapersonal redistribution for its own sake.

Better-directed arguments can be found in the economics literature discussing the operations of the relevant markets and the reasons why they might fail. These need more attention; they are discussed below under the headings of *capital, insurance* and *labour market failures, externality* and *myopia*.


## 2.    Capital Market Failure

If capital markets were perfect, and if there were perfect certainty, then there would indeed be no need for state intervention in life cycle decisions. If income could be smoothly shifted from one period to another, people who became unemployed or went sick could borrow to finance any consequent income losses; similarly, people could save for their retirement. If they chose not to do this, then that is not the fault of the market; it would be a case of 'people' failure rather than market failure.

It seems indisputable that capital markets in the real world are imperfect. Not everyone can borrow freely; indeed it is precisely those people who are unemployed or who face a measurable probability of being unemployed who can find it most difficult to borrow. And small investors may find it difficult to accumulate adequate funds for retirement.

However, as Atkinson (1991) points out, this rather begs the question as to why these markets are imperfect. One possible explanation concerns what is known in the literature as adverse selection: potential borrowers have more information concerning their 'riskiness' than lenders, and hence the latter will adopt lending policies that are too restrictive. Another concerns transaction costs or other sources of economies of scale in savings; these will put higher barriers to savings for small investors. A third concerns the absence of suitable collateral for people with little or no non-human capital; human capital can only act as collateral in a world where slavery is permitted, and the absence of a slave market is a kind of market failure that is better described as a social success.

But of course the biggest reason as to why capital markets on their own are not the solution to life cycle income smoothing is because the world is actually an uncertain place, and, in the presence of uncertainty, it is impossible to save or borrow on a properly informed basis. A market mechanism that has evolved to deal with the problem of uncertainty: insurance. However, this too has its difficulties.

## 3.      Insurance Market Failure

There are a number of conditions that have to be fulfilled if insurance markets are to achieve socially efficient outcomes (Barr, 1993a). They include the absence of: (a) probabilities close to or equal to one; (b) linked probabilities; (c) moral hazard; and (d) adverse selection. The first condition is an obvious one; no insurance company is going to offer insurance against an event that is absolutely certain (or even reasonably) certain to occur. Condition (b) – the absence of linked probabilities – derives from the fact that insurance is a risk-pooling exercise. For the pooling to work, the probability of the insured event occurring to any one individual must be independent of it occurring to any other individual. An example where this condition is not met that is relevant to the concerns of this chapter is the income loss due to the effect of inflation on pensions. In this case, if the event occurs to one individual it will occur to all other insured individuals, thus making risk-pooling and hence the operation of insurance impossible.

However, it should be noted that to describe either of these conditions as ones necessary to avoid market failure in achieving efficiency is a little misleading. In the first case the efficient outcome is for no insurance to be offered – which is precisely the market outcome. If a future income loss is certain then the appropriate way to cover that loss is through saving or borrowing, not through insurance. There may be a number of reasons why this is not possible: individuals may not have the resources to engage in adequate savings or borrowing, or they may be denied access to the relevant institutions. But these would be the consequence of failures in areas other than insurance ones: the failures of markets to achieve an equitable *inter*personal distribution, or failures in capital markets. Both of these are indeed market failures: however, one is market failure to achieve equity rather than social efficiency, and the other we have already considered.

The second case is arguably also one of capital market failure, at least in the pensions case. For if capital markets were operating perfectly, they should offer inflation-proofed instruments, in which insurance companies could invest and hence guarantee inflation-proofed pensions. Even if inflation-proofed investments are not available, this does not provide an argument for the state provision of social security; rather, it is an argument for the government to intervene in the capital market to provide such instruments (index-linked bonds, for example).

Moral hazard and adverse selection (conditions (c) and (d)), on the other hand, are 'genuine' sources of insurance market failure to achieve efficiency. Moral hazard arises when the insured person can costlessly manipulate either the probability of her loss or the size of the loss in a way that cannot be adequately monitored by the insurance company.[2] Examples are people voluntarily making themselves unemployed, or, once unemployed, staying out of work longer than they would if they had had no insurance. Adverse selection arises when insurees have more information concerning their levels of risk than the insurance company. In that case, insurance companies will offer cover based on some notional 'average' which will be too cheap for above-average risks (who will therefore over-insure) and too expensive for the below-average risks (who will under-insure). This process would drive up the premiums charged.

Although these are genuine insurance market failures in theory, there is still a problem about using them to justify state intervention in key areas of intrapersonal redistribution in practice; for they may not always apply to those areas. Unemployment is a relatively simple; for here moral hazard, at least, would appear to be a significant problem. The extra costs of children also pose a moral hazard problem; it is difficult to imagine any insurance company offering insurance against the costs of having children, when the decision is so much a matter of choice. Since people may conceal their health records from the insurance company, adverse selection can be a problem for sickness insurance.

However, pensions are more problematic. People cannot affect their ageing rate; and, although they can affect their time of death (through suicide, for instance), this is hardly costless. Hence moral hazard is unlikely to be a problem. Even if health records are difficult to obtain, insurance companies can acquire information relatively easily on the statistical probabilities of death for different groups, so adverse selection is also unlikely to pose a significant problem. In short, it might be quite difficult to build a case for state intervention at least in the market for pensions. However, the case for markets failing to provide adequate insurance against unemployment, sickness and the extra costs associated with children is much more plausible.

## 4.      Labour Market Failure

This is a relatively new line of argument, and has its beginning in a recent development in the analysis of labour markets: that of 'efficiency wages'. Lazear (1981, 1982) has argued that the need for employers to retain their workforce may lead to a pay structure where employees are paid more than their marginal product at certain periods, and below their marginal product at other times. In particular, employers have an incentive to offer

---

2    If the insurance company could adequately monitor such manipulation, it could make avoiding this behaviour a condition of the insurance contract; in consequence there would be no moral hazard problem.

private pensions and unemployment insurance, so as to encourage employee discipline and loyalty.

But if this is the case, why are not private pensions and private unemployment insurance universally provided? Why does private insurance not emerge spontaneously as part of the labour market contract? To be sure, employer-provided pension schemes are widely prevalent; but even they are far from universal, and employer-provided unemployment insurance is virtually non-existent.[3]

Atkinson (1991) has discussed a number of possible explanations both for the differential coverage of private unemployment and private pension schemes, and for the fact that there is not universal coverage of either. One concerns the role of trade unions. Senior trade union members may not feel themselves at risk from unemployment and therefore not favour the inclusion of unemployment insurance as part of their remuneration package. On the other hand, they do have a strong interest in the payment of pensions and will support the inclusion of private pensions.

Strictly this is not an example of market failure, but of the failure of the collective mechanisms of trade union decision-making (favouring the interests of senior members over those of others more susceptible to the risk of unemployment). Nonetheless it may be a feature of the way that the labour market actually operates, and hence has to be taken into account when discussing the desirability or otherwise of leaving the provision of these kinds of insurance to the workings of that market.

A second possible reason concerns the risk of bankruptcy. Workers may prefer not to have insurance elements included as part of their pay package, since there is a risk that the benefits would not be paid if the firm ran into serious trouble. However, again it is not clear that this is a failure of the labour market. Presumably firms could insure their pension or unemployment funds against such an eventuality; if they do not, then this is because of insurance market failures, not labour market ones. Also, even if there is some kind of market failure in operation here, the appropriate from of government intervention might not be to provide the insurance itself, but to regulate the relevant markets. So, for instance, the pension or unemployment fund could be set up as an entity independent of the firm; indeed, something like this is currently required of pension funds in Britain.

A third reason has been suggested by Atkinson (1991). He argues that under certain circumstances there may be firms where a significant number of workers are employed for short-term contracts (as well as workers on permanent contracts). This is because employers face firm-specific risks, and the availability of short-term contracts is a kind

---

3   Some firms may offer a form of unemployment 'insurance' through guaranteeing to keep employees nominally in employment, even though there is relatively little for them to do. However, such 'job-for-life' schemes are not common in Britain.

of insurance for them that they can cope with a down-turn in demand. In this situation, there is no private unemployment benefit (no permanent workers being laid off in times of recession) and private pensions are only paid to permanent workers. Hence there is a need, on equity grounds at least, for state intervention to provide insurance for the short-term workers.

However, it is not clear that this is a case of labour market failure to achieve efficiency. Given the circumstances postulated, employers seem to be behaving in a rational fashion, and, even if the labour market were operating 'perfectly' in these circumstances, something like this phenomenon would still be occurring. Nor is there anything in this argument on its own that prevents the short-term workers from taking out private insurance or private pensions so as to relieve the precariousness of their situation; if they cannot, then it is due to failures in other markets, such as those described above for capital and insurance, not labour ones.

## 5.     Externality

An externality arises when the production or consumption decisions of individuals affect people who are not directly involved in the decision. If the person or persons concerned are affected adversely, the phenomenon is termed an *external cost*; if they benefit, it is an *external benefit*. A classic example of an external cost is environmental pollution, where an individual making a decision, for instance, to purchase a car does not consider the impact that her driving the car may have on the atmosphere that other people breathe; an example of an external benefit is the decision to get vaccinated against an infectious disease which not only protects the individual vaccinated but also reduces the risk of the disease spreading to others.

Since on the whole people make decisions in markets solely or largely on the basis of the effect on their own interests, and do not take proper account of others who might be affected, markets will not be efficient if externalities are present to a significant extent. More specifically, the market level of provision of a commodity with external benefits will be less than the efficient level; that of a commodity with external costs will be more.

There is at least one kind of externality involved in the life cycle decision. It is an example of external benefits and is therefore likely to cause a sub-optimal ('too little') amount of life cycle redistribution. This is the so-called 'caring' externality, whereby one individual cares for the future welfare of another. One example of this might be parents' concern for their children's higher education. If, as seems plausible, undertaking higher education increases future consumption at the expense of present consumption and if, at the margin, parents value their children's future consumption relative to their present consumption at a higher rate than the children themselves do, then, left to their own devices, children will engage in less higher education than the parents think they should. Suppose further that parents could compensate children for their loss of present consumption (by, for example, paying the fees and paying for their maintenance) and still remain better off (in utility terms). Then, unless such compensation actually takes place, there will be a sub-optimal level of education.

However, this example also illustrates a possible weakness of this argument, at least as part of an efficiency case for state intervention. For, at least in this particular example, compensation almost certainly *would* take place; if parents felt sufficiently strongly about their children's higher education they would be prepared to pay for it. Hence sufficient higher education would be undertaken, even in the absence of state intervention. More generally, voluntary transfers may solve the problem of caring externalities (or indeed of any externality) without the state needing to intervene.

On the other hand, voluntary transfers are subject to the so-called free-rider problem. If an individual's principal reason for engaging in a voluntary transfer is to improve the welfare of the recipient, then she may be tempted to hold back her contribution in the hope that the recipient's welfare will be improved through other people's contributions. Since everyone who is similarly motivated will be similarly tempted, the end result will be too low a level of voluntary transfer. However, both the theoretical and practical significance of the free-rider problem have been questioned (Sugden, 1984).

## 6.    Myopia

This argument is based on the premise that, as Kessler (1989) puts it, individuals' time horizons are 'rather limited'. They do not consider the long term; they plan only on the basis of current events, or on their predictions of the very immediate future; in consequence they do not make sensible savings or insurance decisions. In a word, they are myopic. Myopic individuals, as their life unfolds and they encounter unexpected vicissitudes, such as unemployment or sickness, or even more predictable ones, such as old age, have no personal resources with which to cope with these and experience massive drops in income in consequence.

The problem with describing this as a form of 'market failure' is that it is not the market that apparently fails in this situation. If people actually are myopic in the way described, if they have a short term preference structure, then the market will respond to those preferences in the way it does to any other structure of preferences. If, because of myopia, there is no demand for sickness insurance schemes or for old age pension plans, then the market will not provide them; but that will not be inefficient or sub-optimal, because it is only a response to what people want (or, in this case, to what they do not want). If anything is 'failing' in this situation, it is the individuals themselves who are behaving in a way that outsiders might judge as irrational (although they themselves presumably would not).

The fact that this is a case of 'individual failure' rather than market failure has direct implications for government intervention. For if individuals are myopic, then government may also be myopic. Certainly, there can be no presumption that the distribution of lifetime income as determined by myopic individuals working in a market context will necessarily be worse or more 'irrational' than that which results from intervention by a government elected and run by the same myopic individuals. Indeed, even if governments did behave in a non-myopic fashion, arguably they should not; for to ignore the preferences of their electors would be undemocratic and paternalist.

However, here some of Parfit's arguments have relevance. Parfit's thesis is both weighty and lengthy, and I shall not be able to do justice to it here. However, a helpful guide to some of his reasoning has been provided by John Broome (1985). Combining Broome's insights with my own interpretations, Parfit's argument runs something like this. We normally invoke the concept of personal identity to link a person in one time period with the 'same' person in another, later period. But what does the concept of personal identity actually mean? It presumably does *not* mean what a possible literal interpretation of the words in the phrase personal identity would mean: that is, the person in the first time period is identical in every respect to the person in the second. The person will have aged physically; external factors (such as income or family status) may have changed; tastes may have changed; aspects of personality may have changed. The extent and magnitude of these changes may be small if the distance between the time periods is small, but they are likely to increase with that distance: compare the physique, income, personal relations and personality of an 8 year-old with that of the 'same' person eighty years later.

So if it does not mean actual identity, what does personal identity mean? As Broome describes it, Parfit's answer is a reductionist one: that is, the 'fact' of personal identity can be reduced to some other facts that can be described without using the concept of personal identity. These facts, according to Parfit, are links of a psychological kind, principally those of intention and memory. For instance, a 20-year-old will have memories of her 19-year-old self; and certain features of her current existence will depend on the intentions and actions of that 19-year-old. These links are, according to Parfit, what makes the 20- and 19-year-old the 'same' person. Similar phenomena would link the 8- and 88-year-old mentioned above; but here the phenomena (and therefore the links) would be much attenuated. Hence any argument that was based on the continuity of the self would be much weaker for the eighty year gap than for the one year gap.

What are the implications of this for the myopia argument? Simply that a certain degree of myopia may not be irrational. If people are not 'identical' to their future selves, but only linked to them in certain ways, then it seems quite rational to give those future selves less weight than their present selves. There is no individual 'failure'.

But this in turn means that there *is* a possibility of market failure. For there is now a kind of externality involved. My future self is a 'separate' person who is directly affected by my present decisions in the market. My future self is someone I care about, but not to the same extent as I care about my present self; hence in taking my market decisions I will not give appropriate weight to the interests of my future self, in exactly the same fashion as if the 'externality' applied to a different person. Hence I will tend to save or insure too little from the point of view of optimality.

Again one cannot deduce from this directly that government intervention is necessarily required. For, just as in the case of the irrational myopic individuals, a democratic government will be elected by 'present' individuals who may give too little weight to their future selves in their collective decision-making, just as they do in their market decision-making. So governments may perform as badly as the market.

However, the point is not exactly the same as that for 'irrational' myopia. There a government which over-rode individuals' myopic preferences would be doing so only on the paternalistic grounds that it knew its electorate's interests better than the electorate itself did – a profoundly undemocratic procedure. But, if Parfit's argument is accepted, a government could justify over-riding present individuals' preferences on the *democratic* grounds that other individuals – in particular, the present individuals' future selves – have just as much right for their interests to be respected as present individuals, even if, for obvious reasons, they are not around to be able to express those interests. So there is a market (not individual) failure case (a) for government intervention and (b) for the government when intervening not to rely solely on the preferences of present individuals. Whether in practice it will do so, of course, remains an open question.

## 7.    Conclusion

In short, the arguments derived from capital and labour market failure provide a case for state intervention in intrapersonal redistribution that is good in parts, but does contain significant weaknesses. The argument from insurance failure is rather stronger, at least so far as unemployment insurance and the costs of children are concerned. But perhaps the most convincing of all is the myopic/externality argument derived from the work of Parfit and others, where the state has to act as a representative of people's future selves – people whose interests might be seriously neglected if there were no state-provided social security.

However, the fact that markets fail does not itself necessarily establish the case for state intervention. For it is possible that the state will fail as badly as the market. State social security systems can reduce people's freedom to save or insure as much (or as little) as they want; they may reduce the overall savings rate in the economy as a whole; the taxes necessary to finance them may have damaging effects on the incentive to work. Ultimately the question as to which is the 'best' system for engaging in intrapersonal redistribution is an empirical one: which system fails the least?

Chapter Three

# The Welfare State and Redistribution Between Generations

## John Hills

## 1.    Introduction

The previous two chapters have explored both the development of policy towards state redistribution across the life cycle, and the theoretical justifications for such redistribution. Such redistribution could, in principle, be achieved in two ways. One would be enforced contributions into a fund which would be invested on its contributors' behalf and drawn on when needed – much in the way that private sector pension schemes in fact operate. The second is what has actually occurred in Britain: welfare services like education, health care and social security are financed on a 'Pay As You Go' basis, using the National Insurance contributions and tax payments drawn (largely) from the current working generation to pay for the benefits going (largely) to the non-working generations.

In a steady state, the outcome of these two alternatives might, under certain conditions, be much the same in terms of the payments into the system made by each generation, and the amounts each would receive from it, although outcomes would not necessarily be the same in terms of the nation's stock of capital, savings rates, and so on (see, for instance, Blanchard and Fischer, 1989, Chapter 3 for a discussion of the literature on the 'overlapping generations model' dating back to Samuelson, 1958).

However, looking back over the twentieth century, the British welfare state cannot be described as having been in a steady state, until perhaps the mid-1970s. This can be seen from Figure 3.1, which shows public spending in Great Britain as a percentage of national income for the three areas with which this book is most concerned – education, health and social security. In such a situation, different generations may

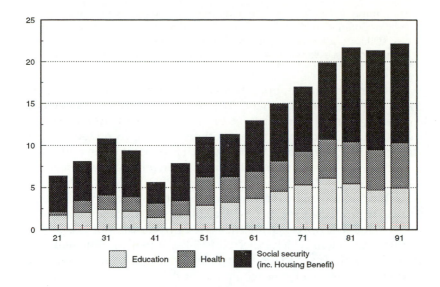

**Figure 3.1** Welfare Spending 1921 to 1991 (% of GDP; GB)

easily be being treated in ways which are more or less favourable than the treatment of others.

Recently demographers and economic historians have started to examine the scale of transfers resulting from the operations of the welfare state between actual generations or age cohorts. This analysis has led to some striking conclusions:

> Seen from a cohort perspective, not only the ups and downs of fertility in the twentieth century but also the workings of social security have created considerable injustices between different generations. If perceived as such, this injustice between the generations could foster discontent with future social policies and, finally, undermine the 'implicit contract' between generations on which the welfare state is based (Johnson, Conrad and Thomson, 1989, p. 1).

In his analysis of the New Zealand welfare state, Thomson (1991, p. 1) puts his findings starkly:

> In New Zealand the big winners in this have been the 'welfare generation' – those born between about 1920 and 1945. Throughout their lives they will make contributions which cover only a fraction of their benefits. For their successors the reverse is true, and the question now is whether such a welfare state has a future.

He also suggests that this finding is not unique to one country:

> The timing and pace of welfare expansion will have created different
> generational imbalances in each modern state, yet the similarities are
> also striking. Analysis ... suggests a comparable erection of youth-states
> in the early post-war years in most developed nations (Thomson, 1989,
> p. 39).

This is clearly an important issue. If the welfare state is creating
generations which are systematically losing from current arrangements,
there certainly may be implications for the future of the welfare state in
its current form. Already in the USA there has been a pressure group,
'Americans for Generational Equity', which proposes cuts in transfers to
the elderly on the grounds that they are no longer poor by comparison
with the young (Johnson and Falkingham, 1992, p. 132). By the same
token, *changes* to existing arrangements which have the effect, for
instance, of reducing the expected receipts of certain generations when
they reach old age, might create imbalances which did not exist before,
and turn generations which expected to 'break-even' in some sense into
net losers. Political conflict between generations over who gets what out
of the welfare state and over who pays for it may come to be added to
the existing conflicts between rich and poor, men and women, South and
North, and so on.

However, the arguments are not clear-cut. First, the use of Pay As
You Go funding does not of itself prove that intergenerational inequity
exists, as is explored below. Second, even if inequity does exist in some
countries, it may not in others. Indeed, Johnson and Falkingham (1988,
p. 144) suggest that, in Britain,

> ... the welfare system has been remarkably neutral in its treatment of the
> young and the old, and in this respect recent trends in Britain have
> clearly been different from those perceived by Preston for the U.S. and
> Thomson for New Zealand.

Third, it is not clear that the kind of analysis used to reach the
conclusions of intergenerational inequity deployed by Thomson and
others proves their case. It may be true that certain forms of welfare
provision which used to favour the young have been cut back, while
others which favour the old have been increased. But this does not, of
itself, prove that there has been a net transfer between particular
generations. That depends on exactly which age cohorts have benefited
when from each part of social spending, and, crucially, on who paid the
tax and National Insurance bills which financed the total.

Fourth, even if one generation is a 'net gainer', this does not, as we
shall see, necessarily mean that successive generations are 'net losers'.
The analogy with an unsustainable chain letter game (Thomson, 1991,
p. 9) may be misleading. The usual kind of chain letter – with the numbers
involved multiplying at each stage – *is* unsustainable: the first
participants may each receive 64 postcards (or £64) from those further
down the chain in return for the one they each sent, but the process cannot

continue indefinitely without the world's entire population becoming involved, after which further participants become hard to find.

Seen from the perspective of the early 1990s, however, the welfare state, in Britain at least, no longer looks to be growing explosively. Rather, it seems – measured as a share of national income – to have grown rapidly in the thirty years after the Second World War, but to have stabilised since the mid-1970s. This process is discussed in detail in Hills (1990), and is summarised in Figure 3.1. There may, indeed, have been winners and losers as the welfare state has grown to maturity (if that is the correct way to describe it), but the approximate stability of the last fifteen years is not so obviously unsustainable as to imply that currently young generations cannot get back something close to what they put in.

This brings up the final point. Since the welfare state does affect people 'from cradle to grave', it may be misleading to look at just one part of their lives – even what seems quite a long period, like thirty years – and conclude that they have gained or lost. The calculation can only really be made standing at the grave-side, looking back over a period of up to a century.

This chapter sets out to explore whether there is evidence for intergenerational inequity – and the existence of a 'welfare generation' – in Britain in the way in which the benefits from and costs of the major components of social spending – education, health and social security – have been distributed since the 1920s. It is, in effect, an exercise in 'generational accounting' of the kind called for by Kotlikoff (1992), in his book of that title, albeit a partial one in that it looks only at the effects of transfers within the welfare state, not at wider definitions of public sector assets and liabilities.[1]

The next section discusses the issues involved in measuring intergenerational equity (or its absence). Section 3 presents the empirical findings for the period up to 1991. Section 4 explores the effects of extending the analysis with projections up to 2041. Section 5 gives some conclusions. The data used and their sources are described in detail in the Appendix to Hills (1992).[2]

---

1   For such a discussion of public sector assets and liabilities on a wider basis, see Hills (1989), which sets the build up of state pension liabilities against, for instance, trends in the scale of public debt and publicly owned physical assets.

2   The data used are updated in three respects from the sources described in Hills (1992). First, spending figures for 1991–92 are based on the revised out-turn estimates given in HM Treasury (1993), Table 2.5, and associated departmental reports. Second, gross domestic product (GDP) per capita is based on revised GDP figures for 1991–92 (ibid., Table 2.1). Third, the population projections used are those published in OPCS (1993b), using a 1991 base, rather than the 1985 base used in the earlier exercise. None of these revisions makes a substantial difference to the broad overall conclusions.

## 2.      What Do We Mean By 'Intergenerational Equity'?

### Adding amounts accruing at different dates

As later chapters discuss, a large part of the operation of the welfare state consists not of net transfers between rich and poor, but of effective transfers between one stage and another in the same people's lives. At any given moment, a particular cohort may be receiving net benefits from or making net payments into the collective pool, but at other times the reverse may be the case. The problem is how to add together the net flows occurring at different times to give a 'lifetime total'.

First, because of inflation, it is clearly incorrect to say that someone who 'paid in' £1 in 1921 and 'got back' £1 in 1991 has broken-even in any meaningful sense. At the very least, we are interested in real, inflation-adjusted, amounts.

Second, even measuring everything in real terms, a problem remains, which can be looked at in two distinct ways. One is that general economic behaviour suggests that the same amount of real purchasing power now is worth more than the same amount at some point in the future. We should therefore discount amounts received at different times by some real interest rate. This could be done by using actual interest rates over any particular period – which would amount to saying that someone was breaking-even if what they got out at one time was equal to the amount which they would have accumulated in some form of investment in the time since they made the original payment in. However, quite apart from the problem of *which* investment to choose, real rates of return have varied considerably over the last seventy years, at times being substantially negative. It is not obvious that it is appropriate to say to those who were making net payments into the system in the late 1960s that these would be balanced by smaller real receipts in the early 1980s, given the high inflation, and negative *ex post* real interest rates in between.

One solution to this would be to use a constant real interest rate over the whole period, perhaps the average of some measure of real returns in the economy as a whole. There is, however, an alternative, more intuitively appealing, way of looking at the problem. That is to say that payments in and out should be taken as balancing if they represent the same value – or sacrifice – in terms of contemporary living standards. If in one year, someone pays in the equivalent of 20 per cent of that year's average per capita income, then this would be balanced by a receipt in a later year equivalent to 20 per cent of the later year's average per capita income.

This is the approach adopted here. Receipts from and payments for the welfare state are measured as percentages of contemporary gross domestic product (GDP) per capita. In 1991–92, GDP per capita in the UK was just over £10,000, while in 1921 it was just under £100 (Hills, 1992,

Table A3).[3] An age cohort which paid £1 million into the welfare state in 1921 would thus be taken as being treated neutrally if, for instance, it got about £100 million out in 1991.

This approach is equivalent to using the real rate of growth in per capita income as the real discount rate. There are some economic arguments for thinking that the two might be similar in the long run. However, the stronger reason for using it is the intuitive appeal of the fact that, measured in this way, a 'steady state' welfare state would be 'generationally neutral'. That is, with successive cohorts of constant size and life expectancy, welfare spending taking a constant percentage of GDP, and no change in the ratios between spending on people of different ages, no generation would be a net gainer or a net loser. Each cohort would make the same tax and National Insurance contributions to pay for welfare services and would receive services and benefits costing the same amount as each other, when measured in units of GDP per capita. Other implicit discount rates would imply that intergenerationally fair welfare states were either unsustainable (if the discount rate was higher than the real per capita growth rate), or were ever-diminishing (if the reverse was true). Neither alternative seems satisfactory. We therefore use this unit of measurement to define the baseline against which we examine actual spending patterns over time for each cohort.

## What is a 'generation'?

A second issue is the definition of what constitutes a 'generation'. On the one hand, the narrower the age range used the better, since even quite small differences in birth dates can, as a result of wars or the economic cycle, be associated with large differences in lifetime circumstances (Johnson and Falkingham, 1992, p. 6). On the other hand, we do not have the data to allocate spending and taxation by very narrow age ranges. The narrowest age bands for which the necessary information is available are five year age cohorts. There are good data on the actual numbers in each five year cohort at each census since 1921 and interpolations can be made for the years in between. The Office of Population Censuses and Surveys (OPCS) also publishes projections for them for the future. In addition, there are relatively good figures for the receipt of social security benefits by five year age groups (see DSS, 1991, for instance). Education spending could be allocated to narrower age groups, but allocating health spending even by five year groups involves some fairly heroic assumptions.

---

3   Although the unit of measurement is taken as UK GDP per capita, the rest of the analysis below is, for data reasons, for spending in and the populations of Great Britain, excluding Northern Ireland.

The cohorts used are described in Table 3.1. They are those in successive five year age groups at each Census (i.e. in April), starting with the cohort born between April 1901 and March 1906. This group – 'Cohort 1' – were aged between 85 and 89 in April 1991. In order to put some flesh on the analysis, the table also lists a 'representative' for each of the cohorts born by 1966. In the case of Cohort 1 this is Sir Alec Douglas-Home, now Lord Home. If David Thomson's identification of a New Zealand 'welfare generation' born between 1920 and 1945 also proved correct for Britain, it would be Cohorts 5 to 9 – the 'Thatcher to Major generation' – which would be the net beneficiaries from the welfare state.

The figures below illustrate the way in which the empirical findings are built up. To keep the diagrams comprehensible, they are results for every third cohort from Cohort 1 to Cohort 16 (born between 1976 and 1981). Tables 3.3 and 3.5 below give the final results for each cohort.

The size of these cohorts varies, and this may affect their fortunes in various ways. Larger cohorts may, for instance, face tougher labour market conditions. As far as this analysis is concerned, one might expect larger cohorts to gain from the way in which they can spread out the financing cost of pensions and other provision for the elderly when they

Table 3.1  Age Cohorts Used in the Analysis

| Cohort | Born[a] | Age in 1991[b] | 'Representative' | Size when 15–19 (m) | Size in 1991 (m) |
|---|---|---|---|---|---|
| 1 | 1901–06 | 85–89 | Alec Douglas-Home | 3.98 | 0.62 |
| 2 | 1906–11 | 80–84 | Barbara Castle | 4.03 | 1.24 |
| 3 | 1911–16 | 75–79 | Harold Wilson | 3.87 | 1.81 |
| 4 | 1916–21 | 70–74 | Denis Healey | 3.55 | 2.22 |
| 5 | 1921–26 | 65–69 | Margaret Thatcher | 3.74 | 2.70 |
| 6 | 1926–31 | 60–64 | Geoffrey Howe | 3.28 | 2.81 |
| 7 | 1931–36 | 55–59 | Michael Heseltine | 3.07 | 2.85 |
| 8 | 1936–41 | 50–54 | John Smith | 3.21 | 3.01 |
| 9 | 1941–46 | 45–49 | John Major | 3.58 | 3.43 |
| 10 | 1946–51 | 40–44 | Gordon Brown | 4.15 | 4.04 |
| 11 | 1951–56 | 35–39 | Tony Blair | 3.70 | 3.68 |
| 12 | 1956–61 | 30–34 | Charles Kennedy | 4.01 | 4.10 |
| 13 | 1961–66 | 25–29 | Matthew Taylor | 4.47 | 4.62 |
| 14 | 1966–71 | 20–24 | - | 4.34 | 4.36 |
| 15 | 1971–76 | 15–19 | - | 3.56 | 3.59 |
| 16 | 1976–81 | 10–14 | - | - | 3.36 |
| 17 | 1981–86 | 5–9 | - | - | 3.53 |
| 18 | 1986–91 | 0–4 | - | - | 3.75 |

Notes:
a    Years starting in April.
b    April 1991.

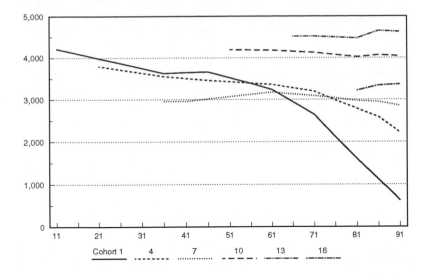

**Figure 3.2** Size of Cohort (Great Britain; 000s)

are young, although this might be offset if smaller successor generations were only prepared to pay less generous pensions to them. For smaller cohorts, the reverse might be true (see Ermisch, 1990, p. 46 for a discussion).

Table 3.1 shows the relative sizes of each cohort as it reached age 15–19, the largest being Cohort 13 born between 1961 and 1966 (the 'Matthew Taylor' cohort), which was nearly 50 per cent larger than Cohort 7 (the 'Heseltine' cohort) born between 1931 and 1936. Figure 3.2 shows how the sizes of the six cohorts used to illustrate the analysis have changed between 1911 and 1991. As well as demonstrating the variation in size between cohorts, it also shows that, even if one covers the whole period from 1911 to 1991, only the first cohort has got near to the end of its life. The others have many years of the welfare state to go (assuming it survives in some form), years which have to be allowed for in some way if we are to make a meaningful comparison of lifetime positions.

### Incidence assumptions

It would be possible to allocate spending (and the taxes which finance it) on a year-by-year basis. To save computation, however, the approach here is to use spending – in units of GDP per capita – in every fifth year as representative of spending levels over a five year period.[4]

---

4  Thus, for instance, spending on pensions in 1991–92 is divided between five year age

Spending is allocated to those on whom it is directly spent and it is valued at the amount which it costs the public sector. Either assumption could be questioned. The true incidence of any benefit may not be on its direct beneficiaries. For instance, education spending is allocated to the children and young people at school or college. It may, however, be that the true beneficiaries of some of this spending are their parents, who would have paid for their children's education themselves, if the state had not. Or the beneficiaries might include a wide range of age cohorts, who gain from the higher level of economic performance resulting from better education and training (including the direct beneficiaries' children and parents); this is a form of the general 'spillover' problem with incidence analysis. Similarly, in the absence of state pensions, working age children might have helped more to support their elderly parents, and so might really be the beneficiaries of part of pensions spending. However, such wider effects are not allowed for here. It seems most consistent to allocate benefits to the individuals who receive the cash or service. To test the sensitivity of this, we do examine the effect on the results to allocation of education to parents rather than their children.

Second, the true value to its beneficiary of a service provided in kind like education or health care might be very different from the amount which it costs the state to provide. Inefficiencies or restricted choices might mean that recipients would put a lower value on services than their cost. Alternatively, the state might be providing – for instance, through the NHS – services which would have a far higher market value than their cost. We have no way of allowing for such differences between cost and value, so are forced to use cost, which should be borne in mind when interpreting the results.

## Looking at entire cohorts

The analysis in this chapter looks at the position of age cohorts *as a whole*. Within each cohort some may do better, and others worse than the cohort average.[5] We investigate such intra-cohort variation and the factors which create it in detail in later chapters, looking at the effects of the welfare state as it was structured in the mid-1980s on the members of a single (synthetic) cohort. Unfortunately, we do not have the longitudinal survey data to look at such variation within actual cohorts over the

---

cohorts according to proportions based on data from *Social Security Statistics* (DSS, 1991). Five times the annual spending on 65–69 year-olds is then added to the previous receipts of Cohort 5, who were 65–69 in April 1991, to give their cumulative receipts by age 70.

5  So that when, to ease presentation, results are presented below in terms of cumulative receipts or costs per survivor in each cohort, these are *averages* for those reaching a certain age, from which the experience of the whole cohort is built up. They do not necessarily represent the experience of any particular member of the cohort.

historical past. However, we can look at the average position of successive cohorts about which such variation takes place.

An alternative approach would be to look at the experience of 'typical' members of each cohort and to work out how they would have been affected by the rules of the benefit and taxation systems at each stage in their lives. While this approach certainly generates some insights, it may be misleading if one cannot identify truly typical life histories. Given the range of varying circumstances involved, to do this accurately one needs a very wide range of different cases – which is why the model, LIFEMOD, described in later chapters looks at 4,000 different life histories to examine variation within a single cohort. As successive cohorts vary in all sorts of ways one would need many different cases for each cohort, which would be an enormous exercise.

However, if one does not allow for variation in circumstances between cohorts, the results in terms of their receipts and tax payments may be misleading. For instance, Figure 3.2 shows that mortality patterns have changed: later cohorts live longer, which means they will collect pensions and benefit from health care over longer periods. Failing to allow for this will understate the relative gains from the pension system for later cohorts, a problem which appears to affect the comparison between the 'Late' and the 'Early' families made in Thomson (1991). While it is of interest to answer the question 'how would someone with the same life history be treated now in comparison with forty years ago?', such an approach does not answer the key question of whether actual cohorts have been net gainers or losers from the operation of the welfare state.

For that reason the aggregate approach used here seems preferable, giving insights of comparable value to other distributional analysis which looks at variations between groups split in one way (such as gender, education or income), abstracting from further variation caused by other factors. In this case the factor on which we concentrate is year of birth. Later chapters in this book look at intra-cohort variations.

## Summary

What is reported below is a fairly standard, first round, incidence exercise looking at the distribution of the benefits of public spending on education, health and social security, and the costs of the taxes which finance them.[6] However, the allocation is not for a single year and

---

6   As discussed below, the taxes allocated are only those required to pay for the three spending areas at each date. One could only go from conclusions reached on the basis of the distribution of these three services to conclusions about public spending as a whole if it was thought that the other activities paid for by taxation were 'intergenerationally neutral' in the sense that their benefits went to each age group in

between different income groups (as in, say, CSO, 1993), but is for a long time period and between successive five year age cohorts.

To be a 'welfare generation', one of these cohorts would have to take out more than it puts in – that is, receive, over its completed lifetime, greater benefits than the taxes it pays to finance the welfare state, with amounts at different dates measured in relation to living standards (GDP per capita) at that point. For a generation which was 'born to pay' – to quote Longman's (1987) title, describing those who will have to pay for US baby-boomers in retirement – the reverse would be true.

## 3.    Intergenerational Distribution 1921 to 1991

### Education

As can be seen from Figure 3.1, public education spending (as a percentage of GDP) in Great Britain had trebled from its inter-war levels by 1976, but has subsequently fallen back. The same is true of the total measured in units of GDP per capita (see Table 3.2). At the same time the shares of this spending going first to secondary education and then to tertiary education have risen, and the age distribution within each tier has changed.

Putting all of this together, and allowing for the different sizes of successive cohorts, Figure 3.3 shows the average cumulative receipts from education spending per survivor at each age in the six illustrative cohorts.[7] Thus, by the time they were 20, members of Cohort 1 had received state education costing an average of 80 per cent of a year's average per capita income. By the same age sixty years later, members of Cohort 13 had received education costing about 300 per cent of a year's per capita income, with more to come in their twenties.

Spending was higher for each successive cohort, with the exception that by age 10, Cohort 16 (born between 1976 and 1981) was in no better position than Cohort 13 at the same age (and Cohort 7 – because of the War – was temporarily behind Cohort 4 at age 15). However, the big difference comes between the pre- and post-War cohorts. If there is an 'education generation', it consists of those of us educated since the War.

---

proportion to the remaining taxes they paid. The true picture could, of course, be rather different from this.

7    The spending figures used start in 1921, but Cohorts 1 and 2 receive some education before then. The amounts allocated to them at earlier ages are based on spending (in per cent of GDP per capita) per survivor of that age in 1921. In other words, 1911 and 1916 spending levels are taken to match those of 1921 in relation to average incomes and numbers at each age. The same is done for health spending. In neither case are the amounts involved, and hence the potential errors from the procedure, very large.

**Table 3.2** Public Spending on Education, Health and Social Security 1921 to 1991[a] (GB)

| | £ million (cash) | | | 000s of GDP per capita[b] | | |
|---|---|---|---|---|---|---|
| | Education | Health | Social Security | Education | Health | Social Security |
| 1921 | 84 | 20 | 212 | 723 | 174 | 1821 |
| 1926 | 86 | 60 | 199 | 887 | 619 | 2043 |
| 1931 | 101 | 72 | 285 | 1072 | 758 | 3007 |
| 1936 | 104 | 80 | 263 | 994 | 772 | 2521 |
| 1941 | 122 | 145 | 213 | 668 | 790 | 1160 |
| 1946 | 166 | 163 | 431 | 823 | 806 | 2130 |
| 1951 | 405 | 481 | 671 | 1393 | 1657 | 2311 |
| 1956 | 653 | 623 | 1034 | 1594 | 1520 | 2525 |
| 1961 | 986 | 867 | 1629 | 1876 | 1650 | 3101 |
| 1966 | 1710 | 1370 | 2580 | 2373 | 1910 | 3589 |
| 1971 | 3050 | 2280 | 4450 | 2860 | 2134 | 4169 |
| 1976 | 7710 | 5850 | 11580 | 3283 | 2492 | 4934 |
| 1981 | 13800 | 12600 | 28600 | 2906 | 2665 | 6038 |
| 1986 | 17700 | 18200 | 45100 | 2757 | 2650 | 6547 |
| 1991 | 27700 | 30400 | 67000 | 2750 | 3017 | 6639 |

**Notes:**

a   Data are for financial years except for education up to 1946 and health up to 1936, which are for calendar years.

b   That is, cash spending in each year divided by that year's GDP per capita.

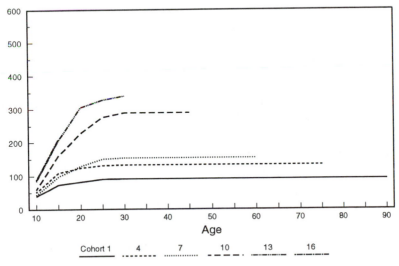

**Note:**
Line for Cohort 16 overlaps with line for Cohort 13.

**Figure 3.3** Cumulative Education Spending per Survivor (% of GDP per capita)

## Health

If anything, public spending on health jumped even more rapidly than education after the War with the establishment of the National Health Service, being nearly double the percentage of GDP in 1951 that it had been between 1931 and 1946. With the exception of the period 1981 to 1986, it has continued to grow more or less steadily since the 1960s (Figure 3.1 and Table 3.2).

Part of this growth reflects, however, not just greater provision for a given age, but also the effects of an ageing population. Unfortunately, few data are available on the relative costs of different age groups to the NHS before the 1980s. Figures 3.4(a) and (b) therefore illustrate the effects of making two different assumptions about the variation in health spending by age and about how this has changed over time (for details see Hills, 1992, Tables A7 and A8). Although the 'high variation' assumptions do result in rather higher lifetime receipts for the minority who survive into their late-eighties and nineties, the difference in the effects of the two assumptions between complete cohorts (most of whom do not survive that long) is not very large. The main analysis of overall effects below uses the 'low variation' figures illustrated in Figure 3.4 (a).

The pattern of health spending through the life cycle is almost the opposite of that of education, with the bulk of it coming after retirement.[8] Again, the members of later cohorts had benefited more by any given age than those from earlier cohorts, but in this case the increase between each was much more even.[9]

## Social security

Social security spending is the largest of the three programmes analysed. Indeed, before the War it was larger than health and education put together, as it has also been since 1981 (Table 3.2). Detailed breakdowns of social security spending by kind of benefit are available, and so are figures which allow its allocation by five-year age group. Total spending

---

8   The costs associated with birth and very young children – which are of increasing importance – are allocated to the children themselves. Again, an alternative assumption could have been made of allocating them to the parents.

9   This is not true of the early 1950s and early 1980s. A by-product of the analysis presented here is a series for health spending per capita in relation to average incomes for any given age group. This gives an approximate index for the volume of health provision in relation to demographic 'need'. This fell for most ages between 1951 and 1956, when total health spending fell in relation to average income (Table 3.2). It also fell between 1981 and 1986, when health spending fell slightly behind average income growth, but demographically adjusted need was rising at an unprecedented rate: a further by-product is an index for 'demographically adjusted need', which rises (using the 'low variation' assumptions) from 92 in 1921 to 115 in 1981, but jumps to 127 by 1991 (the 'high variation' assumptions give an even greater jump).

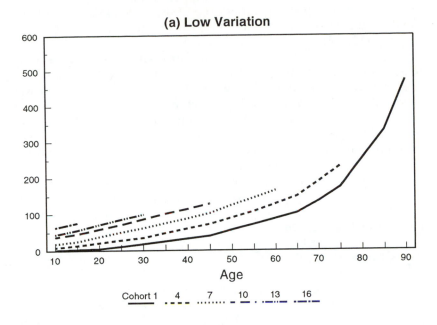

**(a) Low Variation**

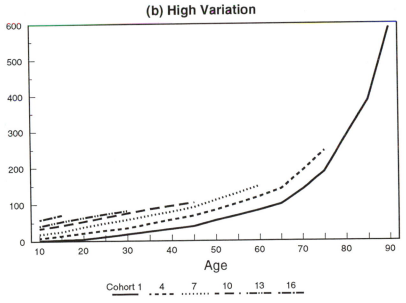

**(b) High Variation**

**Figure 3.4** Cumulative Health Spending per Survivor (% of GDP per capita)

John Hills

rose in the Depression of the 1930s, dipped in the War, rose with the growth in pension spending through the 1950s, 1960s and 1970s, and rose rapidly at the start of the 1980s with the growth of unemployment (Figure 3.1 and Table 3.2).

Figure 3.5 shows that – as with health spending – social security receipts are heavily weighted, as one would expect, towards the over-sixties. As far as the earlier cohorts (1 to 7) are concerned, there was little change in the relative value of pre-retirement social security receipts over the period. However, the later cohorts – born after the War – have been on a higher trajectory as a result of a combination of factors, including the introduction of family allowances (now Child Benefit) and higher unemployment. Note that the average member of Cohort 1 surviving to age 90 would have received social security benefits equivalent to eleven years' worth of average per capita income (compared with less than one year's worth from education and between five and six from health).

### Paying for welfare

Thus far we have shown that benefits from the welfare state have been, by and large, greater at any given age for each successive cohort, with a particularly large jump in education receipts for those educated after the War. However, this tells us only about what each cohort is getting *out* of

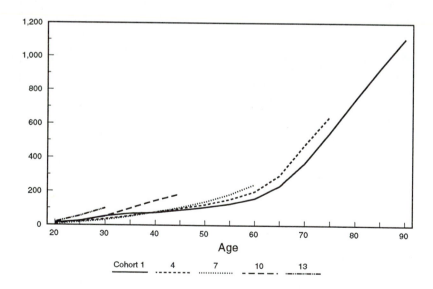

**Figure 3.5** Cumulative Social Security Spending per Survivor (% of GDP per capita)

the system. It does not help us to identify their net positions until we can say something about what they have put into it.

Unfortunately, although there is a series of incidence studies of taxation dating from the 1930s and 1940s (such as Clark, 1938, or Shirras and Rostas, 1942) to 1990 (CSO, 1993), these studies concentrate on the incidence of taxation by income group. There is remarkably little information on relative tax payments by age in Britain. There is not even very much information about incomes by age in a form which could allow estimates of relative tax payments.

The allocation of tax payments to successive cohorts is therefore rather cruder than that of the spending items (for details see Hills, 1992, Appendix). In outline, tax revenues were divided into four categories: employee National Insurance Contributions (NICs); income tax; indirect taxes; and estate duties (or, in each case, their earlier equivalents). Total education, health and social security spending was then assumed to be financed by all employee NICs, and the proportion of the other three categories which was needed to cover the balance.[10] Employee NICs were divided equally between the 20–59-year-old population. Income tax was also divided equally between 20–59-year-olds up to 1941. After then, a rising proportion was also allocated to those aged over 60, the proportion being based on CSO figures for the relative income tax payments of 'retired' and 'non-retired' households since the 1960s. A similar procedure was followed for indirect taxes, although in this case, the retired population was assumed to be carrying part of the burden before the War. Estate duties and their equivalents were assumed to be paid by each cohort as its members die, a kind of payment in arrears for the welfare state.

In view of the relatively unsophisticated nature of this allocation, later in the chapter we examine the sensitivity of the results to making an alternative assumption, allocating the costs of financing the welfare state in proportion to age-related gross incomes which result from our own model, LIFEMOD.

The results of the base assumption are illustrated in Figure 3.6. This puts the increasing receipts of each successive cohort from the welfare state in a rather different light, since the amounts each cohort pays have been rising even more rapidly. Indeed, by age 75 the average survivor in Cohort 4 had already paid more than the average survivor in Cohort 1 had by age 90, and the average survivor in Cohort 7 had paid even more than this by age 60. Later cohorts may get more, but they also pay more.

---

10  In effect, the counterfactual assumption is that, had the welfare state not existed, employee NICs would not exist either, and all other taxes would be equiproportionately lower by the amount equivalent to the balance of welfare spending.

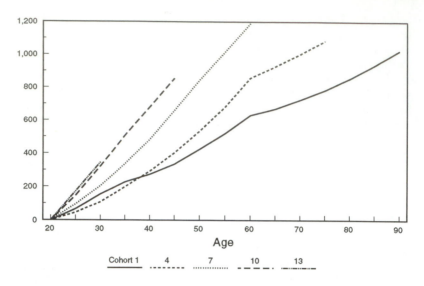

**Figure 3.6** Cumulative Tax Paid per Survivor (% of GDP per capita)

## Net receipts

Figure 3.7 combines the results illustrated in Figures 3.3–3.6 to show the average cumulative net benefits to the survivors in each cohort by the time they receive any given age. For the earliest cohort, cumulative receipts up to age 90 can be shown; for Cohort 16, the picture only extends as far as age 15.

For each cohort, the cumulative net position follows a wave pattern. Up to age 20, people are gaining, mainly through the education system. After that, their accumulated surplus first reduces and then turns into a deficit as average tax payments in people's working lives exceed average health and social security receipts. After retirement, tax payments drop, health and social security receipts rise steeply, and eventually the average cohort member surviving long enough goes into lifetime surplus.

What the diagram shows is that with the increase in the scale of the welfare state in the thirty years after the War, the *amplitude* of this wave has increased. The cumulative net benefits by age 20 are higher for each successive cohort, but so is the accumulated net deficit by age 60.

What the diagram does *not* give us, however, is an answer to the main question under investigation of equity between cohorts. This is first because later cohorts are surviving longer than earlier ones – so the average member may survive long enough to be in a better lifetime position than the average member of an earlier cohort, even if the position at any given age is worse. Secondly, only Cohort 1 has got near to the end

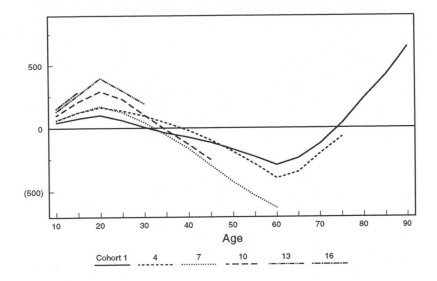

**Figure 3.7** Cumulative Net Gain per Survivor (% of GDP per capita)

of its life. Using data up to 1991, it is not at all clear how later cohorts will end up. Things look bad for Cohort 7, down by the equivalent of more than six years' worth of average income for each survivor aged 60, well below Cohorts 1 and 4 at the same age. But more generous pensions and better funded health care throughout retirement might yet change the end result.

Figure 3.8 shows the cumulative net position of each cohort *as a whole*, built up from the receipts of those surviving to each age, thus allowing for differential survival rates. In this diagram, a 'welfare generation' would end up above the break-even line; those 'born to pay' would end up below it. Table 3.3 gives more detailed figures for the cumulative positions by 1991 of each of the 18 cohorts born between 1901 and 1991.

At this point in the analysis, only one thing is clear: Cohorts 1 and 2 – the Alec Douglas-Home and Barbara Castle cohorts – do appear as net winners. By 1991, these groups' cumulative net receipts from the welfare state had already exceeded their net payments into it. Cohort 3 – the Harold Wilson cohort – had also almost reached break-even by the time its members had reached 80, so it too should end up as a net gainer. Beyond this, it is hard to say anything with certainty. Looking at Figure 3.8, Cohort 4 (Denis Healey's), tracking just below Cohort 1, look as if it too will end up as a net gainer, but for later ones it is hard to tell.

John Hills

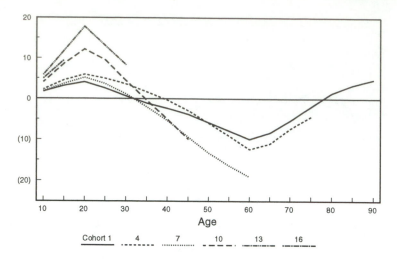

**Figure 3.8** Cumulative Net Gain for Cohort (millions of GDP per capita)

**Table 3.3** Cumulative Net Receipts by Cohort in 1991 (millions of GDP per capita)

| Cohort | Age in 1991 | Education | Health (low variation) | Social Security | Taxes[a] | Net benefit |
|---|---|---|---|---|---|---|
| 1 | 85–89 | 3.8 | 8.2 | 21.6 | -28.8 | +4.8 |
| 2 | 80–84 | 3.9 | 8.8 | 22.6 | -32.8 | +2.7 |
| 3 | 75–79 | 4.2 | 8.4 | 21.0 | -33.8 | -0.2 |
| 4 | 70–74 | 4.8 | 6.8 | 17.6 | -33.7 | -4.4 |
| 5 | 65–69 | 5.2 | 7.0 | 14.6 | -38.8 | -12.1 |
| 6 | 60–64 | 4.6 | 5.7 | 9.5 | -37.4 | -17.6 |
| 7 | 55–59 | 4.6 | 5.0 | 7.3 | -36.0 | -19.1 |
| 8 | 50–54 | 6.7 | 4.7 | 6.8 | -34.1 | -15.9 |
| 9 | 45–49 | 9.6 | 4.7 | 7.0 | -34.1 | -12.7 |
| 10 | 40–44 | 12.0 | 5.3 | 7.5 | -34.6 | -9.9 |
| 11 | 35–39 | 12.1 | 4.2 | 7.2 | -25.9 | -2.4 |
| 12 | 30–34 | 14.7 | 4.3 | 6.4 | -21.6 | +3.9 |
| 13 | 25–29 | 15.3 | 4.5 | 4.6 | -16.0 | +8.3 |
| 14 | 20–24 | 14.3 | 3.9 | 2.5 | -7.6 | +13.1 |
| 15 | 15–19 | 12.0 | 3.0 | 0.5 | - | +15.6 |
| 16 | 10–14 | 7.1 | 2.5 | - | - | +9.5 |
| 17 | 5–9 | 3.4 | 2.2 | - | - | +5.5 |
| 18 | 0–4 | - | 2.1 | - | - | +2.1 |

**Note:**
a    Taxes required to finance welfare services only.

This leads to one firm conclusion: it is very hard to say anything definitive about intergenerational equity on the basis of incomplete life-histories. Unless we project the analysis forward into the future, there is little we can say about cohorts born since the 1920s.

## 4.    Projections of Receipts and Payments to 2041

While the future – particularly over the fifty year period which we need to examine – is clearly highly uncertain, we do have some information to work on. First, we have official projections of the numbers of each cohort surviving to a given age (in this case, those in OPCS, 1993b). Second, we have the Government Actuary's (1990) projections of the future costs of the State Earnings Retirement Pension Scheme (SERPS), which represents the largest change to the future shape of the welfare state about which we already know. Beyond this, we can only work on the basis of current spending patterns.

### The base projection

The base projection here uses spending patterns as they were in relation to average incomes in 1991–92 for each group of a given age, and assumes that groups of the same age benefit from the equivalent level of spending in the future. Thus, 10–14-year-olds were benefiting from annual education spending equivalent to 24 per cent of GDP per capita in 1991–92 (about £2,400), so it is assumed that 10–14-year-olds will continue to benefit from the same level of spending per head relative to average incomes in the future.

The exception to this is that projected SERPS receipts are used rather than those actually being received by particular age groups in 1991–92, and the changing build-up of receipts for different cohorts is allowed for. The net benefits included from greater SERPS receipts are lower than the gross benefits to allow for the increased tax payments and reduced means-tested benefits which will result from them.[11]

The first column of Table 3.4 shows the projected total of spending on education, health and social security as a percentage of GDP which results from this process. Thus, if spending on the three services for people of a given age continued to have the same value in relation to average incomes as it did in 1991, their cost would rise from 22.2 per cent of GDP in 1991 to 26.3 per cent in 2041. This 4.1 percentage point increase

---

11  The results do not allow for the proposed increase in women's pension age to 65 after 2010.

**Table 3.4** Projected Total Spending on Education, Health and Social Security 1991 to 2041 (% of GDP; GB)

|        | 1991 spending patterns[a] | Social security price-linked[b] | Health spending rises by 0.5% p.a. above GDP p.c.[c] |
|--------|:---:|:---:|:---:|
| 1991   | 22.2 | 22.2 | 22.2 |
| 1996   | 22.3 | 21.4 | 22.5 |
| 2001   | 22.6 | 20.9 | 23.0 |
| 2006   | 22.9 | 20.6 | 23.5 |
| 2011   | 23.5 | 20.3 | 24.3 |
| 2016   | 24.0 | 20.1 | 25.1 |
| 2021   | 24.5 | 19.8 | 25.8 |
| 2026   | 25.2 | 19.7 | 26.9 |
| 2031   | 25.9 | 19.6 | 27.9 |
| 2036   | 26.3 | 19.3 | 28.7 |
| 2041   | 26.3 | 18.8 | 29.1 |

Notes:
a    Allowing for build-up of net receipts from SERPS (on 'earnings-linked' basis).
b    Allowing for net receipts from SERPS (on 'price-linked' basis).
c    And using high variation of health by age.

in the share of national income needed to finance the welfare state over a fifty year period contrasts with the 16.6 percentage point increase over the previous fifty years shown in Figure 3.1. The bulk of the increase comes from demographic factors – the ageing population.

This increased cost of the three services is assumed to be met by greater tax and national insurance payments by all age groups, with the relativities between individuals of each age staying as they were in 1991.[12]

### Results from the base projection

Figures 3.9 and 3.10 and Table 3.5 give the results of using projections on this basis. From Figure 3.9 it can be seen that, at any given age from 30, the position of surviving members of Cohort 7 is worse than that of those from any of the other cohorts. For later cohorts, the relative decline in position is reversed, although the later cohorts do not end up in as favourable a position as Cohorts 1 and 4.

---

12   This is not entirely satisfactory, as it does not allow for the rising relative income – and hence tax – levels of part of the elderly population which can be expected from greater occupational pension receipts in the future. This could imply that the net lifetime gains of Cohorts 7 to 10 are somewhat exaggerated (for later cohorts the lower tax payments at earlier ages and higher payments in retirement would roughly cancel out).

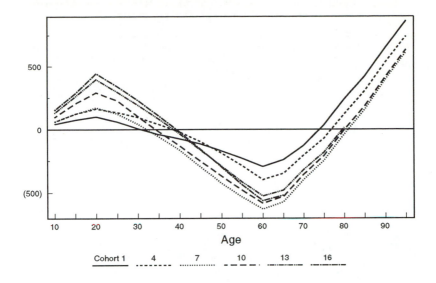

**Figure 3.9** Projected Cumulative Net Gain per Survivor (1991 spending patterns; % of GDP per capita)

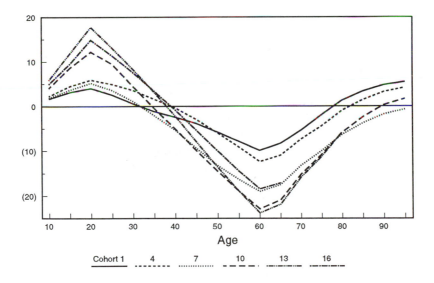

**Figure 3.10** Projected Cumulative Net Gain for Cohort (1991 spending patterns; million GDP per capita)

**Table 3.5** Cumulative Net Receipts by Cohort in 2041 (1991 spending pattern maintained; millions of GDP per capita)

| Cohort | Age in 2041 | Education | Health (low varation) | Social Security | Taxes[a] | Net benefit |
|--------|-------------|-----------|-----------------------|-----------------|----------|-------------|
| 1  | -     | 3.8  | 8.7  | 22.2 | -29.2 | 5.5   |
| 2  | -     | 3.9  | 10.4 | 24.6 | -33.8 | 5.2   |
| 3  | -     | 4.2  | 11.3 | 25.5 | -36.0 | 5.0   |
| 4  | -     | 4.8  | 11.5 | 25.6 | -37.6 | 4.4   |
| 5  | -     | 5.2  | 13.1 | 27.6 | -45.1 | 0.8   |
| 6  | -     | 4.6  | 12.9 | 28.1 | -45.8 | -0.2  |
| 7  | -     | 4.6  | 12.9 | 29.7 | -46.7 | 0.5   |
| 8  | -     | 6.7  | 13.9 | 32.7 | -51.0 | 2.4   |
| 9  | -     | 9.6  | 16.2 | 38.6 | -59.8 | 4.6   |
| 10 | 90–94 | 12.0 | 19.5 | 45.7 | -72.3 | 4.9   |
| 11 | 85–89 | 12.1 | 16.2 | 41.2 | -65.9 | 3.6   |
| 12 | 80–84 | 14.7 | 16.0 | 43.0 | -72.5 | 1.3   |
| 13 | 75–79 | 15.3 | 16.1 | 43.0 | -79.9 | -5.5  |
| 14 | 70–74 | 14.8 | 13.0 | 35.2 | -74.6 | -11.6 |
| 15 | 65-69 | 13.4 | 10.0 | 24.2 | -61.5 | -14.0 |
| 16 | 60–64 | 12.7 | 8.2  | 16.7 | -56.6 | -19.0 |
| 17 | 55–59 | 13.7 | 8.0  | 13.6 | -57.4 | -22.1 |
| 18 | 50–54 | 14.6 | 7.9  | 12.1 | -53.5 | -19.0 |

**Note:**

a    Taxes required to finance welfare services only. Tax receipts resulting from rise in SERPS netted out of social security.

However, later cohorts are surviving longer. The population projections used suggest a median life-span of 73 for Cohort 1, 77 for Cohort 4, 81 for Cohort 7 and 83 for Cohort 10. In each case, these ages are remarkably close to the break-even point at which cumulative net benefits become positive.

Figure 3.10 shows results for cohorts as a whole up to age 95 (beyond which there are too few survivors to make any appreciable difference). Cohorts 1 and 4 end up as net gainers, Cohort 7 breaks even, but Cohort 10 ends up as net gainers, longer life expectancy having a noticeable effect after age 80. Even projecting forward to 2041 is not long enough to give a definitive result for Cohorts 13 and 16, but they too look as if they will end up narrowly as net gainers.

Perhaps the most striking feature of the diagram, however, is the closeness of the end-positions to break-even. By and large, each cohort gets out something close to what it puts in. In contrast to the statements about 'considerable injustices between different generations' and about the unsustainability of the welfare state quoted at the start of this paper, the British welfare state comes out of this analysis as remarkably well-balanced.

Table 3.5 shows more detailed results for all of the cohorts born between 1901 and 1991.[13] The first four cohorts – Douglas-Home to Healey – are net gainers, ending up with a cumulative net benefit for each five year age group of roughly 5 million units of GDP per capita (or, at current population sizes, something under 10 per cent of one year's total GDP). The next three (Thatcher to Heseltine) make small net losses or gains. After that, Cohorts 8 to 12 (Smith to Kennedy) end up as net gainers, and it looks as if Cohort 13 (Taylor) will do so too.

On this base projection, therefore, the conclusion is very different from that described by Thomson for New Zealand. The only apparent losers – and only narrowly – is the cohort born between 1926 and 1931. The clearest 'welfare generation' is those born between 1901 and 1921.

Those born between 1921 and 1936 do not do so well. This partly reflects the timing of the expansion of the welfare state. Cohorts 6 and 7 are also two of the smallest cohorts. This gives some support to the idea that smaller cohorts lose out from having few members amongst whom to spread the costs of paying for welfare when they are of working age.

Table 3.6 shows the same results recalculated to express the position of the cohort as a whole as an average per member of the cohort alive at age 15–19. It shows how lifetime gross receipts per member build up from the equivalent of just under nine years' worth of GDP per capita for the earliest cohort to over eighteen for Cohort 10. Tax payments to finance the welfare state also grow towards the same level, but the growth comes a little later (and from a slightly lower base). The result of this is that the earliest cohorts – gaining from the rise in receipts but not affected so much by the rise in tax – end up as net gainers, to the extent of an average of something over one year's worth of GDP per capita for each member.

However, the scale of these net gains and losses is not enormous. The final column of the table shows the receipts of each cohort as a percentage of the tax it pays. Apart from the first four, the receipts of each of the cohorts with complete projected lifetimes is within eight per cent of the tax which it pays. Even the first four cohorts 'pay for' between 80 and 90 per cent of the benefits which they receive. Again, this is a long way from being generations which 'make contributions which cover only a fraction of their benefits' (Thomson, 1991, p. 1).

To summarise, what appears to have happened is the following. During this century, public spending on education, health and social security has grown from a low level to around 22 per cent of national

---

13 Projections were also made for later cohorts, so that the cost of spending on them could enter the calculation of tax liabilities for the cohorts in which we are interested. The same was done with spending on cohorts born before 1901.

income. If levels of provision for any age were to remain unchanged relative to average incomes (apart from SERPS), their total cost would grow to just over 26 per cent of national income over the next fifty years.[14] This spending is financed mainly by the working population at any time. Because the benefits of the welfare state are – for obvious reasons – weighted towards the latter parts of people's lives, there is a generation born in the early years of the century which has benefited from the expansion in the welfare state in their own retirement, but whose lifetime tax payments reflected the somewhat smaller levels of provision for their parents' generation. Later generations roughly break-even.

### Alternative assumptions about the future

All of this is based on the idea that the welfare state has reached some kind of maturity, and that relative levels of provision will now remain constant for any given age group. This is not, of course, necessarily so.

**Table 3.6** Projected Lifetime Receipts and Tax Payments Until 2041 (1991 spending pattern maintained[a])

| Cohort | Born | Age in 1991 | Size when 15–19 (m) | Cumulative receipts and payments (GDP per capita per member at 15–19) | | | Receipts as % tax |
| --- | --- | --- | --- | --- | --- | --- | --- |
| | | | | Receipts | Tax | Net gain | |
| 1 | 1901–06 | 85–89 | 4.0 | 8.7 | 7.3 | 1.4 | 119 |
| 2 | 1906–11 | 80–84 | 4.0 | 9.7 | 8.4 | 1.3 | 115 |
| 3 | 1911–16 | 75–79 | 3.9 | 10.6 | 9.3 | 1.3 | 114 |
| 4 | 1916–21 | 70–74 | 3.6 | 11.8 | 10.6 | 1.2 | 112 |
| 5 | 1921–26 | 65–69 | 3.7 | 12.3 | 12.1 | 0.2 | 102 |
| 6 | 1926–31 | 60–64 | 3.2 | 13.9 | 14.0 | -0.1 | 100 |
| 7 | 1931–36 | 55–59 | 3.1 | 15.4 | 15.2 | 0.2 | 101 |
| 8 | 1936–41 | 50–54 | 3.2 | 16.6 | 15.9 | 0.7 | 105 |
| 9 | 1941–46 | 45–49 | 3.6 | 18.0 | 16.7 | 1.3 | 108 |
| 10 | 1946–51 | 40–44 | 4.1 | 18.6 | 17.4 | 1.2 | 107 |
| Incomplete lifetimes | | | | | | | |
| 11 (to 90) | 1951–56 | 35–39 | 3.7 | 18.8 | 17.8 | 1.0 | 105 |
| 12 (to 85) | 1956–61 | 30–34 | 4.0 | 18.4 | 18.1 | 0.3 | 102 |
| 13 (to 80) | 1961–66 | 25–29 | 4.5 | 16.7 | 17.9 | -1.2[b] | 93 |

Notes:
a    But allowing for build-up of net receipts from SERPS (on 'earnings-linked' basis). Health on 'low variation' basis.
b    Cohort 13 is in a slightly less favourable position at age 80 than was Cohort 10 at the same age.

---

14 Of course, the economic cycle and changing unemployment may be superimposed on – and at times be larger than – these demographic and structural effects. In effect, the projections assume constant age-related unemployment from 1991–92.

First, current government policy is not to link social security benefits to current living standards as the base projection assumes, but to link them to prices. Benefits will thus gradually lose value in terms of average incomes and the accounting unit – GDP per capita – used here. The second column of Table 3.4 shows the effect on the overall total of government spending if this policy was followed for the next fifty years (assuming annual real per capita growth of 1.5 per cent, in line with the assumption made by the Government Actuary, 1990). In this case, the cost of the three services falls from 22 per cent of GDP in 1991 to 19 per cent in 2041.

Alternatively, there may be pressures for the welfare state to grow. For instance, spending on health care for given age groups has risen more rapidly than average incomes for much of the period since the War (and when it did not in the early 1980s, the strains were apparent). Also, the 'low variation' assumption made about health spending by age might understate growth in spending as the population ages. The third column of Table 3.4 therefore shows the effects of adding an annual 0.5 per cent rise in the cost of health care[15] to the base projection, and of assuming that the 'high variation' in health spending with age is correct. In this case, the total cost of welfare spending reaches more than 29 per cent of GDP by 2041.

These alternatives represent significantly different paths for the welfare state: in the first, it is rolled back from its current scale, while in the second it resumes growth. As a test of the sensitivity of the base results, Table 3.7 shows the effects of these alternative projections on the position of the cohorts born up to 1966 in the same form as Table 3.6.

The first part of the table shows the effects of price-linking social security. For the four earliest cohorts, there is little effect by comparison with the base projection: the 1.5 per cent per year relative decline in the value of social security payments makes little difference until after most of their members have died. However, the change pushes cohorts from Cohort 5 (the Thatcher cohort) onwards into making net losses, although they still receive back over 90 per cent of the tax they pay.

What would happen, as the welfare state scaled down in this way, would be that those currently in middle age would receive significantly lower pensions themselves in thirty or so years' time, but would not save very much in tax from only slightly reduced pensions paid to their parents' generation. If they wanted to maintain their relative living standards in retirement, they would have to pay more privately towards their own pensions at the same time as paying the tax bill for those currently retired. Eventually, for much later cohorts, social security

---

15  Say, because of medical advance. Demographic factors and maintaining the relative pay of health workers are already accounted for.

(apart, as it happens, from SERPS, which is in certain ways linked to average earnings) would cease to have very much importance either way and the system would return to some kind of lower level intergenerational balance. In short, the current price-linking policy is of most disadvantage to those cohorts who are currently middle-aged.

As one might expect, Table 3.7 shows that the alternative scenario of a gradual build-up of health costs while the relative values of other items remained the same would have the reverse effect. The gains of the first few cohorts are increased by comparison with the base case because the 'high variation' assumption about health spending allocates more of the spending in the 1980s and 1990s to them. The position of subsequent cohorts is also improved, although none of them reaches as favourable a position as the first four.

### Alternative allocations of benefits and taxes

As mentioned above, it is possible to allocate the benefits from and costs of the welfare state in alternative ways to those used in the base case. It might be that the conclusions reached would be different if those alternatives had been used. Table 3.8 presents a sensitivity analysis

**Table 3.7** Projected Lifetime Receipts and Tax Payments Until 2041 (variations to 1991 spending pattern)

| | (a) Social security price-linked[a] | | | | (b) Health spending rises 0.5% p.a. above GDP p.c.[b] | | | |
|---|---|---|---|---|---|---|---|---|
| | Cumulative receipts and payments (GDP p.c. per member at age 15–19) | | | Receipt as % tax | Cumulative receipts and payments (GDP p.c. per member at age 15–19) | | | Receipt at % tax |
| Cohort | Receipts | Tax | Net | | Receipts | Tax | Net | |
| 1 | 8.7 | 7.3 | 1.4 | 119 | 9.1 | 7.3 | 1.7 | 124 |
| 2 | 9.6 | 8.4 | 1.2 | 115 | 10.1 | 8.4 | 1.7 | 120 |
| 3 | 10.5 | 9.2 | 1.2 | 113 | 11.1 | 9.3 | 1.8 | 119 |
| 4 | 11.5 | 10.5 | 1.0 | 110 | 12.4 | 10.6 | 1.8 | 117 |
| 5 | 11.7 | 11.9 | -0.2 | 98 | 12.9 | 12.1 | 0.8 | 107 |
| 6 | 13.0 | 13.7 | -0.7 | 95 | 14.7 | 14.0 | 0.7 | 105 |
| 7 | 14.0 | 14.8 | -0.8 | 94 | 16.3 | 15.3 | 1.0 | 107 |
| 8 | 14.8 | 15.3 | -0.5 | 97 | 17.7 | 16.1 | 1.6 | 110 |
| 9 | 15.6 | 15.9 | -0.2 | 99 | 19.2 | 17.0 | 2.3 | 113 |
| 10 | 15.8 | 16.3 | -0.5 | 97 | 19.9 | 17.8 | 2.2 | 112 |
| Incomplete lifetimes | | | | | | | | |
| 11 (to 90) | 15.8 | 16.4 | -0.6 | 96 | 19.8 | 18.2 | 1.6 | 109 |
| 12 (to 85) | 15.2 | 16.3 | -1.1 | 93 | 19.1 | 18.6 | 0.5 | 103 |
| 13 (to 80) | 13.5 | 15.8 | -2.2 | 86 | 17.2 | 18.5 | -1.3 | 93 |

**Notes:**
a    Assuming to fall by 1.5% in relation to GDP p.c. Allows for 'price-linked' SERPS.
b    With 'high variation' in health receipts with age.

showing the receipts of each cohort as a percentage of the taxes they pay under seven variations by comparison with the base case.

The first two of these are those already presented in Table 3.7. Variation C incorporates the same assumptions as the base case, but allocates all of the benefits of education to parents[16] rather than to those being educated. This would be appropriate if it was assumed that, in the absence of state provision, parents would have paid for just as much education for their children. Its effect is to bring the benefits of the post-War expansion of education forward to earlier cohorts, increasing the gains of the earliest cohorts, and turning Cohorts 5–9 into net gainers to the tune of 10 to over 20 per cent of the tax they pay. After that, the balance stabilises again.

Table 3.8 Sensitivity Analysis: Receipts of Cohorts as Percentage of Tax Paid

|  | Base case | Variation A | B | C | D | E | F |
|---|---|---|---|---|---|---|---|
| Tax | As base | As base | As base | As base | Alt. | Alt. | Alt. |
| Health variation | Low | Low | High | Low | Low | High | High |
| Future social security linked | Earnings | Prices | Earnings | Earnings | Earnings | Earnings | Prices |
| Future health costs | As base | As base | Rising | As base | As base | As base | As base |
| Education allocated to | Children | Children | Children | Parents | Children | Parents | Parents |
| 1 | 119 | 119 | 124 | 122 | 110 | 117 | 117 |
| 2 | 115 | 115 | 120 | 117 | 109 | 116 | 115 |
| 3 | 114 | 113 | 119 | 121 | 108 | 119 | 118 |
| 4 | 112 | 110 | 117 | 124 | 109 | 126 | 124 |
| 5 | 102 | 98 | 107 | 117 | 102 | 121 | 118 |
| 6 | 100 | 95 | 105 | 116 | 100 | 120 | 116 |
| 7 | 101 | 94 | 107 | 123 | 102 | 127 | 121 |
| 8 | 105 | 97 | 110 | 121 | 106 | 126 | 118 |
| 9 | 108 | 99 | 113 | 116 | 109 | 120 | 112 |
| 10 | 107 | 97 | 112 | 109 | 108 | 112 | 103 |
| Incomplete lifetimes |  |  |  |  |  |  |  |
| 11 | 105 | 96 | 109 | 106 | 106 | 108 | 99 |
| 12 | 102 | 93 | 103 | 100 | 101 | 99 | 92 |
| 13 | 93 | 86 | 93 | 92 | 92 | 90 | 83 |

The next variation, D, is like the base case, except that in this case taxes are allocated in an alternative to the way described in section 2, which might put too much of the burden on the working population, and which allows for little variation within either the working or retired populations. Instead, taxes are allocated simply in proportion to the gross

16 To be precise, the age group 25 years older than the direct beneficiaries of education.

incomes of those of different ages, using the relativities of gross incomes by age which are generated by LIFEMOD using the 1991 tax and social security systems (see Chapter 5). This shifts the tax burden onto later ages by comparison with the base case. In terms of its effect on different cohorts, it has the opposite effect to variation C, reducing the net gains of the earlier three cohorts by comparison with the base case. For later cohorts the effect of using the alternative tax assumption is slight.

The other two columns show the effects of making various combinations of the alternative assumptions – Variation E combining the allocation of education to parents, the alternative tax assumption, and the 'high variation' assumption about health costs, while Variation F adds the assumption that social security payments will continue to be price-rather than earnings-linked. The table shows that the use of different assumptions can clearly affect the precise position of any of the cohorts, but none of the combinations suggests the presence of a cohort only paying for a 'fraction of its benefits', or only receiving back a fraction of the taxes it pays. While there may be 'welfare generations' to the extent of receiving net gains of up to 25 per cent of the tax they pay, the greatest net loss for those with completed lives by 2041 does not exceed 6 per cent of the taxes they pay under any of the scenarios.[17] It is thus hard to identify a generation which is 'born to pay' to any great extent.

## 5.     Conclusions

This chapter describes an exercise to allocate the benefits from education, health and social security, and the taxes required to finance them in Britain from 1921 to 2041 between five year age cohorts of the population. The aim was to investigate whether different cohorts taken as a whole end up as net gainers or net losers from the operation of the welfare state.

First, it appears that those born between 1901 and 1921 will get more out of the welfare state than they put in, although even this generation will have 'paid for' 80 to 90 per cent of what they receive under most assumptions. Of course individual members may fare far better or far worse than this average.

Second, it is not possible to reach conclusions about later cohorts unless one makes a projection of what will happen in the future. If one assumes that education, health and social security will (with the exception of allowing for the build-up of SERPS receipts) maintain their current values in relation to contemporary living standards over the next

---

17  The net loss for cohorts 12 and 13 by age 80 exceeds this in some cases, but the scale of net receipts between 80 and 95 is such that the cohorts are likely to come back much more closely into balance by the end of their lifetimes.

fifty years, cohorts born between 1921 and 1966 will end up roughly breaking-even, generally making small gains. This picture would be little changed if, on top of the effects of demographic change, health spending for people of a given age grew somewhat faster than average incomes.

However, if social security payments continued to be price- rather than income-linked over the next fifty years, the picture would deteriorate for those born after 1921, and all the subsequent cohorts examined would end up as net losers, albeit narrowly (they would still get back more than 90 per cent of what they would have 'put in').

Alternative ways of allocating education and health benefits and the tax required to finance spending also increase or decrease the estimated net gains or losses for particular cohorts, but they do not affect the overall conclusion: for most cohorts aggregate lifetime benefits are not very different from aggregate lifetime taxes, and it is hard to identify a 'born to pay' generation which gets back significantly less than it puts in.

It was suggested above that the analogy of an explosive – and unstable – 'chain letter' game was misleading as a description of the operation of the British welfare state. A better analogy might be the following. A single line of people – stretching indefinitely into the distance – sit next to one another on chairs. Each has a box of chocolates. When the game starts, each in turn passes their box of chocolates to the person on the left. The person at the far left-hand end of the line ends up a net gainer, with two boxes of chocolates. Every one else eventually breaks-even, ending up with a single box of chocolates, *provided* that the line carries on indefinitely and that no one changes the rules. However, if someone down the line was to panic in the interval between passing on their original box and receiving their neighbour's, and say that the game ought to be stopped, it is they who would end up as the only losers.

In the case of the British welfare state, those born in the early years of the century are the equivalent of the person at the left-hand end of the line, and they end up as clear net gainers. Given that they lived through the Depression of the 1930s and were the generation who had to fight the Second World War, it might be thought churlish to begrudge them this gain; after all, intergenerational equity is not just about the welfare state.

Those of us born later are the equivalent of those further down the line. In the end we shall generally get back what we put in – *provided* that we do not start calling the game off by abolishing or substantially scaling down the welfare state. However, individual members of a particular cohort may well have very different interests from its average member. Date of birth is only one of the many characteristics determining how the welfare state affects people. For individuals, the differences in the net lifetime effects of the welfare state which result from their income levels, gender, and family circumstances may be much more important. While this chapter has abstracted from all these other differences, it is such intra-cohort variation which we explore in the chapters which follow.

Chapter Four

# Simulating Lifetime Income Distribution and Redistribution

## Jane Falkingham, Ann Harding and Carli Lessof

As Chapter One has discussed, the idea that social policy, and in particular social security systems, can be viewed as a kind of counter-life cycle device has a long pedigree dating from Rowntree onwards. Beveridge himself was explicit in his aim that social insurance was not an attempt to take money from the rich and give to the poor but rather it should provide a mechanism to smooth out the average person's income from periods of comparative plenty to periods of want (Evans and Glennerster, 1993).

However, despite these explicit goals, evaluation of the redistributive effect of social security systems has largely been limited to cross-sectional studies with attempts to examine *lifetime* income distribution and redistribution being few and far between.[1] Although annual net fiscal incidence studies are useful for measuring the extent of income redistribution at any one point in time, they tell us very little about what to expect over lifetimes. Programmes that on an annual basis appear to be very successful in redistributing income towards the poor may result in more varied outcomes when viewed across a longer period. For example, at any single point in time, a large proportion of those on low incomes are retirees who might have enjoyed high incomes in the past. Others are low income students who will probably earn much higher incomes in the future. Thus taken over a lifetime, incomes might be much more equally distributed than on a cross-sectional basis.

Similarly, whilst taxes may appear progressive in standard fiscal incidence studies it is likely that the cash transfer recipients of today were

---

1 To our knowledge, comprehensive attempts to quantify the redistributive impact of social security over the lifetime are to date limited to Harding (1993) for Australia, and Nelissen (1994) for the Netherlands.

the high taxpayers of yesterday. It may be that, as Beveridge envisaged, over a lifetime all of the redistribution achieved by taxation and expenditure programs is intrapersonal rather than interpersonal.

To disentangle the relative strengths of these different types of redistribution requires information about the same people to be collected regularly throughout their lives. As Atkinson points out the 'immediate problem with the lifetime approach is that of obtaining the required data' (1983, p. 45). In contrast to the wealth of cross-sectional data, there is a comparative dearth of lifetime information. Although there are some longitudinal data available in the UK[2] none is entirely appropriate. The scarce data that are available are incomplete for any cohorts except those that have now reached the oldest ages of the population. Even if a complete panel were available, problems would still remain in reaching conclusions about the effects of the *current* social security system, as taxes and benefits in earlier parts of people's lives will have been paid and received under different systems. Given these limitations, an alternative is to simulate lifetime profiles. There are a number of possible methods available to simulate lifetime income data.

## 1.    Simulating Longitudinal Data

Economists and econometricians in the past have used a range of techniques to simulate lifetime income profiles. A common approach is to simulate particular features of the life cycle such as the distribution of earnings or of labour supply over the entire life cycle. Blinder (1974) pioneered a life cycle model of consumer behaviour for the US, simulating earnings and inheritance for individuals with different taste parameters (e.g. between labour and leisure), whilst Blomquist (1976) used wage rate, labour supply, assets, inheritance and tax functions to simulate the distribution of lifetime income in Sweden.

Such models may utilise longitudinal data collected over several time periods and use these to estimate lifetime earnings, labour supply or other functions (Lillard, 1977). Others may use several cross-sectional surveys to produce *pseudo cohorts* (Winter, 1991), whilst some may simply employ cross-sectional data for one year and create *synthetic cohorts* (Ghez and Becker, 1975; Miller, 1981). Here the characteristics of those captured in the single sample survey are attributed to the simulated cohort.

Whilst the above approaches shed light on particular aspects of lifetime profiles they all fail, to a greater or lesser degree, to capture the

---

2    For example, the 1946 MRC National Survey of Health and Development; the 1958 National Child Development Study; the 1970 British Cohort Study; and the OPCS Longitudinal Survey 1971–1991. The latter has the critical limitation of not including income data. In the future, data will be available from the new British Household Panel Survey.

enormous degree of change in the circumstances of individuals over time. For example, plotting the lifetime earnings profile of married men fails to take into account the fact that very few men remain constantly married and constantly in the labour force for their entire married lives. From longitudinal data we know that families are constantly dissolving and reforming; that earnings vary enormously from year to year, even for those who are employed full-time full-year; and that there is frequent movement in and out of the labour force and between full- and part-time work (particularly for women). All of this results in substantial relative income mobility, with individuals and families moving up and down the income distribution from year to year.

Recognition of this diversity and change in individuals' circumstances during the life cycle is therefore essential if we are to build up any picture of lifetime welfare. The relatively recent technique of *dynamic microsimulation* offers such an approach. Microsimulation models were pioneered by Guy Orcutt in the US in the late 1950s and 1960s (Orcutt, 1957; Orcutt *et al.*, 1961, 1976). The defining quality of such models is that they deal with the characteristics and behaviour of micro-units, such as individuals, families or households.

There are three major types of microsimulation models: static models; dynamic population models; and dynamic cohort models.[3] The type of simulation model which is applicable is dependent on the question which needs to be answered.

The most widely used are *static simulation models.* These are used for estimating the immediate impact of policy changes by systematically varying certain behavioural relations and/or institutional conditions of a microdata base. Such models take as their microdata base cross-sectional information on a representative sample of the population of a country e.g. both TAXBEN (Johnson *et al.*, 1990) and POLIMOD[4] are based on data from the Family Expenditure Survey (FES).

*Dynamic population models* also take a sample of the population as their initial microdata base. However, in this instance the sample is then projected forward through time. *Ageing* of the cohort is achieved through explicit modelling of demographic and socio-economic process. Because the attributes of each person at time *t+1* are determined using the attributes at time *t*, the cohort can be said to be aged 'dynamically' rather than 'statically'. The simulation of events is accomplished by the use of streams of randomly generated numbers combined with a Monte Carlo selection process and the relevant transition probabilities. For example, when simulating mortality, a randomly generated number ranging from 0 to 1, drawn from a uniform distribution, can be assigned to the record

---

3   For a full account of the different types of microsimulation models and their applications, see Harding (1993, Chapter 2).
4   POLIMOD has been constructed by the Microsimulation Unit, University of Cambridge.

of each individual for every period. If this randomly generated number is less than the probability of dying in that year, given the age and gender of the person, then the individual is selected to die and their records are terminated. However, where the random number exceeds or equals the mortality probability, the person survives to the next year of life. In this way, they become part of the pool 'at risk of death' in the following year, when they are subject to the same procedure (with a new probability of death and different random numbers).

The occurrence of other demographic events may also be simulated. For example, a family unit could be diminished in size through divorce or augmented through the birth of a child during the simulation process. By the process of dynamic demographic ageing, the size of the cross-section under investigation will be altered. Dynamic population models are therefore particularly useful for forecasting the future characteristics of the population and thus for modelling the effects of policy change over the *longer* period. For example, in the US the dynamic population model, DYNASIM, has been used to estimate both the needs of the elderly in the twenty-first century and the long-range effects of social security amendments (Zedlewski, 1990); whilst in Britain PENSIM is being developed to look at the influences on the income distribution of pensioners up to 2030 (Hancock, Mallendar and Pudney, 1992).

*Dynamic cohort models* employ the same dynamic ageing process as population models. However, the microdata base is not underpinned by the characteristics of a real sample unit; rather the simulation process itself creates 'synthetic' micro-units and forecasts the whole life cycle from birth to death. The advantage of this type of microsimulation is the availability of information about the *complete* life histories of each cohort member. In contrast, dynamic population models typically produce incomplete life histories, mapping only a few decades of the lives of individuals from many different age groups (although the same lifetime profiles could be generated using a dynamic population model, where the micro-unit is children aged 0 and the simulation period 100 years!). Dynamic cohort models, with their ability to take into account the degree of change over time of each individual's personal circumstances, are thus particularly suitable for addressing questions concerned with lifetimes and the life cycle, for example analyses of times of want and plenty.

Existing examples of such dynamic cohort models are very limited. They include DEMOGEN within Statistics Canada (Wolfson, 1988), the German SFB3 model (Hain and Helberger, 1986) and the Australian HARDING model (Harding, 1993). The results in subsequent sections of this book are based upon LIFEMOD – a dynamic cohort microsimulation model constructed by the Welfare State Programme at the London School of Economics over the period 1989–93.[5] Below we describe the key

---

5   LIFEMOD benefited enormously from watching the earlier development of

characteristics of LIFEMOD and discuss some of the problems and limitations.

## 2.     LIFEMOD – A Dynamic Cohort Microsimulation Model

LIFEMOD is an example of dynamic cohort microsimulation, simulating the life histories of a cohort of 2,000 males and 2,000 females. Each individual is followed from birth through to death, experiencing major life events such as schooling, marriage, childbirth, children leaving home, employment and retirement.

The LIFEMOD cohort is 'born' in 1985, and subsequently lives for up to 95 years in a world that remains the same as it was in their birth year. Thus the model is not a representation of the *actual* British population in 1985. Nor does not attempt to predict what the actual experience of the cohort born in Britain in 1985 will be. Instead it represents what would happen to a single cohort if they lived their entire lives under the demographic and economic conditions as they were in Britain in that year.

A striking example of the effect of the steady state assumption is provided by Figure 4.1, which compares the LIFEMOD and 1985 population structures. The most prominent feature is the much greater proportion of persons of older ages in LIFEMOD than in the observed population. This is because the theoretical cohort has been exposed to significantly lower risks of mortality over the entire life-course than is the case for current generations who have reached old age. For example, a surviving 85-year-old in 1985 was born in the year 1900. Infant mortality rates were much higher then those observed in 1985, being around 150 per 1,000 at the turn of the century compared with 11–13 per 1,000 in the 1980s. Likewise adult mortality rates in the 1920s and 1930s when this person was in their twenties and thirties were again much higher than contemporary rates. Mortality rates for persons aged 25–34 in the late 1920s were 3–4 per 1,000 in contrast to less than 1 per 1,000 today. Thus the real cohort born in 1900 were less likely to survive than those in the model cohort. Figure 3.2 above indicates how mortality patterns with age have changed over the century.

Throughout the discussion of the model result, it should be appreciated that this is a hypothetical population; the model *shows what the population would look like if the demographic, labour force, income and other characteristics of the population and all government policies in force in 1985 remained unchanged for 95 years.*

---

HARDING, also at the LSE, and learning where it was safe to tread.

Proportionate Age Structure Pyramid for Population of Britain 1985

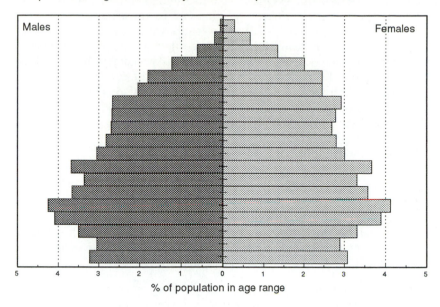

Proportionate Age Structure Pyramid for Population of LIFEMOD

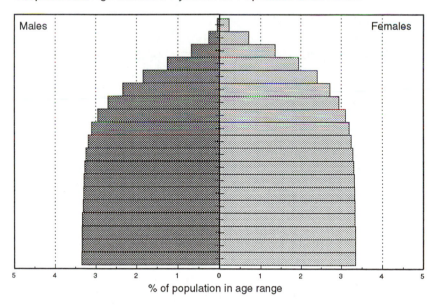

**Figure 4.1** Age Structure Pyramids

Although the steady state assumption results in a highly stylized 'population' it nevertheless provides a useful benchmark against which current government policies, and changes to those policies, can be evaluated. It allows us to abstract from the influences of period and cohort effects and to analyse the lifetime effects of the tax and benefit system as they were structured at one particular moment in time; thus controlling for the patterns of variation between cohort experiences discussed in Chapter 3. Such a steady state world is also assumed in other dynamic cohort models such as HARDING (1990, 1993), DEMOGEN (Wolfson, 1990) and SFB3 (Galler and Wagner, 1986).

**The structure of LIFEMOD**

Figure 4.2 illustrates the processes simulated by LIFEMOD which generate the results presented in the remainder of this book. The construction of the model is described in detail in Falkingham and Lessof (1991, 1992), Falkingham *et al.* (1993), Hills and Lessof (1993), Propper and Upward (1993) and Winter (forthcoming). In outline, the 'life histories' of each individual are built up as follows:

- Half the members of the sample are designated as men, half as women, and they are allocated a parental social class (with proportions matching the actual social class distribution of parents in 1985).
- Their *length of life* is determined.
- Their *educational* histories are built up, with probabilities of receiving private or state education, staying on at school, participating in youth training, going on to University or other tertiary education, returning to education as a mature student, and so on depending on parental social class and previous educational history. This includes allocation of the public cost of each of these. Student grants are also allocated at this stage (with amounts received depending on parental social class).
- *Family* histories are built up. Cohort members form couples (through marriage or 'serious' cohabitation), get divorced, remarry and so on. That is, in each time period, a proportion of unattached individuals are selected at random to form unions, and a proportion of existing unions to dissolve. The probabilities of these events depend on age and previous marital status. Partners come from within the sample (allowing the determination of joint incomes for couples), and there is a degree of 'assortative mating', based on educational background.
- Women have *children*, with probabilities of giving birth varying with marital status (some become lone parents without first being married or cohabiting), previous births and age, again reflecting actual fertility patterns in 1985. Children stay with the mother when marriages dissolve (so that widowers are the only male lone parents),

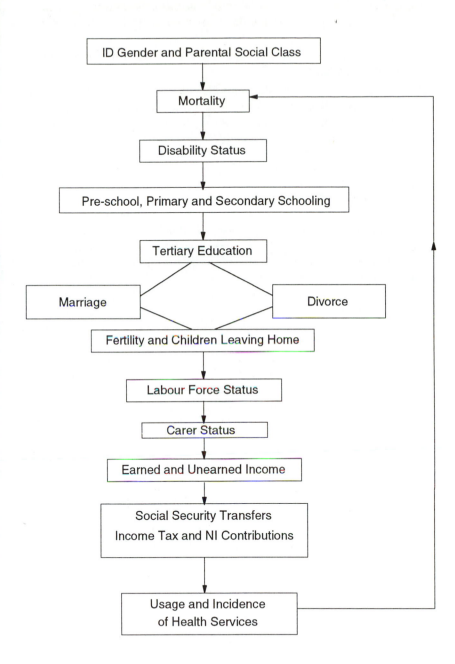

**Figure 4.2** The Structure of LIFEMOD

and leave home (for benefit and income calculation purposes) between ages 16 and 18 (depending on the educational history of their parents).

- A history of the use (and cost) of *health* services is built up, as well as a history of *disability*.

- After assignment of *carer* status and family status determined above, the model calculates *labour force* participation and status – employed full time, employed part time, self-employed, unemployed and out of the labour force. Individuals move between different states with transition probabilities drawn from Labour Force Survey data (OPCS, 1993a, and earlier equivalents). These can vary in certain ways within a year with, for instance, some weeks of unemployment and others of employment. For simplicity, people are assumed not to work after pension age (60 for women, 65 for men). *Earnings* depend on an initial random factor ('talent'), education, gender, age, family status and labour force status. They also depend on previous earnings, with a 'random walk' element as well as career progression. Individuals are also assigned a history of investment income.

- On the basis of all of this information, the model calculates the *tax and benefit position* of each individual for each year from age 16 under the rules of the 1985 social security and direct tax system. We also examine the effects of the systems as they were structured in 1991. Components include: (i) *Contingent benefits*, which depend on circumstances rather than income, including Child Benefit and One Parent Benefit, maternity benefits, sickness and disability benefits, and Unemployment Benefit (allowing for recent employment history in a way which mimics the effects of contribution conditions); (ii) *National Insurance and pension contributions*, which depend on earnings, and which also build up rights to the basic state retirement pension, the State Earnings Related Pension Scheme, and occupational pensions. Some are within public sector pension schemes, others within private schemes, and a final group do not have occupational pensions at all; (iii) *State and private pensions and widows benefits*, depending on contribution records, and allowing for inheritance of state and occupational pension rights by widows (and of SERPS rights by widowers); (iv) *Income tax*, allowing for joint taxation of legally married couples (in the 1985 system); (v) *Means-tested benefits*, including Family Income Supplement (Family Credit in the 1991 system), Supplementary Benefit (Income Support in 1991), and 'passported' benefits. This allows for the division of years into periods of employment and unemployment (as these benefits are calculated on a weekly, rather than an annual basis), for joint assessment of married and cohabiting couples, and for a probability of non-take up (depending on the size of entitlement); (vi) *Maintenance* payments are made from ex-partners to lone parents with children aged under 19 and in full-time education (the probability of payment being made depending on the benefit status of both ex-partners).

The simulation process requires transition probabilities or behavioural equations as inputs for every variable that is generated. The various probabilities of demographic and other events occurring to people in LIFEMOD are estimated from an enormous range of data sources but most notably published official statistics, especially the demographic series produced by OPCS (OPCS, 1986a, 1986b); and secondary analysis of the three major sample social surveys in Britain – the Family Expenditure Survey, General Household Survey and Labour Force Survey. As far as possible all input data were calculated for the year 1985. Where probabilities of transitions between states are required, for example, for labour force participation, data on status in 1984, 1985 and 1986 were used.

## 3.    Caveats, Qualifications and Health Warnings

The use of microsimulation models in distributional analysis of the kind presented in the following chapters involves a number of difficult issues whose significance should be fully appreciated when interpreting the ensuing results. Undoubtedly the main problem confronting microsimulation modellers is data. As stated above, the probabilities of moving between various states in LIFEMOD are estimated from cross-sectional data. While every attempt was made realistically to simulate transitions there is no way of validating the model. Since no one will actually live out their life in a perpetual 1985 world, we simply cannot know how well the resultant dynamic profiles match the lifepaths of individuals.

There are also a number of other major issues which should be born in mind.

### Indirect taxes, local government and benefits in kind

Firstly, LIFEMOD currently ignores indirect taxes and is limited to the major cash transfers and benefits in kind received from education and health. Local government taxes and transfers are also omitted, with the single exception of local authority administered student maintenance grants. The results outlined in this book therefore only deal with the lifetime redistribution of cash income and certain benefits in kind, financed by personal income tax transfers.

The inclusion of expenditure taxes, local government taxes and other tax revenues could make a substantial difference to the findings. In the UK in 1985, income taxes and National Insurance Contributions amounted to only 52 per cent of central government revenues. During the 1980s the British government has pursued a policy of shifting the tax burden from one of 'tax as you earn' to 'tax as you spend' and this has obvious implications for redistribution. In order to allow for this, some of the results look at the whole personal tax system, taken as a percentage of gross income (see Chapter 7).

Benefits in kind from other government funded services and other non-cash incomes will also affect lifetime redistribution. For example, Evandrou *et al.* (1993) show that for renters, there is a clear decline in average housing subsidies as one rises through the income distribution, while imputed rents to owner occupiers show the opposite pattern (Hills, 1991). However, although in an ideal world one would like to include benefits in kind received from both housing and other social services, the sectors we cover – education, health and social security – together accounted for 87 per cent of total welfare spending in 1985/6 (Table 8A.2 in Le Grand, 1990). Thus, despite these caveats, the analysis presented below is still very instructive, given that these are the main tools designed to achieve income redistribution objectives in modern societies.

**The question of the counterfactual**

A second issue is that in assessing the impact of the tax or social security system upon the distribution of income, the distribution *after* intervention necessarily has to be compared with the distribution *before* intervention. This immediately raises the question of what the most appropriate 'before' benchmark – or counterfactual – is. In what follows we observe convention and measure the redistributive effect of the tax and social security systems against the original distribution of pre-tax and pre-transfer income. While it is clearly invalid to assume that the pattern of factor incomes would remain the same if there was no government, such an assumption is implicit in this study as there are no data available indicating how the lifetime distribution of factor income in Britain would change if the government miraculously disappeared.

**Assumed incidence of transfers and taxes**

A third difficulty concerns the assumed incidence of transfers and income taxes. The benefit of cash transfers is assumed to be fully incident upon those to whom they are paid. This assumption is not uncontroversial. It is arguable that the benefit of Child Benefit is incident equally upon a husband and wife, or indeed upon the children, rather than solely upon the person who is the formal recipient. Yet alternative assumptions are also not straightforward. The mother has been made the recipient of Child Benefit (family allowances) precisely because of doubts as to who received the benefit when it was paid to the husband. Similarly it is not clear that the benefits are fully incident upon children (Barro, 1974). Thus, while sensitivity analysis can be conducted on the impact of different incidence assumptions, the results in this book use the standard incidence assumptions; with Child Benefit incident on the female partner and supplementary benefit on the male, if present.[6]

Likewise, the burden of taxation is assumed to be fully incident upon those legally liable to pay it. Those with liabilities are also assumed to pay them in full and no account is taken of possible tax evasion or of the underground economy. However, full compliance is not mirrored in the case of benefit receipt, and the model incorporates assumptions as to take-up rates. In LIFEMOD take-up of means-tested benefits is related to the size of entitlement; the higher the entitlement the greater the likelihood of the individual claiming it.

The benefits of education and health services have been assumed to be wholly incident upon those using the services and their value has been assumed to be equal to their cost of provision. Again, these assumptions could be queried (see the discussion in Chapter 3 above).

### Real economic growth

A fourth issue is whether and how to allow for real economic growth. The 'unit of account' in LIFEMOD is based on *current* earnings levels. One could allow for real earnings growth as well as career progression in earnings as people become older, but one would then also have to discount for the lower value of later receipts. Implicitly the approach adopted assumes that the effects of overall real economic growth and a real discount rate cancel each other out. However, occupational pensions and payments under SERPS do not keep pace with average earnings once people retire. This means that, *once in payment*, benefits which are indexed to *prices* rather than earnings, such as SERPS rights in retirement, are assumed to slip back each year by the *difference* between prices and earnings movements. Their levels in the model thus decline with age; more rapidly in the case of private occupational pensions and Guaranteed Minimum Pensions, which do not even keep pace with inflation, let alone earnings. Implicitly other benefit rates, including the basic state pension, are assumed to maintain their relationship with average earnings. This has not, in fact, been British government policy since 1979, but what we are modelling is the effect of the 1985 *system*, not making a projection of what will happen under current policies (see Chapter 3 for a discussion of the effects on actual cohorts of price-linking social security).

---

6   Where calculations are based on equivalent income (see below) and the assumption is made of equal sharing between partners, the initial incidence of taxes and transfers between partners makes no difference.

In Chapters 8 and 11 assumptions concerning real earnings growth and interest rates are introduced. Increases to wage rates due to economic growth are imposed *in addition* to those due to age and experience. For these chapters the tax scales (i.e. lower and upper earnings limits) have also been amended to reflect the rising real wages. Elsewhere in the book, with the exception of pensions in payment, the results abstract from economic growth.

## 4.     Measuring Income and Welfare

The processes described above allow us to construct a number of different measures of income and welfare that are widely used in the following chapters.

*Original income* is income received from market, or private, sources and is calculated from labour income (earnings from employment and self-employment), investment income, occupational and personal pension receipts, and maintenance payments. Maintenance payments are treated as positive additions to original income for recipients but count as a negative item, reducing original income, for those paying it. Original income measures the resources available to individuals before the intervention of the state and it has been assumed that it is an appropriate standard against which to measure the redistributive effect of government taxes and expenditures. This implies that the original distribution of income would remain the same if no public sector existed. It is likely that in the absence of the welfare state people would behave differently, particularly in respect of savings behaviour and participation in pensions schemes; but in the absence of data on how Britons in 1985 would have behaved if the government and Mrs Thatcher had not existed the distribution of original income remains the best, albeit imperfect, counterfactual.

*Gross income* comprises original income plus *cash benefits*. Cash benefits in turn are composed of all cash transfers under the social security system, contributory and non-contributory, as well as local authority student grants.

*Net income* measures the amount of income individuals actually have available to spend each year. It is calculated as gross income minus all direct taxes (income tax and National Insurance Contributions). Although compulsory, local authority taxes are not included and so net income here is not a true measure of disposable income. The unit of analysis throughout is the individual. Where there is joint taxation of (legally married) couples, the joint liabilities of husbands and wives are apportioned between them in proportion to their contributions to their joint taxable income, so that all income tax payments are ultimately made on an individual basis.

*Final income* is net income plus the imputed benefit from services in kind. The benefit is proportional to the cost of their provision. Here this *in kind income* is limited to imputed income from utilisation of government-funded education and health services.

While such individual income measures are of great interest, they take no account of the effects on living standards of (i) the economies of scale experienced by couples and (ii) the presence of children. A single high earning man is likely to have a very different standard of living from a married man with the same earnings, two children and a wife with no original income. In order to allow direct comparisons across individuals living in families of different size and composition it is now common practice to use measures of *equivalent income* (CSO, 1993). Income is aggregated across the income unit (normally taken to be a family or household) and then divided by an equivalence scale, which summarises the differences in income required by various types of families to achieve comparable standards of living.

While the need to use equivalence scales is now widely accepted, there is still a major debate about which scale to use, or indeed whether a single set of scales is equally applicable to both high and low income families (Whiteford, 1985; Coulter *et al.*, 1992). The main results presented here use the *McClements equivalence scale*, rescaled so that a single adult takes the value of 1.00. However, we also explore the sensitivity of the results to the scale used, applying the *'OECD'* (Organization for Economic Co-operation and Development) scale, which gives a generally higher weight to children. The values of both these scales are shown in Table 4.1. Note that four separate equivalent income measures are used in the following analysis; equivalent original income, equivalent gross income, equivalent net income, and equivalent final income. When constructing the latter it was assumed that benefit from 'in kind' income is limited to the recipient. With this assumption, it is not appropriate to apply an equivalence scale to that proportion of income, so equivalent final income here is simply the sum of equivalent net income and the unadjusted value of benefits in kind.[7]

Implicit in the use of equivalence scales is the assumption that each person in a family experiences the same standard of living, i.e. that *income is shared equally within the family*. Research by Vogler (1989) and Pahl (1989) suggests this is not always the case. Consequently we have also included in the analysis two variations on this 50/50 assumption.[8] The

---

7   Again, alternative assumptions could be made such as that in the absence of state provision private insurance or other payments would be made out of *family* income. The benefit of not having to do this thus accrues to the family as whole. With this assumption equalising benefits in kind *would* be appropriate.

8   Under the central case of equal sharing, the equivalent net income (EQNET) of both husbands and wives is the same and is given by
    $$EQNET = (NET_h + NET_w)/EQS$$
    where EQS is the equivalence scale for the family unit. Under the assumption of

Table 4.1 Alternative Equivalence Scales

| Family type | | Equivalence value | |
|---|---|---|---|
| | | McClements scale | OECD scale |
| Single adult | | 1.0 | 1 |
| Additional adult | | 0.64 | 0.7 |
| Child | aged under 2 | 0.15 | 0.5 |
| | 2–4 years | 0.30 | 0.5 |
| | 5–7 years | 0.34 | 0.5 |
| | 8–10 years | 0.38 | 0.5 |
| | 11–12 years | 0.41 | 0.5 |
| | 13–15 years | 0.44 | 0.5 |
| | 16–17 years[a] | 0.59 | 0.5 |

Note:
a    in full-time education and living at home.

first variant is that each member of a couple contributes only 80 per cent of the net income they receive into the pool. The male partner retains 20 per cent of his income and this is not subject to an equivalising factor since only he gets the benefit of this. However, the female partner is assumed to continue to share the 20 per cent of her income she retains with the remaining members of the household, i.e. children. The second variant is that once again all income is pooled but the man gets 60 per cent of that pooled income compared with the woman's 40 per cent.

Finally in measuring *lifetime* welfare it is necessary not just to take into account individuals' changing family circumstances over their lifetimes, but also their length of life.[9] If unadjusted measures of total lifetime income are used, this may lead to individuals being located in the upper part of the income distribution purely because they have a long life and so have longest to accumulate total income. It is a moot point whether individuals gain greater utility purely by virtue of having lived longer. Subsequent results use *annualised lifetime equivalent net income* as the measure for ranking people. Lifetime income is annualised by averaging total lifetime equivalent income over each year of life from age 16. It provides a measure of average standard of living over each year of adult life.

---

unequal *pooling* the incomes of husband and wife are now given by
$$EQNET_h = (0.2*NET_h) + (0.8*(NET_h + NET_w))/EQS \text{ and}$$
$$EQNET_w = ((0.2*NET_w)/(EQS\text{-}0.6)) + (0.8*(NET_h + NET_w))/EQS$$
and under the assumption of unequal *sharing* of pooled income, incomes are now given by
$$EQNET_h = (1.2*(NET_h + NET_w))/EQS \text{ and}$$
$$EQNET_w = (0.8*(NET_h + NET_w))/EQS.$$

9   See Harding (1993, p. 47) for a fuller description of why the annualising procedure is important.

## 5.       Example Life Histories

Figures 4.3 and 4.4 give an impression of how the different income measures discussed above are simulated, illustrating the interactions between the social security and tax system, household composition, spouse's income and the individual's own income over the life cycle. Data are presented for two couples, the first of whom have relatively low lifetime incomes, the second relatively high.

### Man 1000 and Woman 2310

The top panel of Figure 4.3 shows the composition of gross income for Man 1000 and Woman 2310, and the lower panel the corresponding levels of their net income and equivalent net income.

Man 1000 has a poor employment record. He leaves school at 16, and being unable to find regular employment, receives Supplementary Benefit (SB) from age 16 to 20. Because of his interrupted work history he only receives Unemployment Benefit (UB) in the years when he is 23 and 24 (during which entitlement runs out) and when he is 38; at all other times when he is out of the labour market he is reliant on SB. The only time he pays significant amounts of tax, reducing his net income below his gross income is during his mid-30s.

Meanwhile Woman 2310 leaves school at 16, does not claim SB in that year (after which the capital from which she derives a small income rules out entitlement), she works from age 18 to 24, and between the ages of 22 and 24 she takes a degree course, following which she has one year of better paid full-time employment. At age 26 she has a child and lives as a lone parent receiving Child Benefit and One Parent Benefit and working part-time until she is 36, after which she works full-time for three years before going part-time again. She earns enough to pay significant amounts of tax, depressing her net income, and after her child is born her equivalent net income is, of course, below her unequivalised net income.

The two marry when he is 43 and she is 41. Her child stays with them for another three years before leaving home. Marriage seems to have a galvanising effect on him, and he has a relatively good stretch of employment between 42 and 51. He again has a bad patch, receiving UB when 52–53, and again when 62. By contrast she works full-time when 43, works three more years part-time, and then exits the labour market. At age 54 she receives Invalid Care Allowance reflecting her work as a carer. Her capital still rules out SB entitlement, so they have very low incomes indeed, particularly when he is 55 and 61.

When they reach pension age, things become more stable. At age 60 she receives a partial basic state pension of £1,540 per year, and an Additional Pension (AP) under SERPS of £1,060 (benefiting from the 'best 20 years rule' and from home responsibility years). From age 65 he

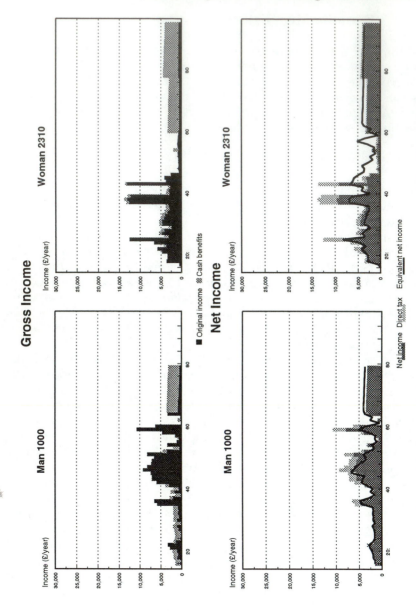

Figure 4.3  Gross and Net Income for Man 1000 and Woman 2310 (1985 system)

receives the full basic pension of £1,870, an Additional Pension of £630, and an occupational pension of £1,000 the result of his work in his forties and early fifties (through a private employer's occupational scheme).

He dies when he is 79. At this point her basic state retirement pension is made up to the full amount, £1,870, her Additional Pension is augmented by inheritance of his SERPS rights, taking the total to £1,650, and she inherits half of his occupational pension, although low rates of indexation in the fifteen years since he retired have reduced its relative value, and it only adds £260 to her income. At this point her gross income is as high as in all but a few years of her working life. Her equivalent net income stays much the same as before his death. She eventually dies after completing 95 years (the longest survival allowed in the model).

Looking at their entire lifetimes, he has an average net equivalent income per year of life from 16 of £3,025, while hers is £3,615. This puts him in the second lowest decile group of lifetime income for the whole LIFEMOD population, and her in the third lowest decile group.

**Man 1065 and Woman 4000**

The fortunes of the second couple are in complete contrast, as can be seen from Figure 4.4. He is in full-time education until age 20 and receives a student grant. He begins earning at age 21, is never unemployed, and works to age 64 in jobs with generally rising income year by year, and with private sector occupational pensions. He also receives a small amount of investment income.

Meanwhile she stays in full-time education only for one year beyond compulsory schooling, is unemployed receiving SB when she is 17, 18 and all but two weeks of the year she is 19. For the next three years she works for part of the year, receiving SB in the other part (her capital is relatively small, so she is entitled to SB).

They marry when he is 26 and she is 24, and have three children by the time she is 32 (who eventually leave home by the time she is 48). She receives Maternity Allowance when the first and third children are born (but not the second, as her employment record was not good enough at that point). She receives Child Benefit while the children are at home and in education. After age 29 she mainly works part-time, but does have a few years of full-time employment. At age 59 she is unemployed for part of the year and receives some Unemployment Benefit.

Note that she works full-time at age 55 when he is near the peak of his career, which takes their incomes to a high enough level to select 'wife's earnings election' for income tax assessment.

At age 60 she receives a full basic pension of £1,870, an Additional Pension of £350, and an occupational pension of £1,350. At age 65 he also gets the full basic pension, an Additional Pension of £1,270, and an occupational pension of £4,130 (whose value gradually slips behind

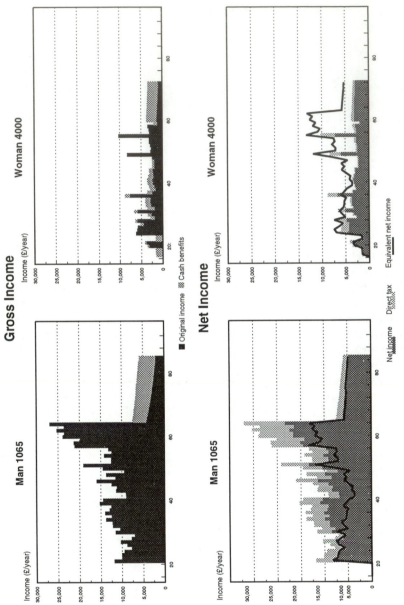

Figure 4.4 Gross and Net Income for Man 1065 and Woman 4000 (1985 system)

general living standards). She dies when she is 72, at which point he inherits half of her Additional Pension (and his living standard rises slightly).

Throughout the period of their marriage his equivalent net income is below his net income, while her equivalent net income is above her net and gross incomes in all but two years. This reflects the effects of the assumed equal sharing within couples, as well as the presence of their children.

Their average lifetime equivalent net incomes per year from age 16 are roughly twice those of the first couple – £6,110 for him and £6,150 for her – putting them in the eighth decile group of the model population's lifetime income distribution, that is, within the top 30 per cent.

**Lifetime total incomes**

Table 4.2 illustrates the measures of lifetime income discussed above. Man 1065 has roughly four times the original income of the others, mainly resulting from his high earnings, but also from his occupational pension. For cash benefits the position is rather different, with Woman 2310 (who lives to age 95) receiving the largest amounts of both basic and additional pensions. Direct tax payments are progressive, with Man 1065 paying 26 per cent of lifetime gross income in tax, while the others pay between 12 and 15 per cent.

The end result of this is that lifetime net incomes are less unequal than original incomes, with that of Man 1065 being somewhat more than double that of the others. Man 1065 is a net loser from the net effects of cash benefits and direct taxes, while the other three – particularly Woman 2310 – are net gainers.

For the first couple the effects of sharing during the period when they are married are fairly limited, although her equivalent net income is about a tenth higher than the net income she receives in her own right. For the second couple, there is a more dramatic effect, with a substantial effective transfer from him to her. Note that in both cases the gain from sharing by the woman exceeds the loss by the man – the effects of economies of scale of living together implied by the equivalence scale more than offsetting the effect on living standards of children.

The data also illustrate the effects of annualising income. Woman 2310 has a total lifetime equivalent net income four-fifths that of Woman 4000. However, she survived to age 95 whereas Woman 4000 died at 72 and so *per year of adult life* the former's average standard of living as measured by equivalent net income was significantly even lower. Interestingly, Woman 2310 accumulates the greatest income from in kind benefits, making extensive use of the health service in her later years.

Jane Falkingham, Ann Harding and Carli Lessof

**Table 4.2** Lifetime Incomes, Tax Payments and Benefit Receipts: Example Cases

|  | Man 1000 | Woman 2310 | Man 1065 | Woman 4000 |
|---|---|---|---|---|
| Earnings | 149 | 143 | 602 | 130 |
| Investment income | - | 46 | 13 | 6 |
| Occupational pensions | 11 | 3 | 60 | 14 |
| *Original income* | 160 | 193 | 675 | 150 |
| Basic pension | 28 | 62 | 39 | 24 |
| Additional pension | 11 | 44 | 36 | 5 |
| Other benefits | 27 | 12 | - | 27 |
| *Total cash benefits* | 65 | 117 | 75 | 56 |
| *Gross income* | 226 | 310 | 750 | 206 |
| Income tax | 18 | 34 | 158 | 20 |
| NICs | 10 | 11 | 34 | 6 |
| *Net income* | 199 | 265 | 558 | 180 |
| *Equivalent net income* | 194 | 289 | 428 | 350 |
| Income from benefits in kind | 43 | 68 | 56 | 23 |
| *Final income* | 237 | 357 | 484 | 373 |
| *Annualised equivalent net income* | (3027) | (3615) | (6112) | (6148) |
| Net lifetime gain: |  |  |  |  |
| – Tax and benefits[a] | +38 | +72 | -117 | +30 |
| – Sharing[b] | -5 | +25 | -130 | +170 |

**Notes:**

a    Net income minus original income.

b    Equivalent income minus net income.

These life histories serve as just a few examples of the mass of data that is accumulated during the modelling process. They demonstrate that despite the necessary simplifications, the dynamic cohort microsimulation model captures remarkable complexity. LIFEMOD is not a piece of software as many models are. Instead, a series of programs construct one large data set containing full *lifetime* profiles of 2000 men and 2000 women with key demographic, labour force and income characteristics. While LIFEMOD is simplified and stylised, it nevertheless provides one of the few available strategies for exploring important and barely explored questions about distribution over the lifetime.

**Chapter Five**

UK
D91
HSS
H23

# The Effects of the Welfare State over the Life Cycle

## Jane Falkingham and John Hills

Results from LIFEMOD can be used in three different ways:

(a) They can be used to give *life histories* showing how incomes change with age, averaged over the whole population or for particular groups. This allows, for instance, analysis of the effects of ageing abstracted from the complicating effects of changing economic conditions over real time (that is, abstracting from period effects).

(b) The results for each of the 4,000 individuals in each year they are alive (from age 16) can be treated as a separate observation (a total of over 230,000 of them). These observations can then be analysed as if they represented a *cross-section* through a population of all ages, analogous to analysis of surveys like the *Family Expenditure Survey*.

(c) Income, benefit receipts in cash and kind, and tax payments can be totalled over all years of each individual's life to give a picture of *lifetime* distribution.

In this chapter we concentrate on the first of these; the second and third are explored in subsequent chapters. We use results from the model to look at average (mean) incomes, benefits and taxation by age. We do this for different sub-groups of the model population, broken down between men and women and between different categories of 'life history' (for which we can use information about what happens to model individuals over their entire lives). In doing so we attempt to address two main sets of questions:

- First, how do original incomes from the market vary over the life cycle, that is with age? Original income includes earnings (discussed in Section 1), occupational pensions, investment income and the positive or negative contribution of maintenance payments.

Allowing for family circumstances and sharing within couples gives 'equivalent original income', the patterns of which are described in Section 2.

• Second, how do the welfare state (in the form of cash benefits, education and health services) and the taxes required to finance it modify this picture (Section 3)? To what extent does it act to 'smooth out' the peaks and troughs of original incomes? What are the implications of this for the cumulative net receipts from or payments into the system at a given age (Section 4)?

The main parts of the analysis are based on the tax and social security system as it was structured in 1985. Section 5 explores the effects of the important changes in the structures and relative generosity of the systems between then and 1991.

## 1.    Earnings and the Life Cycle

Income within LIFEMOD, as in real life, is dominated by earnings. The way in which earnings are modelled is described in detail in Winter (1994). First, the model simulates labour force participation trajectories for each individual between age 16 and statutory pension age.[1] Individuals can be employed full-time, employed part-time (women only), self-employed (men only), unemployed or out of the labour force.[2] They move between these states with transition probabilities based on *Labour Force Survey* data. These can vary in certain ways within the year with, for instance, individuals experiencing some weeks of employment and others of unemployment within the same year.

Second, the earnings of individuals over their lives follow a pattern determined by equations based on the way in which earnings varied with age, qualifications, gender, family status and labour force status in 1985 (derived from that year's *Family Expenditure Survey*). The general career progression suggested by these equations is varied by an initial factor ('talent', related to educational attainment, but whose effects can be removed by subsequent experiences like unemployment). They also follow a subsequent 'random walk' in which earnings in one year depend

---

1   For simplicity, earnings after statutory pension age (60 for women or 65 for men) are not allowed for in LIFEMOD. Model results do not incorporate recent proposals for the raising of women's pension ages.

2   This is clearly an over-simplification, made in order to keep the size of the model within bounds. In fact, nearly a quarter of the self-employed in 1986 were women (Brown, 1992, Table 1.1) and 10 per cent of part-time employees in 1986 were men (*Labour Force Survey*).

on those in the previous year, but with a degree of variation reflecting the actual variability in the population in the mid-1980s.

Figure 5.1 shows average full-time weekly earnings (for those working full-time all year) by age for men and women in the model divided into six groups by lifetime educational achievement. For a given age and educational level, men's earnings are higher than women's. Within the groups, earnings initially rise with age, but then flatten out and eventually fall (with the exception of women who go straight from school to university, whose peak earnings are at age 55–59). The higher the educational group, the steeper the career progression and – generally speaking – the later the levelling out and eventual decline. Thus women who leave school at 16 and have no further education reach average full-time earnings of nearly £130 per week (at 1985 prices) in their late twenties. By contrast, men going straight to university reach a peak of full-time earnings of £380 per week in their early fifties. As one might expect, the career progression of those who return to university or further education (FE) is particularly steep. These general patterns are consistent with other studies of earnings by age and education, matching closely those presented in Bennett, Glennerster and Nevison (1992c), Figure 2.

Figure 5.2 compares the average earnings for men and women who work full-time at different ages in the LIFEMOD population with average earnings for the actual population in 1985 (drawn from the *New Earnings Survey*). For men, the figures are quite close. In both LIFEMOD and in the actual 1985 cross-section of the population, earnings rise rapidly for men in their twenties and thirties, but flatten out at later ages. Before age 30, the LIFEMOD results are slightly below those of the actual population, but they are generally higher later on. For women working full-time, the LIFEMOD results show higher earnings from age 20.

The main reason for the differences is that the actual cohorts making up people in their forties and fifties in 1985 were less qualified than their juniors. Although their age and experience boosted their earnings, their lower level of qualifications tended to reduce them. By contrast, the LIFEMOD results represent the experience of a single cohort, whose qualifications throughout life reflect those being gained by young people in the mid-1980s. The LIFEMOD results show what Summers (1956, quoted in Atkinson, Bourguignon, and Morrison, 1992, p. 29) describes as the 'latent earnings distribution', which abstracts from the effects of varying qualifications and other differences between cohorts.[3]

---

3   The implicit assumption made here is that age and qualifications in themselves are the principal factors affecting earnings, so that a population better qualified overall will have higher earnings. An alternative would be that qualifications simply determine an individual's ranking within a fixed overall distribution. In that case, earnings of a better qualified population would be no different from those of a less well qualified one. In a modern, open, economy the former assumption seems more

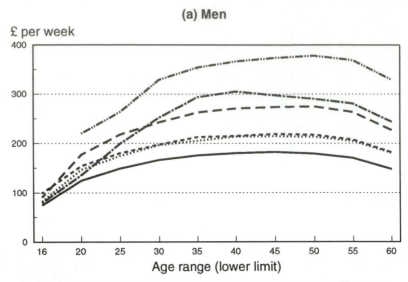

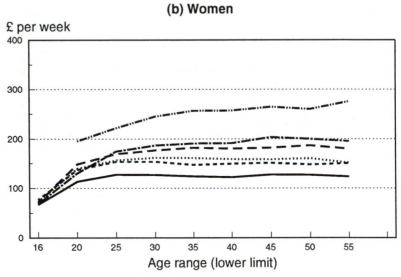

**Note:**
Individuals working full-time all year.

**Figure 5.1** Full-time Earnings by Education

**(a) Men**

£ per week

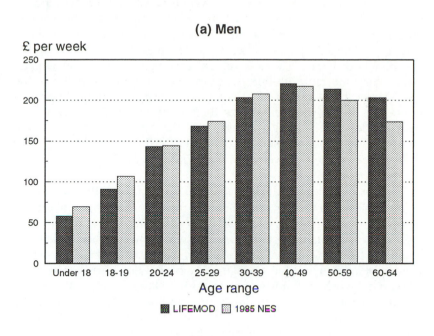

**(b) Women**

£ per week

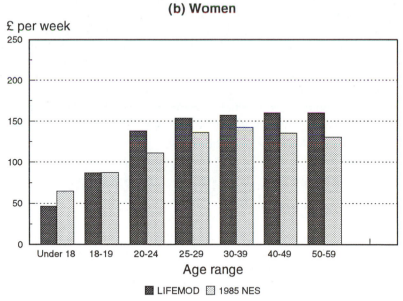

**Figure 5.2** Earnings in LIFEMOD and 1985 *New Earnings Survey*

This discussion relates to average weekly earnings for those who are in work full-time. However, actual annual earnings are also affected by unemployment, non-participation in the labour market, and – for women only in LIFEMOD – part-time working. The highest (solid) lines in the two panels of Figure 5.3 show annual earnings for men and women respectively working full-time all year. These follow the patterns one would expect from Figure 5.1. For men a peak of around £12,000 is reached in their forties; for women the pattern is very flat after age 25, with the level remaining just above £8,000. Even abstracting from differences in labour force participation there is thus a 'gender gap', with women's earnings 10 per cent below men's at age 20–24, and over 30 per cent lower at age 45–50.

The next lines (dashed) show average earnings over the whole year for all those employed for at least part of the year – unemployment and non-participation during parts of the year bring down the average slightly for men and these, with part-time work, lower it substantially for women. The third (dotted) lines show average earnings for *all* men or women of a given age, the average being pulled down further by those who do not work at all during the year, for instance because of full-time education, long term unemployment, child-care, invalidity or early retirement. Averaged over all women, mean annual earnings decline slowly from a peak of £4,700 reached by age 25–29. By contrast, for all men the peak of nearly £10,000 is not reached until 45–49.

Putting all this together, the combined effects of differential labour force participation and the gender gap in full-time earnings mean that earnings for all men in the model for each year of life between 16 and 65 average £7,840 per year, but those for women between 16 and 60 average only £4,150. Women's shorter working lives mean that *total lifetime* earnings for women are only half those of men (see Tables 6.5 and 6.6 in the next chapter), an even bigger gender gap than this gap in annual earnings.

## 2.    Original Incomes and the Effects of Family Circumstances

Figure 5.4 reproduces the annual earnings progressions for all men and women from the previous figure (the dotted lines). It also shows total *original income* (the dashed line), adding in the effects of occupational pensions (which depend on pre-retirement earnings, and on the kind of

---

plausible when choosing between the two.

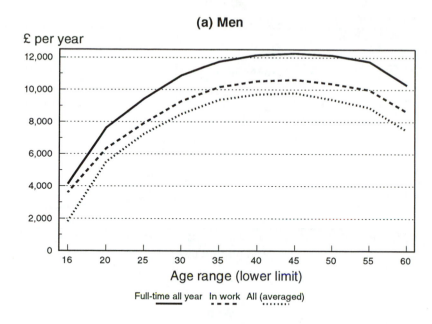

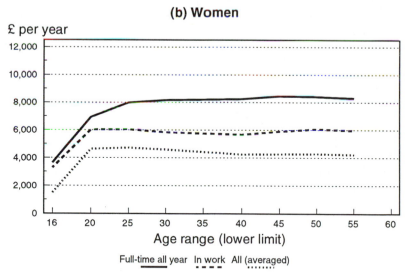

**Figure 5.3** Earnings by Age

## (a) Men

£ per year

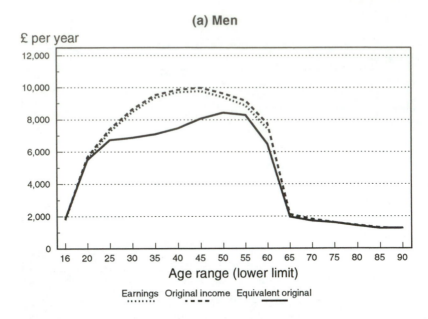

Earnings   Original income   Equivalent original

## (b) Women

£ per year

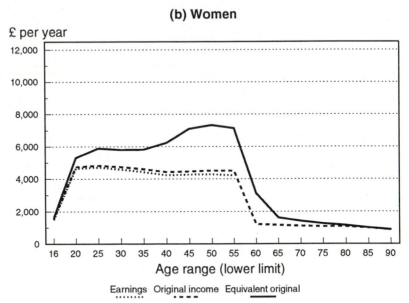

Earnings   Original income   Equivalent original

**Notes:**
Equal sharing; McClements equivalence scale.

**Figure 5.4** Original Incomes by Age

employer), investment income,[4] and maintenance payments (positive for women, negative for men). It is only after retirement age that mean original incomes differ greatly from mean earnings.

The diagram also shows levels of *equivalent original income*, allowing for the effects on living standards of income pooling by couples and of the presence of children. [5] Equivalent original income measures the resources available to people before the intervention of the state, and as such is an indicator of their potential standards of living in the absence of the welfare state, albeit an imperfect one. The general pattern is clear: men's equivalent original incomes are below their own unadjusted original incomes, whereas for women, the reverse is the case. Sharing within the family – if income is shared equally – has a substantial equalising effect between men and women. None the less, even on this assumption, women's equivalent original incomes are still below those of men.

Finally, Figure 5.5 combines the results for men and women to show the variation with age in earnings, original incomes and equivalent original incomes, for the whole model population. By comparison with unadjusted original incomes, allowing for the effects of children depresses equivalent original incomes in people's thirties, but advantages from sharing boost them in their fifties. This produces a pronounced pattern over the life cycle. Readers of *Le Petit Prince* will recognise it as the shape of an anaconda which has swallowed an elephant. Equivalent original incomes rise rapidly for people in their twenties (climbing up the tail end of the elephant), level out as people have children (going along its back), rise again to reach a peak before retirement (the head), fall at retirement and then gradually decline (going down the trunk end). It is this variation with which the welfare state has to cope in its role of smoothing out living standards over the life cycle.

## 3.    The Impact of the Welfare State

Table 5.1 shows how the components of income including benefits and direct taxes vary on average with age for all model individuals. As we have seen, average **original income**, dominated by earnings, increases with age until people are about 50. After pension age, it falls sharply by about three-quarters, and continues to fall during retirement.

---

4    As a result of modelling difficulties, investment income is a relatively unsophisticated part of the model, and we would not place a great deal of weight on results heavily dependent upon it.

5    See p.75, Chapter 4, for details of derivation of equivalent income measures.

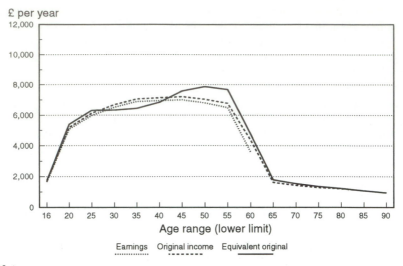

£ per year

Earnings    Original income    Equivalent original

**Note:**
Equal sharing; McClements equivalence scale.

**Figure 5.5** Original Incomes by Age: All

The rest of the table shows the effects of the welfare state. **Cash benefits**, dominated by pension receipts, follow the opposite pattern to original income, with cash benefits after age 65 being about three times the average for all years of life. Before retirement, the total of cash benefits changes little with age, the fall in means-tested benefits and student grants being offset by the rise in contributory benefits (such as Invalidity Benefit) and – between 25 and 44, at least – that in Child Benefit and One Parent Benefit (OPB). Note that receipts of Additional Pensions under the State Earnings Related Pension Scheme (SERPS) are based on its pre-1988 rules, carried through to maturity. This results in average payments under SERPS reaching three-quarters of the size of basic pension. The effects of changes since 1985 in the rules of SERPS and other parts of the tax–benefit system are discussed below.

Cash benefits therefore reduce the drop in average **gross income** (original income plus cash benefits) on reaching pension age to about a quarter, cushioning the 'shock' of loss of earnings.

**Direct taxes** – income tax and employee (and self-employed) National Insurance Contributions (NICs) – follow a similar pattern to gross income, but with the trends with age somewhat more exaggerated. Their effect is further to moderate the picture, so that **net income** (gross income minus direct taxes) in retirement starts at about five-sixths of the level it had been.

**Table 5.1** Composition of Individual Income by Age Group (1985 system; equal sharing; McClements; £/year)

| | Age group | | | | | | | | All |
|---|---|---|---|---|---|---|---|---|---|
| | 16–24 | 25–34 | 35–44 | 45–54 | 55–64 | 65–74 | 75–84 | 85–95 | |
| Earnings | 3550 | 6250 | 6910 | 6890 | 5070 | - | - | - | 4600 |
| Maintenance (net) | - | - | - | - | - | - | - | - | - |
| Investment income | 80 | 140 | 160 | 190 | 260 | 280 | 300 | 250 | 190 |
| Occupational pensions | - | - | 10 | 30 | 270 | 1250 | 960 | 790 | 280 |
| Total original income | 3640 | 6390 | 7080 | 7120 | 5600 | 1520 | 1250 | 1040 | 5070 |
| | | | | | | | | | |
| Student grants | 50 | 10 | - | - | - | - | - | - | 10 |
| Retirement pension | - | - | - | - | 440 | 1800 | 1830 | 1860 | 430 |
| SERPS (AP) | - | - | 10 | 20 | 310 | 1380 | 1530 | 1530 | 340 |
| Contributory benefits | 30 | 60 | 70 | 100 | 110 | - | - | - | 60 |
| Child Benefit/OPB | 50 | 230 | 240 | 50 | - | - | - | - | 100 |
| Disability benefits | 20 | 30 | 40 | 60 | 90 | 30 | - | - | 40 |
| Means-tested benefits | 260 | 160 | 150 | 130 | 110 | - | - | - | 130 |
| Total cash benefits | 410 | 490 | 500 | 370 | 1060 | 3220 | 3360 | 3390 | 1110 |
| | | | | | | | | | |
| Gross income | 4050 | 6880 | 7590 | 7480 | 6660 | 4740 | 4610 | 4430 | 6180 |
| Income tax | 620 | 1230 | 1430 | 1480 | 1230 | 550 | 540 | 520 | 1070 |
| NICs | 260 | 440 | 470 | 460 | 350 | - | - | - | 320 |
| Direct taxes | 880 | 1670 | 1900 | 1940 | 1580 | 550 | 540 | 520 | 1390 |
| | | | | | | | | | |
| Net income | 3180 | 5210 | 5690 | 5540 | 5090 | 4200 | 4070 | 3910 | 4790 |
| Equivalent net income | 3260 | 5070 | 5270 | 5990 | 5720 | 4650 | 4290 | 3940 | 4950 |
| Education | 440 | 50 | 10 | - | - | - | - | - | 80 |
| Health | 120 | 130 | 130 | 240 | 260 | 500 | 1010 | 1690 | 300 |
| Equivalent final income | 3820 | 5250 | 5410 | 6240 | 5980 | 5150 | 5310 | 5640 | 5320 |
| Equivalent original income | 3770 | 6320 | 6640 | 7720 | 6260 | 1670 | 1310 | 1040 | 5220 |

Allowing for family circumstances (assuming equal sharing and using the McClements scale for the moment) gives **equivalent net income**. This is somewhat lower than unadjusted net income for those between 25 and 44 (when there are the most children at home) but is higher at other ages (reflecting the economies of scale of income sharing between couples).

Allowing for **benefits in kind** from education and health services substantially alters the pattern of income by age. Education is concentrated on the youngest age group,[6] while health care is concentrated on those over 65, particularly those over 85. For those aged 85 to 95, the average value of public spending on their health care comes to nearly £1,700 per year, which is larger than their average original

6    In the totals for *lifetime* health and education discussed in the next chapter, we allow for education and health benefits received before age 16. Note that what we are doing here is to assume that benefits in kind from education and health accrue to the individuals involved, without their value being affected by family circumstances.

income and almost as large as their average receipt from the basic state pension.

Adding benefits in kind to equivalent net income gives **equivalent final income**, the penultimate line of the table. Because benefits in kind are so concentrated at the top and bottom of the age range, the path of equivalent final income with age is much flatter than that of equivalent net income.

For comparison, the final line of the table shows original income adjusted for family circumstances to give **equivalent original income**. The difference between the two shows the extent to which the welfare state and direct taxes act to moderate the effects of age on income. As can be seen, the system – at least as it was structured in 1985 – is very successful in doing this, with the variation in equivalent final incomes with age being far less than that of equivalent original incomes.

As a measure of relative *living standards* at a given age, equivalent net income is superior to equivalent final income: the latter incorporates, for instance, the value of NHS services needed to cope with increased medical needs for those in later life. When examining the *net transfers* implied by the welfare state, it is equivalent final income which matters. In the analyses below we therefore use whichever of the two definitions is appropriate.

**Differences for men and women**

The effects of taxes and benefits are somewhat different for men and women. Figure 5.6 shows average equivalent original incomes (the solid lines, as in Figure 5.4), equivalent net income (the dashed lines) and equivalent final income (dotted) at different ages for all men and all women separately.

Four points stand out:

- As we have seen, men's equivalent original incomes are higher than women's (resulting both from higher earnings and greater labour force participation), even if one assumes equal sharing by couples.
- Apart from the youngest age group, before retirement average equivalent net incomes are below original incomes, but after retirement net incomes are higher.
- The age variation in net incomes is much smaller than that of original incomes. Again excluding those aged below 20, average equivalent net incomes for both men and women stay within a range of just below £4,000 to just above £6,000; while average equivalent original incomes range between £1,000 and over £8,000.
- The important differences when allowing for benefits in kind to give equivalent final incomes comes for the youngest group (from

**(a) Men**

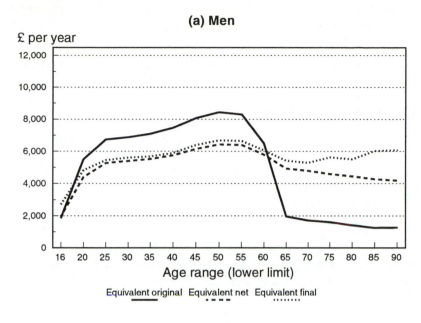

**(b) Women**

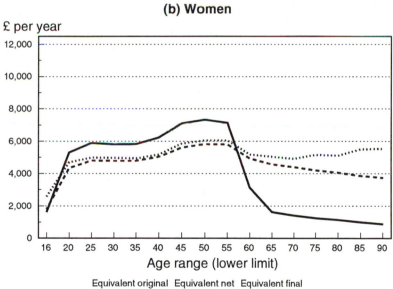

**Notes:**
1985 tax and social security systems; equal sharing; McClements equivalence scale.

**Figure 5.6** Equivalent Incomes by Age

education) and after retirement (with increased use of health services). As a result, equivalent final incomes vary even less than net incomes with age.

In summary, it is clear that the welfare state has a substantial effect in 'smoothing out' the peaks and troughs of income by age.

## The effects of different life histories

The results presented above are averages for men and women which mask a plethora of varied life histories. It is not just age and gender, but also other characteristics which influence the pattern of income over the life cycle. An advantage of LIFEMOD is that, because we have data for complete life histories, we are able to 'stand by the grave-side' and look back over each individual's life history to allocate him or her to different lifetime experience categories.

Table 5.2 shows how living standards (as measured by equivalent net income) vary with age for thirteen illustrative sub-groups of the model population whose life histories fall into different (exhaustive) categories. Figure 5.7 shows the same information graphically for some of these groups (with narrower age bands).

From these it can be seen that being married at some point, but never having children, tends to raise the equivalent net income of men compared with those who never marry. Marriage with children depresses equivalent net incomes between ages 25 and 50, but raises it for older groups. After retirement, both groups of ever-married men are better off than those who never marry by a similar margin.

Ever-married, never divorced women have substantially higher equivalent net incomes than those who never marry, even after allowing for the presence of children. However, because the group of 'never married, never lone parent' women is small – 3 per cent of the total sample – we would not read too much into their comparative position.

During the time when couples have children, the equivalent net incomes of both men and women are depressed compared with couples who never have children. It is notable, however, that this shows up more as a *delay* in rising living standards with age over working lifetimes (the flat 'elephant's back' in the diagrams), rather than as a *fall* in living standards, except in the case of women experiencing more than five years as lone parents, whose living standards clearly drop between ages 25 and 35.

Overall, young adults have the lowest incomes, and there is a fall in equivalent net income after pension age. The best off groups are men aged 35–59 who never have children (whether or not they marry), men reaching their fifties who ever do have children (i.e. when the children leave home), and the women to whom these men are married.

**Table 5.2** Equivalent Net Income by Age and Life History Type (1985 system; £ per year)

| Age | Life history type | | | | | | |
|---|---|---|---|---|---|---|---|
| | Never married or lone parent | Ever married/never lone parent | | | | Ever lone parent | |
| | | No divorce | | Ever divorced | | 1-4 years | 5+ years |
| | | No child | Children | No child | Children | | |
| **(a) Men** | | | | | | | |
| 16–24 | 3320 | 3260 | 3340 | 3310 | 3300 | - | - |
| 25–34 | 5430 | 5590 | 5160 | 5870 | 5420 | 4850 | - |
| 35–44 | 6300 | 6590 | 5050 | 7130 | 5750 | 4330 | - |
| 45–54 | 6270 | 6740 | 6030 | 7300 | 6450 | 4270 | - |
| 55–64 | 5420 | 6180 | 6180 | 6410 | 6260 | 4160 | - |
| 65–74 | 4270 | 5090 | 5020 | 4530 | 4910 | - | - |
| 75–84 | 3880 | 4710 | 4730 | 4230 | 4570 | - | - |
| 85–95 | 3370 | - | 4500 | - | 4500 | - | - |
| Percentage of all individuals in group | 7 | 4 | 21 | 2 | 15 | 1 | |
| **(b) Women** | | | | | | | |
| 16–24 | 2920 | 3050 | 3270 | 3170 | 3390 | 3330 | 3190 |
| 25–34 | 4120 | 4790 | 5150 | 4780 | 5200 | 4840 | 4420 |
| 35–44 | 4080 | 6030 | 5120 | 5140 | 5270 | 5000 | 4170 |
| 45–54 | 3780 | 6690 | 6250 | 5300 | 5730 | 6090 | 4930 |
| 55–64 | 3320 | 6040 | 6010 | 4640 | 4680 | 5850 | 4810 |
| 65–74 | 2840 | 4890 | 4920 | 4010 | 3920 | 4800 | 4160 |
| 75–84 | 2700 | 4470 | 4540 | 3760 | 3520 | 4480 | 3820 |
| 85–95 | 2680 | 4140 | 4220 | - | 3370 | 4050 | 3550 |
| Percentage of all individuals in group | 3 | 6 | 17 | 3 | 2 | 5 | 13 |

**Note:**
Results based on less than 150 observations omitted.

This is a rather different pattern from Rowntree's finding – discussed in Chapter 1 – of 'five alternating periods of want and comparative plenty' (1902, pp. 169–71) at the end of the last century, the periods of want being childhood, having a family of one's own and old age. 'Young adulthood' between 15 and 25 no longer appears as a time of 'comparative plenty', and the dip in living standards while there are children in the family between 30 and 40 is not at all pronounced. Late middle age (the 'empty nest') appears as the clearest time of comparative plenty. This important change appears to reflect the much greater premiums for age and experience now incorporated in wages than at the turn of the century, smaller family sizes and the 'smoothing' effects of the

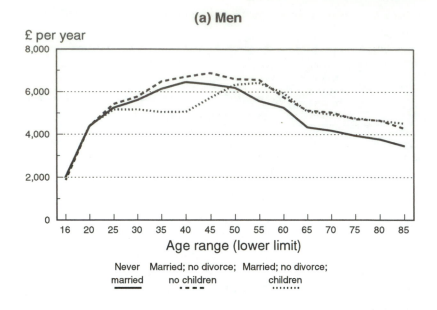

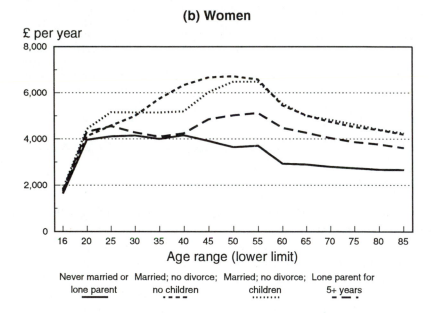

**Notes:**
1985 tax and social security system; equal sharing; McClements equivalence scale.

**Figure 5.7** Equivalent Net Incomes by Age: Selected Life History Types

welfare state itself through taxation and social security which we have been examining.

Finally, the table makes clear the much lower average lifetime incomes of women who experience five or more years as a lone parent (26 per cent of women in the model) than those who marry, but are never divorced. Table 5.2 suggests that those who experience divorce, but not lone parenthood, tend not to be so badly off before pension age, but are actually worse off in retirement than those experiencing lone parenthood. This may reflect the timing of divorce in the two cases – the non-lone parent group getting divorced *later*, and so having lower chances of remarriage. By contrast, men who divorce emerge as a well-off group in late middle age (despite the allowance for maintenance built into the calculations). The impact of lone parenthood, its timing and duration, is further examined in Chapter 9.

## Sensitivity to sharing assumptions and equivalence scale

These patterns of living standards by age could, in part, reflect the assumptions we have made about equal sharing of incomes between couples and the use of the McClements equivalence scale, which gives comparatively little weight to the effects of young children on living standards. Figure 5.8 shows the effects on average equivalent net incomes for men and women at different ages of making alternative assumptions by comparison with our base assumptions of equal sharing and the McClements scale (the solid line).[7]

The first variation (the short dashed line) assumes that each member of a couple contributes only 80 per cent of the original income they receive into the equally shared pool. Only pooled income is equivalised using the McClements scale, as only this income benefits from the economies of scale of sharing. This means that couples starting with unequal original incomes (usually with the man receiving more) end up with unequal net incomes. Compared with the base case, the effect is a rise in equivalent net incomes for men in their thirties and forties, and a fall for women up to retirement age.

The second variation (the dotted line) assumes that all income within each couple is pooled, but that the man receives 60 per cent of the pooled result, and the woman only 40 per cent (regardless of which of them received the original income). This has more of an effect, increasing incomes for men between 25 and 60 by about £1,000 per year and reducing them for women at the same ages by corresponding amounts.

---

7    See pages 75–76 for a discussion of the derivation of these alternative income sharing assumptions.

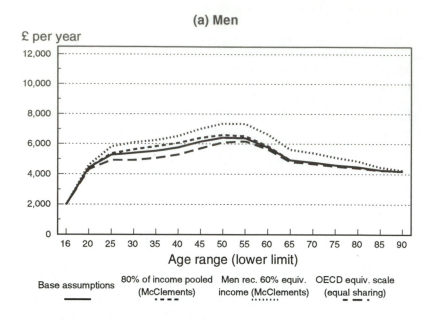

**(a) Men**

£ per year

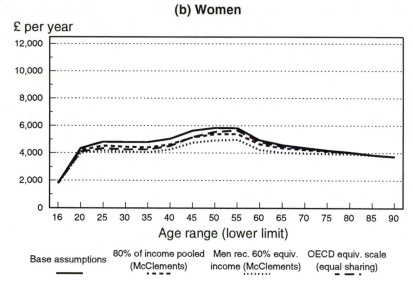

**(b) Women**

£ per year

**Note:**
1985 tax and social security systems

**Figure 5.8** Equivalent Net Incomes: Alternative Assumptions

Finally, the line with long dashes shows the effects of using the 'OECD' equivalence scale, which puts more weight on the effects of children than the McClements scale (but assuming equal sharing by couples).[8] Compared with the base case, the flattening out of living standards between ages 25 and 40 is more pronounced for both men and women, but in neither case does an actual 'dip' in living standards appear at this level of aggregation.

Overall, then, the figure shows that the general findings – of a flattening out rather than fall in living standards when people are in their thirties and of a single peak in late middle age – are not very sensitive to alternative assumptions about sharing and the equivalence scale used.[9]

## 4. Cumulative Net Gains from the Welfare State by Age

The welfare state and the tax system thus combine to shift resources across the life cycle, essentially succeeding in the aim of adding to incomes at times of 'want' through transfers from the times of 'plenty'. As we have already seen in Chapter 3, the result of this process is a pronounced age-related pattern in whether people are cumulatively 'in credit' or 'in debt' to the system.

Figure 5.9 shows, for the 'LIFEMOD cohort', the cumulative receipts by each age from cash benefits, education and health services net of the taxes required to finance them. As the average amount of direct tax paid in the model under the 1985 system does not equal the total of benefits in cash and kind, the net receipts shown in the figure are based on direct tax payments rescaled so that they equal the spending to be financed.[10] This assumes that over its complete life cycle, the cohort as a whole finances the benefits it receives, in other words there is no redistribution

---

8 Under the OECD equivalence scale, a weight of 1.0 is given for the first adult, 0.7 for other adults, and 0.5 for children.

9 As Coulter *et al.* (1992) show, the use of just one alternative equivalence scale is not enough to demonstrate complete robustness. However, in this case, the direction and scale of change are clear. It would require children to be given much the same weight as the first adult – in other words to look at *per capita* incomes – to create a noticeable dip in the diagrams.

10 All employee NICs plus the equivalent of 132 per cent of income tax payments calculated under the 1985 system are required to pay for all benefits including health and education received before 16. Welfare spending is not, of course, necessarily financed only by direct taxes. The issues involved in how welfare benefits are financed are explored in more detail in Chapter 7, including looking at the effects of an alternative, equivalent to assuming financing from the whole tax system. This makes an important difference in terms of distribution by income group. However, for the age-related analysis here, the difference is less important.

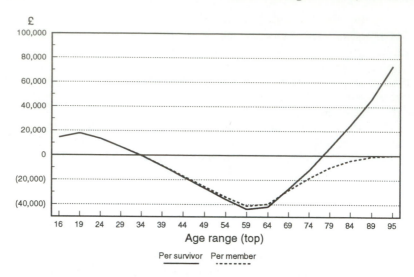

**Figure 5.9** Cumulative Net Receipts from Welfare (direct tax finance: 1985 tax and social security)

to or from any other cohort. As we saw in Chapter 3, this is not always exactly the case in reality.

The first line in the figure shows the cumulative net gain *per survivor* at each age. Thus those surviving to age 16 would have received an average of £14,500 from education and health services. With more education, cumulative net receipts rise for a while, but then fall back as tax payments to pay for welfare outstrip receipts. By age 34, survivors have, on average, paid as much tax as they have received in benefits. By age 59, they have put in nearly £50,000 more than they have received. Thereafter receipts from pensions and health services outstrip tax payments, so that those surviving to age 79 have once again got as much out as they put in. Those surviving longer end up, on average, as net gainers – by more than £70,000 for those surviving to age 95. In effect, those dying before age 79 on average make a net transfer to those dying after then.

The second line shows the cumulative position by age for the cohort as a whole (including those who do not survive), with the net position expressed as an average amount per member. This confirms that by the time age 95 is reached (at which age all surviving cohort members are assumed to die), the cumulative net gain is zero (tax payments having been scaled to achieve this result).

## 5.    Effects of Changes to Tax and Social Security by 1991

Between 1985 and 1991 the British tax and social security systems went through substantial changes. The 'Fowler' reforms of 1988 (DHSS, 1985) changed the system of means-tested benefits (with Income Support replacing Supplementary Benefit and Family Credit replacing Family Income Supplement). They also substantially modified the rules of the State Earnings Related Pension Scheme (SERPS), cutting the benefits which will accrue under it in the long run. Over the period benefit levels in general became less generous in relation to earnings, mostly being uprated each year in line with the growth in prices rather than incomes (and in some cases, like Child Benefit, losing value in real terms as well). Finally, the direct tax system was changed in various ways, with income tax rates cut in the 1988 Budget (particularly for those with the highest incomes) and with simplifications to the structure of employee National Insurance Contributions. The fall in the value of the upper earnings limit for NICs relative to average earnings also reduced benefits accruing under SERPS and reduced the progressivity of NICs at the top end of the earnings distribution.

We examined the lifetime effects of these changes on the LIFEMOD population by replacing the 1985 direct tax and social security system with the 1991 system (with parameters such as benefit rates and tax thresholds adjusted back to 1985 values in line with the change in average earnings between April 1985 and April 1991).[11] Note that we did not change the demographic or earnings structure of the model – the results described below compare the effects of the two tax-transfer systems on the same 1985-based population. There were not the same kind of structural changes for *utilisation* of health and education services between the two dates, so the estimates of benefits in kind from them are not revised in what follows.

Figure 5.10 presents, using the 1991 system, the same information as Figure 5.6 did for the 1985 system (and still at 1985 prices). The first point to note is that equivalent original incomes in retirement are slightly higher than under the 1985 system. This is because the 1986 Social Security Act shortened the minimum qualifying service for preserved occupational pensions to two years, so those who change jobs frequently end up with somewhat better pensions. Second, as far as men are concerned, comparison of the top panel with its equivalent in Figure 5.6 shows that their equivalent net and final incomes are higher before

---

11  In both 1985 and 1991 systems, we used the systems as they were in April. For most benefits and taxes, the systems applied for the whole of the financial years 1985/6 and 1991/2. The one or two features changed in mid-year were not incorporated.

**(a) Men**

£ per year (1985 prices)

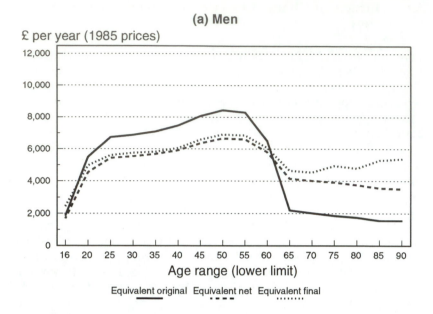

Equivalent original  Equivalent net  Equivalent final

**(b) Women**

£ per year (1985 prices)

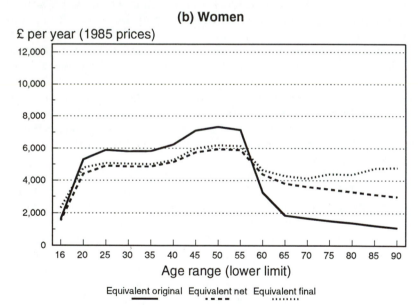

Equivalent original  Equivalent net  Equivalent final

**Note:**
1991 tax and social security systems; equal sharing; McClements equivalence scale.

**Figure 5.10** Equivalent Incomes by Age: 1991 System

retirement by up to £200 per year, but after retirement they are lower by as much as £700 per year. For women, equivalent net and final incomes before retirement are only slightly higher than with the 1985 system; after retirement the reduction is as much as £800 per year, leaving them about 20 per cent lower.

The 1991 system is examined further in Chapters 6 and 7. The effect of its less generous social security benefits (particularly pensions under SERPS) and less progressive direct tax rates is to raise net and final incomes for men before retirement (and, through sharing within the family, for women on average too), but to reduce incomes after retirement. The system as it is now structured is clearly somewhat less effective at 'smoothing out' variations in life cycle incomes than was the 1985 system.

Finally, Figure 5.11 shows cumulative net receipts from welfare spending net of the taxes required to finance it[12] in the same way as Figure 5.9. The key difference between the two is in the *amplitude* of the 'wave pattern' of cumulative net receipts. The cumulative net loss to survivors reaching 59 is reduced to just over £30,000, while the cumulative net gain

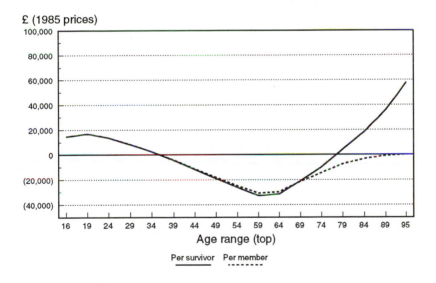

£ (1985 prices)

Age range (top)

Per survivor    Per member

**Figure 5.11** Cumulative Net Receipts from Welfare (direct tax finance: 1991 tax and social security system)

---

12  In this case, financing is assumed to come from all of employee NICs and 121 per cent of income tax liabilities calculated under the 1991 system's rules.

to those reaching 95 is reduced to below £60,000 (at 1985 prices).[13] The welfare state is doing 'less work' in terms of smoothing income over the life cycle under the 1991 rules, and so the cumulative credits from or debts to it at different ages become smaller.

## Summary

- Annual earnings for all men in the model between 16 and 65 average £7,840 per year, with a peak reached in their late forties.

- For women between 16 and 60 the average is only £4,150, and earnings are flat after their mid-twenties. Total lifetime earnings for women are only half those of men.

- Equivalent original incomes rise rapidly for people in their twenties, level out as people have children, rise again to reach a peak before retirement, fall at retirement, and then gradually decline.

- Welfare spending and taxation as structured in 1985 were very successful in smoothing incomes over the life cycle, with the variation in equivalent final incomes with age being far less than that of equivalent original incomes.

- Apart from the youngest age group, before retirement average equivalent net incomes are below original incomes, but after it net incomes are higher.

- The pattern of equivalent net incomes over the life cycle does not show the clear 'alternating periods of want and comparative plenty' found by Rowntree at the end of the last century. The premiums now put on age and experience in the labour market and the welfare state itself substantially moderate the effects of family formation and retirement on living standards.

- These general patterns are robust to alternative assumptions about sharing and the equivalence scale used.

- Women who experience five or more years as a lone parent have much lower incomes over their lives than those who marry, but are

---

13 The pattern in Figure 5.11 has roughly the same shape as those for recently born cohorts discussed in Chapter 3 (see Figure 3.9), also based on future SERPS receipts under the post-1988 rules (Figure 5.10 illustrates the effects of more generous earlier rules and so shows greater gains to those surviving well after pension age). The units used here are 1985 pounds; LIFEMOD does not generate a figure for 'GDP per capita' to give comparability with the earlier diagrams, but it can be noted that average original income per capita in the model is around £5,000 and GDP per capita would exceed this, so the amplitude of the 'wave' pattern is of similar magnitude to the results in Chapter 3.

never divorced. By contrast, men who divorce emerge as a well-off group in late middle age.

- If one looks at the cumulative effects of the 1985 system, those surviving to age 59 would on average have put in nearly £50,000 more to pay for welfare benefits than they have received; by age 79 cumulative receipts overtake cumulative payments; those surviving to age 95 longer end up, on average, with a net gain of over £70,000.

- The 1991 tax and social security system incorporates less generous cash benefits (particularly pensions under SERPS) and less progressive direct tax rates. This raises net and final incomes before retirement but reduces incomes after retirement. The 1991 system is thus less effective at 'smoothing out' variations in life cycle incomes than that of 1985.

- Under the 1991 system, the cumulative net loss to survivors reaching 59 is reduced to just over £30,000, while the cumulative net gain to those reaching 95 is reduced to below £60,000 (at 1985 prices).

Chapter Six

# Lifetime Incomes and the Welfare State

UK
HSS
H23
D31

## Jane Falkingham and John Hills

The previous chapter showed how incomes vary with age. It also demonstrated how the welfare state 'smooths out' some of the variations, transferring resources from times of comparative plenty to those of comparative need. A result of these transfers is that, looking at a cross-section of the whole population in a single year, incomes after taking account of the effects of the welfare state are much less unequally distributed than original incomes. This is illustrated by the Central Statistical Office's annual analysis of the effects of taxes and benefits on household income, based on the Family Expenditure Survey (CSO, 1993).

From the perspective of annual incomes on a cross-sectional basis, some redistribution of this kind would be seen even if the *only* effect of the welfare state was life cycle, or in*tra*personal, redistribution. In any year we may see relatively poor elderly people gaining from state pensions, for instance, and relatively well-off people in work paying more in taxes than they receive in benefits. But the picture may look very different from the perspective of complete lifetimes. Pensioners may simply be getting back what they each themselves put into the system at an earlier stage, with no redistribution between individuals (in*ter*personal redistribution) taking place at all on a lifetime basis.

This chapter uses LIFEMOD results to look at the effects of the welfare state and direct taxes over cohort individuals' complete lifetimes. It uses lifetime totals of incomes, benefits in cash and kind, and direct taxes to explore the extent to which the inequalities between the 'lifetime poor' and 'lifetime rich' are reduced, and to examine which income groups are the lifetime 'gainers and losers' from the system. Chapter 7 looks in more detail at the question of how much of what the welfare state does can be ascribed to different kinds of redistribution.

## 1.    Cross-sectional Distribution

To set the lifetime results in a more familiar perspective, Table 6.1 shows the results of the model used to give an analogue of a cross-sectional survey. In the table, each year of life of the model individuals from age 16 is treated as a separate observation. Thus someone dying at age 76 contributes sixty observations to the results, each treated for the moment as unrelated. The 234,000 observations generated are split into tenths, or decile groups, the richest being the tenth. They are ranked in order of equivalent net income.[1] This averages £1,040 per year (at 1985 prices) for the bottom decile group of observations and £10,860 for the top decile group (the range for the top decile group being from £8,500 to £36,600).

Total *original* income, mainly consisting of earnings, is distributed very unequally, with the average for the top group being seventy times that of the bottom group.[2] The highest observation for a single year is £66,000, while the lowest is zero. Net maintenance payments average zero (the negative figures for men matching the positive receipts by women), but represent a small net transfer from higher to lower income groups.

*Cash benefits* have their highest value for the fourth and fifth decile groups, and their lowest for the top group. In addition:

- The bottom income group does *not* receive the greatest amounts of cash benefits. This is partly because some model individuals (like real ones) are entitled to means-tested benefits, but fail to claim them. Others are not entitled to social security benefits, for instance, young people including those in full-time education, although some of these do receive student grants (which have the greatest value for the poorest group on this cross-sectional basis).

- Means-tested benefits are, none the less, strongly skewed towards the poorest two groups.

- Pensions are concentrated in the middle of the income distribution. In part this is because the scale of receipts under the mature State Earnings Related Pension Scheme (under 1985 rules) means that most pensioners are not in the poorest groups.

- Family benefits (Child Benefit and One Parent Benefit) are rather more skewed towards the bottom half of the annual income

---

1   Unless otherwise indicated, results are for decile groups ordered by equivalent net income – there is no 're-ranking' in terms of the other income measures. Of our income measures, equivalent net income best captures relative living standards. However, we do examine below some of the differences ranking by original income.

2   If ranked by equivalent *original* income, the bottom decile group derives nearly all of its income from state benefits and has negligible original income; average original income for the top group on this ranking is £14,100.

**Table 6.1** Composition of Income by Cross-sectional Distribution (1985 system; equal sharing; McClements; £/year)

| | Decile group of individuals by lifetime equivalent net income per year | | | | | | | | | | |
|---|---|---|---|---|---|---|---|---|---|---|---|
| | Bottom | 2 | 3 | 4 | 5 | 6 | 7 | 8 | 9 | Top | All |
| Earnings | 120 | 1260 | 2280 | 2550 | 2960 | 3630 | 4920 | 6440 | 8680 | 13190 | 4600 |
| Maintenance (net) | - | 20 | 10 | - | - | - | - | - | -10 | -10 | - |
| Investment income | 80 | 80 | 90 | 100 | 120 | 130 | 160 | 230 | 290 | 600 | 190 |
| Occupational pensions | - | 20 | 90 | 180 | 330 | 540 | 610 | 520 | 330 | 140 | 280 |
| *Total original income* | 200 | 1380 | 2470 | 2830 | 3420 | 4300 | 5690 | 7180 | 9290 | 13930 | 5070 |
| Student grants | 40 | 30 | 10 | - | - | - | - | - | - | - | 10 |
| Retirement pension | - | 290 | 570 | 800 | 810 | 730 | 540 | 360 | 180 | 70 | 430 |
| SERPS (AP) | - | 110 | 360 | 730 | 700 | 610 | 440 | 280 | 150 | 70 | 340 |
| Contributory benefits | 40 | 140 | 90 | 50 | 50 | 50 | 50 | 50 | 50 | 40 | 60 |
| Child benefit/OPB | 40 | 160 | 130 | 110 | 100 | 100 | 100 | 90 | 80 | 40 | 100 |
| Disability benefits | 10 | 30 | 60 | 20 | 30 | 40 | 50 | 50 | 60 | 40 | 40 |
| Means-tested benefits | 730 | 420 | 90 | 30 | 10 | 10 | - | - | - | 70 | 130 |
| *Total cash benefits* | 860 | 1180 | 1310 | 1740 | 1700 | 1520 | 1180 | 830 | 520 | 300 | 1110 |
| *Gross income* | 1060 | 2550 | 3770 | 4570 | 5120 | 5820 | 6860 | 8020 | 9810 | 14220 | 6180 |
| Income tax | 10 | 70 | 310 | 530 | 660 | 860 | 1180 | 1520 | 2050 | 3510 | 1070 |
| NICs | 10 | 70 | 150 | 180 | 220 | 270 | 360 | 470 | 620 | 820 | 320 |
| *Direct taxes* | 20 | 140 | 460 | 710 | 880 | 1130 | 1550 | 1990 | 2670 | 4330 | 1390 |
| *Net income* | 1050 | 2410 | 3310 | 3860 | 4240 | 4690 | 5320 | 6030 | 7140 | 9900 | 4790 |
| *Equivalent net income* | 1040 | 2550 | 3160 | 3790 | 4290 | 4830 | 5440 | 6280 | 7570 | 10860 | 4950 |
| Education[a] | 520 | 110 | 40 | 30 | 20 | 10 | 10 | 10 | - | - | 80 |
| Health[a] | 170 | 270 | 360 | 450 | 400 | 360 | 290 | 250 | 210 | 190 | 300 |
| *Equivalent final income* | 1730 | 2630 | 3560 | 4270 | 4710 | 5200 | 5740 | 6530 | 7790 | 11050 | 5320 |
| Average age | 31.1 | 42.4 | 47.1 | 52.8 | 52.8 | 51.7 | 48.5 | 46.6 | 44.9 | 45.8 | 46.4 |
| % women | 58 | 59 | 58 | 57 | 54 | 52 | 50 | 47 | 45 | 43 | 52 |

**Note:**
a   Excludes receipts before 16.

distribution than pensions, but much less so than means-tested benefits. The poorest group receives little from them.

Overall, cash benefits are of greatest relative importance at the bottom of the distribution, and reduce the disparity in *gross* incomes between top and bottom groups to 13 to 1. By contrast, *direct taxes* rise steeply through the distribution, reducing the disparity in *net* incomes to 9 to 1.

The next line of the table takes account of the effects of family circumstances on living standards, adjusting net incomes in line with the 'McClements' equivalence scale, and assuming that net income is equally shared within families. Doing this suggests that the benefits from income sharing outweigh the costs of children by greater amounts at the top than at the bottom of the distribution, so that the disparity in *equivalent net* incomes between top and bottom is increased to 10 to 1.

Benefits in kind from *education* (as the table is for adults, this is post-16 education only here) are strongly concentrated on the poorest decile group on a cross-sectional basis. This is unsurprising, as they are also the youngest on average, containing, for instance, most of the students. By contrast *health* benefits are spread out across the distribution, with, like pensions, a pronounced 'hump' around the fourth and fifth decile groups, which can be seen to have the highest average ages.

Together, these benefits in kind are worth almost twice as much on average (£470 per year) for the bottom half of the distribution as for the top half (£270 per year). Adding them to equivalent net income to give *equivalent final* income shows a further reduction in inequality, with the ratio between top and bottom groups reduced to 6 to 1.

This picture is summarised in Figure 6.1. The top panel shows the way in which cash benefits are of greater relative importance for the lower income groups, while direct taxation (the difference between net and gross income) has the greatest relative effect at the top. Net incomes for the bottom six decile groups are thus above original incomes, while the reverse is true for the top four. The lower panel shows the effects of family composition in raising equivalent net incomes at the top of the distribution, but reducing them somewhat at the bottom. This indicates that there are more families with children at the lower end of the income distribution. Benefits in kind are of generally declining size for higher incomes, and equivalent final incomes are less unequally spread than net incomes, although considerable inequality remains.

Another way of looking at the effects of taxes and benefits on distribution is to look at the Gini coefficients[3] of income measured in different ways (see Table 6.3). These fall from 0.57 for original income, to

---

3   The Gini coefficient measures the inequality of a distribution, taking a value of zero for a completely equal distribution, and of one for a distribution where only one member of the population has all of the income (or whatever is being measured).

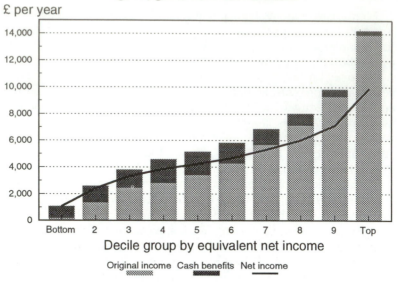

**Original, gross and net incomes**

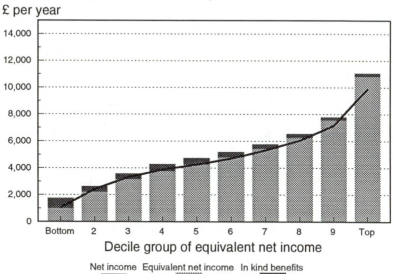

**Net, equivalent net and equivalent final income**

**Notes:**
1985 tax and social security systems; equal sharing; McClements equivalence scale.

**Figure 6.1** Annual Incomes on Cross-sectional Basis

0.42 for gross income, 0.37 for net income, 0.30 for equivalent net income and 0.28 for equivalent final income. Social security, education, health, the direct tax system and the assumed sharing within the family thus halve inequality measured in this way.

In line with the pattern of life cycle incomes explored in Chapter 5, Table 6.1 shows that the poorest income group is also the youngest, while those in the middle have the highest average age. It also shows a clear gender bias, even with assumed equal sharing between couples. The proportion of women in each income group falls continuously from the second to the top groups. Individuals in the bottom half of the distribution are more likely to be women than the average for all cases; for the top half, the reverse is true.[4]

## Comparison with the actual 1985 population

This 'pseudo cross-section' can be compared with a cross-section of the actual 1985 population. Unfortunately, the CSO's analysis of the 1985 FES does not include the information to do so directly. First, the CSO's results are on a household rather than an individual basis. Second, for that year the CSO analysis was still on an 'unequivalised' basis, not allowing for the effects of household size on living standards.

None the less, the CSO's general picture (1986, Table 3) shows a similar pattern. For households ranked by disposable income, the ratios of unequivalised household income between top and bottom decile groups are: 76 to 1 (original income), 11 to 1 (gross income) and 9 to 1 (disposable income).[5]

These ratios are similar to or a little higher than those from the LIFEMOD cross-section. However, households in the top part of the actual income distribution in 1985 had significantly more adults in them than those at the bottom when ranked by original income (CSO, 1986, Table A), and the same would probably be true if the ranking was by disposable income. Ratios of income per adult – more comparable with these LIFEMOD results – would then be lower (but equivalisation and ranking by individual income would affect them as well).

---

4   The 58 per cent of the poorest tenth found to be women compare, for instance, with Wright's (1992) FES-based calculation suggesting that – with assumed equal sharing within the family – 53 per cent of the poorest 13 per cent of the adult population ranked by disposable equivalent income were women in 1986, and Jenkins and Cowell's (1993) finding that women made up 57 per cent of the adults in the poorest fifth of the distribution of all individuals by equivalent disposable incomes in 1988 and 1989 (pooled).

5   The CSO's 'disposable' income differs from our 'net' income in that it includes rent rebates and allowances. The 'final incomes' presented by the CSO in its results are not comparable with ours, as the CSO deducts estimates of indirect tax payments, and includes other benefits in kind. It includes education for those under 16 (allocated to their parents), but excludes education for students living away from home.

The CSO analysis of the actual 1985 income distribution by households gives Gini coefficients of 0.51 for original income, 0.38 for gross income, 0.35 for disposable income (CSO, 1987, Table C) and 0.29 for equivalent disposable income (CSO, 1993, Appendix 4, Table 2). As one might expect, the coefficients for unequivalised household incomes are slightly lower than those given above for the LIFEMOD individual incomes, household composition being a source of variation in income distribution. The coefficients for equivalised net (LIFEMOD) and disposable incomes (CSO) – which do allow for household composition – are remarkably close (0.30 and 0.29, respectively).

A comparison can also be made between average incomes for the LIFEMOD population and average incomes per adult from the FES results (in £/year per individual adult):

|                        | LIFEMOD | FES  |
|------------------------|---------|------|
| Original income        | 5070    | 4535 |
| Cash benefits          | 1110    | 850  |
| Direct tax             | 1390    | 965  |
| Net/disposable income  | 4790    | 4420 |

Original incomes for the better educated LIFEMOD population average 12 per cent more than those for the actual 1985 population (despite the greater proportion of pensioners in the LIFEMOD population). Cash benefits are also higher, mainly because of the higher receipt of basic state pensions (the LIFEMOD cross-section is older than that of 1985) and an average value of £340 per adult for the Additional Pension payable under the mature State Earnings Related Pension Scheme under 1985 rules embodied in the LIFEMOD results (compared with a negligible actual figure in 1985). Partly as a result of higher gross incomes (and also because LIFEMOD does not allow for mortgage tax relief), direct taxes are also higher in the LIFEMOD results, leaving net incomes some 8 per cent above those from the FES.

The results from analysing LIFEMOD as if it were a cross-section of individuals of different ages thus compare well with those drawn from a cross-section of the actual 1985 population. The inequality of incomes defined in various ways is comparable, and while the LIFEMOD population has somewhat higher average incomes, this reflects its higher education level (and the effects of a mature SERPS under its 1985 rules) in the ways one would expect. We can therefore turn to examining what the model's results suggest for total lifetime incomes constructed from a plausible base of annual components.

## 2. Total Lifetime Incomes

Table 6.2 and Figure 6.2 show parallel information to that in Table 6.1 and Figure 6.1, but on the basis of *lifetime* totals of income, benefits and taxes. In this table each individual in the model generates a single observation, so there are 3,983 observations in all.[6] Total original income summed over all the model individuals' complete lifetimes (from age 16) averages £298,000 (at 1985 prices), to which cash benefits add £66,000, but direct taxes subtract £82,000, giving average net income of £282,000. Adjustment for family circumstances and pooling of resources raises average lifetime total equivalent net income to £291,000. Adding benefits in kind (including those received before age 16) from state education and health care gives total equivalent final income of £327,000.

The individuals are ranked into decile groups by a measure of lifetime living standards. Rather than use total lifetime income to do this, the ranking uses each individual's equivalent net income averaged over each year of life from age 16. This 'annualised' basis avoids putting people into the top of the income distribution just because they have a long life, and so have longest to accumulate total income.[7]

The bottom decile group – the 'lifetime poor' – have average equivalent net incomes of £2,750 per year. This, the average for their whole adult lives, compares with the 1985 single person's Supplementary Benefit 'scale rate' of just under £1,500 (allowing for 'passported' benefits, but not housing costs). Meanwhile, the 'lifetime rich' in the top decile group have average equivalent net income of £8,060 per year (with a range for this group from £6,910 to £16,070).

It is immediately apparent from the table and figure that lifetime total incomes are considerably less unequally distributed than incomes analysed on an annual cross-sectional basis. Table 6.3 summarises the comparison between the two distributions, showing the extent to which the gradients in the lifetime totals are dramatically lower than those on an annual basis. Going from one end of the analysis to the other, while the top decile group's *annual original* incomes are 70 times the size of those of the bottom group, the corresponding ratio for *lifetime equivalent final* incomes is only 2.6 to 1. The corresponding Gini coefficients fall from 0.57 to 0.19. For most definitions, the reduction in Gini coefficients going from

---

6 The seventeen model individuals who die before they are 16 are excluded from the results, as they do not live long enough to have an average post-16 living standard calculated. The costs of their education and health provision are, however, allowed for in calculating the taxes required to finance welfare services in Chapter 7.

7 Note that the ratio between top and bottom for annualised equivalent net income is less than that for total net income. This is because those with high incomes have longer lives than those with low incomes – 58.1 years of life after age 16 for the top decile group, compared with 56.7 years for the bottom group.

**Table 6.2** Composition of Income by Lifetime Income Distribution (1985 system; equal sharing; McClements; £000s)

| | Bottom | 2 | 3 | 4 | 5 | 6 | 7 | 8 | 9 | Top | All |
|---|---|---|---|---|---|---|---|---|---|---|---|
| | | | | | | | | | | | |
| Earnings | 108 | 160 | 195 | 212 | 241 | 257 | 298 | 331 | 384 | 519 | 271 |
| Maintenance (net) | 0.8 | 0.5 | 0.2 | 0.1 | -0.1 | -0.1 | - | -0.3 | -0.4 | -0.4 | - |
| Investment income | 4 | 5 | 6 | 5 | 6 | 8 | 9 | 13 | 15 | 40 | 11 |
| Occupational pensions | 4 | 6 | 8 | 13 | 14 | 16 | 20 | 21 | 26 | 34 | 16 |
| *Total original income* | 117 | 173 | 209 | 230 | 261 | 281 | 327 | 365 | 425 | 592 | 298 |
| | | | | | | | | | | | |
| Student grants | 0.3 | 0.2 | 0.2 | 0.3 | 0.3 | 0.3 | 0.5 | 0.7 | 0.8 | 1.3 | 0.5 |
| Retirement pension | 25 | 25 | 26 | 27 | 25 | 28 | 26 | 27 | 24 | 22 | 26 |
| SERPS (AP) | 11 | 15 | 18 | 21 | 21 | 25 | 23 | 26 | 22 | 21 | 20 |
| Contributory benefits | 3 | 3 | 3 | 4 | 4 | 4 | 4 | 4 | 3 | 3 | 3 |
| Child benefit/OPB | 6 | 7 | 6 | 6 | 6 | 6 | 5 | 5 | 4 | 3 | 6 |
| Disability benefits | 2 | 3 | 2 | 2 | 2 | 2 | 3 | 2 | 3 | 4 | 2 |
| Means-tested benefits | 17 | 11 | 9 | 8 | 7 | 5 | 6 | 5 | 4 | 4 | 8 |
| *Total cash benefits* | 65 | 64 | 65 | 68 | 66 | 71 | 66 | 71 | 60 | 58 | 66 |
| | | | | | | | | | | | |
| *Gross income* | 182 | 236 | 273 | 298 | 327 | 352 | 393 | 436 | 485 | 651 | 363 |
| | | | | | | | | | | | |
| Income tax | 17 | 28 | 36 | 42 | 50 | 56 | 68 | 81 | 97 | 153 | 63 |
| NICs | 8 | 12 | 14 | 15 | 18 | 19 | 21 | 23 | 26 | 30 | 19 |
| *Direct taxes* | 25 | 40 | 51 | 57 | 68 | 75 | 89 | 105 | 123 | 183 | 82 |
| | | | | | | | | | | | |
| *Net income* | 157 | 196 | 222 | 241 | 259 | 277 | 304 | 331 | 362 | 468 | 282 |
| | | | | | | | | | | | |
| *Equivalent net income* | 159 | 204 | 231 | 255 | 269 | 293 | 312 | 347 | 373 | 468 | 291 |
| | | | | | | | | | | | |
| Education | 13 | 13 | 13 | 13 | 14 | 13 | 15 | 16 | 17 | 20 | 15 |
| Health | 22 | 21 | 22 | 22 | 21 | 23 | 22 | 22 | 20 | 20 | 22 |
| *Equivalent final income* | 195 | 239 | 266 | 290 | 304 | 329 | 349 | 385 | 410 | 508 | 327 |
| | | | | | | | | | | | |
| Annualised equivalent net income (£/year) | 2750 | 3550 | 3940 | 4260 | 4560 | 4870 | 5260 | 5750 | 6430 | 8060 | 4940 |
| Average age at death | 72.7 | 73.7 | 74.8 | 75.8 | 74.9 | 76.1 | 75.4 | 76.3 | 74.0 | 74.1 | 74.8 |

Decile group of individuals by lifetime equivalent net income (annualised)

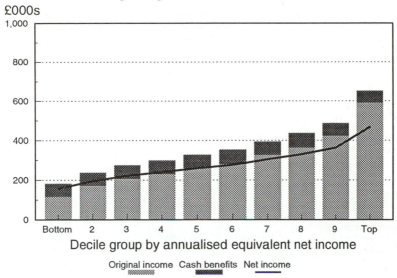

Figure: Original, gross and net incomes

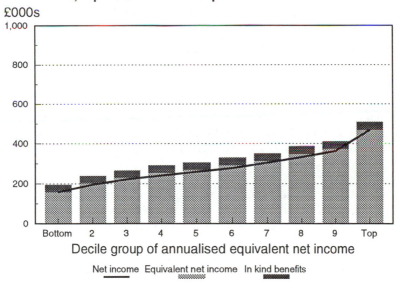

Figure: Net, equivalent net and equivalent final income

**Notes:**
1985 tax and social security systems; equal sharing; McClements equivalence scale.

**Figure 6.2** Lifetime Total Incomes

**Table 6.3** Cross-sectional and Lifetime Income Distribution: Summary (equal sharing; McClements; 1985 system)

| Income measure | Cross-sectional results | Lifetime totals |
|---|---|---|
| (a) *Ratio of top decile group average to bottom decile group average*[a] | | |
| Original | 69.7 | 5.1 |
| Gross | 13.4 | 3.6 |
| Net | 9.4 | 3.0 |
| Equivalent original | n.a. | 4.8 |
| Equivalent net | 10.4 | 2.9 |
| Equivalent final | 6.4 | 2.6 |
| Equivalent original (annualised) | - | 4.7 |
| Equivalent net (annualised) | - | 2.9 |
| (b) *Gini coefficient*[b] | | |
| Original | 0.57 | 0.33 |
| Gross | 0.42 | 0.27 |
| Net | 0.37 | 0.25 |
| Equivalent original | 0.50 | 0.25 |
| Equivalent net | 0.30 | 0.20 |
| Equivalent final | 0.28 | 0.19 |
| Equivalent original (annualised) | - | 0.24 |
| Equivalent net (annualised) | - | 0.17 |

**Notes:**
a   Cross-sectional results ranked by equivalent net income. Lifetime results ranked by lifetime equivalent net income (annualised).
b   Calculated using INEQ program developed by F. Cowell. Cross-sectional results calculated from means of 1,000 groups of results in each case.

annual to lifetime incomes suggested by our results (Table 6.3) is at least as large as Blinder's (1974) suggestion of 30 per cent referred to in Chapter 1; the reduction for original and equivalent original incomes is more like 50 per cent.

While these results suggest that a considerable part of the inequality we observe in cross-sectional distributions can be attributed to life cycle factors, inequality still remains on a lifetime basis. At the same time, sharing within the family, the welfare state and direct taxes clearly have a major effect in reducing inequality. The Gini coefficient of lifetime original incomes is 0.33. This falls to 0.25 when family circumstances are allowed for (assuming equal sharing by couples here) to give equivalent original incomes. Allowing for benefits in cash and kind and direct taxes to give equivalent final incomes, it falls further to 0.19.

## 3. How Are Lifetime and Annual Distributions Related?

Given the strength of the 'life cycle' influences on the cross-sectional distribution shown in Table 6.1, it is natural to ask whether there is much relationship between someone's positions within a particular year, and within the lifetime distribution shown in Table 6.2. The issue is very important for policy. People who appear poor or rich in a particular year may only be so temporarily. Appropriate policy responses may well be different for such groups from those aimed at people who are not only poor in a single year, but who are also poor on a lifetime basis.

Table 6.4 shows where the individuals generating observations in each quintile group (fifth) of *cross-sectional* income can be found in the *lifetime* distribution, also by quintile group (both distributions calculated assuming equal sharing between couples and using the McClements equivalence scale). Thus, for instance, 33 per cent of observations in the second quintile group of the cross-sectional distribution relate to individuals who come in the bottom quintile group of lifetime income.

If annual and lifetime incomes were perfectly correlated, all the observations would fall in the leading diagonal – only the lifetime poor would be poor on an annual basis, and only the lifetime rich would be rich on an annual basis. On the other hand, if the two were unrelated, 20 per cent of each row would fall in each column.[8]

**Table 6.4** Lifetime versus Cross-sectional Distributions: Composition of Cross-sectional Quintile Groups by Lifetime Quintile Groups (%)[a]

| Cross-sectional quintile group[b] | Lifetime quintile group[c] | | | | | |
|---|---|---|---|---|---|---|
| | Bottom | 2 | 3 | 4 | 5 | All |
| Bottom | 40 | 21 | 15 | 13 | 11 | 100 |
| 2 | 33 | 29 | 19 | 12 | 6 | 100 |
| 3 | 14 | 27 | 28 | 21 | 10 | 100 |
| 4 | 8 | 18 | 25 | 28 | 21 | 100 |
| 5 | 2 | 6 | 14 | 27 | 51 | 100 |
| All | 19.4 | 20.2 | 20.3 | 20.4 | 19.7 | 100 |

**Notes:**
a   1985 system; equal sharing; McClements equivalence scale.
b   Quintile groups of individuals by equivalent net income per year.
c   Quintile groups of individuals by annualised lifetime equivalent net income.

---

8   It can be seen that the total proportion of annual income observations falling into each lifetime income quintile group does not exactly equal 20 per cent. This is because those with low lifetime incomes tend to have shorter lives and therefore generate fewer cross-sectional income observations than those with higher lifetime incomes.

In fact, the pattern is somewhere between these two, with 35 per cent of all observations lying on the leading diagonal. At the bottom, 40 per cent of the observations of 'annual poverty' do relate to individuals who are 'lifetime poor' (that is, in the bottom fifth). At the top, 51 per cent of the observations of being rich on an annual basis relate to individuals who are 'lifetime rich' (in the top fifth).

However, the correlation is not perfect. Strikingly, 11 per cent of the observations in the bottom quintile group of annual income relate to individuals in the *top* lifetime quintile group. These are people who are poor in certain years, but are well-off over their lifetimes taken as a whole. By contrast, only 2 per cent of the observations in the top quintile group of the annual income distribution relate to individuals who are 'lifetime poor' (that is, exceptionally good years which turn out to be flashes in the pan). This asymmetry about the leading diagonal was found by Harding in her parallel work on Australia (Harding, 1993, Table 6.5). It implies that high income in one year is a better indicator of high lifetime income, than is low income in one year of low lifetime income.

A main reason for individuals who are actually lifetime rich showing up as poor on a cross-sectional basis is that they are young and/or in full-time education. Looking at the characteristics of the individuals generating the observations corresponding to the top right hand cell of Table 6.4, these 'temporarily poor' individuals have an average age of 27 (compared with 34 for the bottom quintile group of cross-sectional income as a whole) and 38 per cent of them are in full-time education (compared with 16 per cent). On the other hand, being a lone parent is associated with *both* low income on a cross-sectional basis, *and* being lifetime poor: 8 per cent of the observations in the top left hand cell of Table 6.4 (current *and* lifetime poor) are for current lone parents compared to under 3 per cent of all observations.

Thus some characteristics associated with low incomes on a cross-sectional basis – like lone parenthood – are also associated with low lifetime incomes, while others – like being in full-time education – are not. We examine some implications of this in Chapters 8 and 9.

## 4.      How are Lifetime Incomes Made Up?

The picture of lifetime incomes in Table 6.2 has certain differences from the cross-sectional picture in Table 6.1. First, even the bottom decile group has significant lifetime earnings. Indeed these represent over half of their equivalent final incomes, compared to the corresponding figure of under 12 per cent in the cross-sectional results. Second, occupational pensions are even more skewed towards the top of the distribution than lifetime earnings. Allowing for maintenance (at the levels being paid in the 1980s) increases the lifetime incomes of the bottom four groups (disproportionately containing women who experience lone parenthood) but reduces those of the top three groups (containing many of their ex-partners).

The distribution of cash benefits also looks rather different on a lifetime basis. First, lifetime total cash benefits, in contrast to the cross-sectional results, are relatively flat across the whole income distribution (with a slight rise in the middle, but more pronounced dip at the top). This does not stop them being redistributive, given the much greater *relative* importance of a fixed lump sum at the bottom, and if they are financed by taxes which rise with income. In terms of absolute differences in net incomes, it is, however, direct taxes rather than cash benefits which have the greater effect.

Some of the most interesting contrasts with the cross-sectional picture can be seen for the separate kinds of cash benefits. Student grants are concentrated at the top of the lifetime distribution, in contrast to their cross-sectional distribution. Receipt of the basic state retirement pension is virtually flat (the smaller receipts at the very top of the distribution reflect the greater preponderance of men – with shorter lives and pension periods – in it than women). The Additional Pension payable under SERPS is of least importance to the bottom two lifetime income groups, reaches a peak in the sixth, seventh and eighth groups, and then falls back a little for the top two groups.

Like the basic pension, contributory benefits (Unemployment, Invalidity and Sickness Benefits, maternity and widows benefits) are evenly distributed across lifetime income groups. Meanwhile, family benefits have a somewhat greater value for the bottom half of the lifetime income distribution than for the top half. Whereas on a cross-sectional basis the poorest income group did not receive much from family benefits, the 'lifetime poorest' receive the average amount.

By contrast, means-tested benefits, while still of much greater value at the bottom of the distribution than the top, are somewhat *less* concentrated at the bottom when analysed on a lifetime than on an annual basis. This reflects what they are designed to do: they are payable when income is very low at one particular time (on a weekly basis in the model). People with fluctuating incomes may be poor in one year – and so benefit from them – but may be relatively well off over their lifetimes as a whole.

## Differences between men and women

As already seen in Chapter 5, there are profound differences between the levels and patterns of men's and women's incomes over their life cycles. These generate great differences between their lifetime total incomes, which can be seen in Tables 6.5 and 6.6. These show the lifetime average incomes and their composition for the men and women in each decile group of the *overall* income distribution on the same basis as Table 6.2.

As well as the income data, the tables also show the gender composition of each decile group of the overall distribution. Strikingly, 71 per cent of the lifetime poorest group are women, with their share in each decile group falling almost continuously as one moves upwards through the distribution to constitute only 35 per cent of the top group. This gradient is far steeper than that observed in the cross-sectional results shown in Table 6.1.

The tables also show average age at death for each income group. The separate patterns for men and women are clearer than those for the combined population. Women live, on average, over five years more than men. Men and women at the bottom of the distribution have shorter lives than the average, especially men in the bottom group. While age at death generally rises with lifetime income, it falls back for men and women in the top two groups. This pattern reflects causality running in two ways. Those with higher incomes when in work tend to live longer, but long periods of retirement tend to pull down *average* lifetime living standards.[9]

Overall, women have lower lifetime average living standards than men, even with the strong assumption here of equal sharing of resources when they are in couples and allowing for the equalising effects of the welfare state and direct taxes. Average annualised equivalent net income is £4,690 per year for women, 10 per cent below the £5,190 per year for men. However, this difference is a fraction of that between men and women in original incomes, i.e. before allowing for family sharing, benefits and taxation. With lower earnings when in full-time work, part-time working, interrupted labour market participation and earlier retirement, women's average lifetime earnings and original incomes are less than half those of men.

Each subsequent stage of redistribution shown in the tables contributes to reducing the difference in original incomes. Lifetime cash benefits – dominated by pensions – are worth two-thirds more for women than for men. With their greater original incomes, men pay nearly twice as much direct tax as women. The effect of allowing for family circumstances is to raise women's net incomes by a quarter, but to reduce that of men by over 10 per cent.[10] While education is worth

9   It is a moot point whether someone who lives longer, but with a low average standard of living, is 'worse' or 'better' off than someone who has a shorter life, but a merrier one, or at least a higher average income. To compare the welfare of the two one might want to use some combination of both average income per year and length of life (see Atkinson and Bourguignon, 1983, pp. 48–9). However, for our purposes annualised lifetime income seems the most appropriate way of ranking the population, without getting into a multiplicity of alternative methodologies.

10  The sensitivity of these results to the assumptions about sharing within couples is explored below. Even with the least favourable assumption for women – that men

**Table 6.5** Composition of Lifetime Total Income by Lifetime Income Distribution: Men (1985 system; equal sharing; McClements; £000s)

| | Decile group of all individuals by lifetime equivalent net income (annualised) | | | | | | | | | | |
|---|---|---|---|---|---|---|---|---|---|---|---|
| | Bottom | 2 | 3 | 4 | 5 | 6 | 7 | 8 | 9 | Top | All |
| Earnings | 136 | 214 | 252 | 273 | 308 | 333 | 372 | 421 | 479 | 618 | 363 |
| Maintenance | -0.4 | -0.7 | -0.8 | -0.8 | -1.0 | -0.9 | -0.6 | -1.0 | -1.0 | -0.9 | -0.8 |
| Investment income | 4 | 5 | 6 | 6 | 6 | 7 | 10 | 13 | 17 | 41 | 13 |
| Occupational pensions | 3 | 5 | 7 | 10 | 12 | 13 | 17 | 17 | 22 | 29 | 15 |
| *Total original income* | 142 | 223 | 265 | 288 | 326 | 352 | 398 | 450 | 517 | 687 | 390 |
| Student grants | 0.1 | 0.2 | 0.1 | 0.2 | 0.3 | 0.4 | 0.6 | 0.7 | 0.9 | 1.5 | 0.6 |
| Retirement pension | 14 | 16 | 18 | 19 | 18 | 20 | 20 | 20 | 18 | 18 | 18 |
| SERPS (AP) | 6 | 11 | 14 | 14 | 15 | 18 | 18 | 20 | 17 | 17 | 16 |
| Contributory benefits | 2 | 3 | 4 | 3 | 3 | 3 | 3 | 3 | 3 | 3 | 3 |
| Child benefit/OPB | - | - | - | - | - | - | - | - | - | - | - |
| Disability benefits | 5 | 3 | 2 | 2 | 2 | 3 | 3 | 3 | 5 | 5 | 3 |
| Means-tested benefits | 16 | 13 | 10 | 10 | 8 | 7 | 7 | 6 | 5 | 4 | 8 |
| *Total cash benefits* | 44 | 46 | 49 | 49 | 48 | 51 | 52 | 51 | 48 | 48 | 49 |
| *Gross income* | 186 | 269 | 314 | 337 | 373 | 403 | 449 | 501 | 565 | 736 | 439 |
| Income tax | 20 | 37 | 45 | 51 | 60 | 68 | 81 | 98 | 117 | 177 | 82 |
| NICs | 10 | 16 | 19 | 20 | 22 | 24 | 26 | 29 | 31 | 35 | 24 |
| *Direct taxes* | 30 | 53 | 64 | 71 | 83 | 92 | 107 | 127 | 149 | 211 | 107 |
| *Net income* | 156 | 217 | 250 | 266 | 291 | 311 | 342 | 374 | 416 | 524 | 332 |
| *Equivalent net income* | 141 | 192 | 222 | 244 | 257 | 280 | 302 | 332 | 362 | 460 | 294 |
| Education | 13 | 13 | 12 | 12 | 13 | 13 | 16 | 17 | 18 | 21 | 15 |
| Health | 19 | 19 | 20 | 20 | 20 | 20 | 20 | 20 | 19 | 19 | 20 |
| *Equivalent final income* | 173 | 224 | 254 | 276 | 291 | 312 | 338 | 369 | 398 | 500 | 329 |
| Annualised equivalent net income (£/year) | 2800 | 3570 | 3930 | 4250 | 4560 | 4880 | 5260 | 5750 | 6440 | 8070 | 5190 |
| Men as a percentage of group | 29 | 41 | 49 | 48 | 50 | 48 | 57 | 54 | 59 | 65 | 50 |
| Average age at death | 63.6 | 69.9 | 72.6 | 73.3 | 72.4 | 73.4 | 73.4 | 73.8 | 72.2 | 73.0 | 72.2 |

**Table 6.6** Composition of Lifetime Total Income by Lifetime Income Distribution: Women (1985 system; equal sharing; McClements; £000s)

| | Decile group of all individuals by lifetime equivalent net income (annualised) | | | | | | | | | | |
|---|---|---|---|---|---|---|---|---|---|---|---|
| | Bottom | 2 | 3 | 4 | 5 | 6 | 7 | 8 | 9 | Top | All |
| Earnings | 96 | 123 | 139 | 154 | 175 | 186 | 202 | 228 | 252 | 339 | 178 |
| Maintenance | 1.2 | 1.3 | 1.1 | 0.8 | 0.8 | 0.7 | 0.8 | 0.5 | 0.5 | 0.4 | 0.9 |
| Investment income | 4 | 5 | 5 | 4 | 5 | 8 | 7 | 14 | 12 | 38 | 9 |
| Occupational pensions | 4 | 7 | 9 | 16 | 17 | 19 | 25 | 25 | 31 | 43 | 18 |
| *Total original income* | 106 | 137 | 154 | 175 | 198 | 214 | 235 | 268 | 295 | 420 | 206 |
| Student grants | 0.3 | 0.3 | 0.3 | 0.4 | 0.4 | 0.3 | 0.4 | 0.6 | 0.7 | 1.0 | 0.4 |
| Retirement pension | 30 | 32 | 32 | 35 | 33 | 35 | 34 | 36 | 32 | 31 | 33 |
| SERPS (AP) | 13 | 18 | 23 | 27 | 27 | 31 | 29 | 34 | 28 | 27 | 25 |
| Contributory benefits | 4 | 3 | 3 | 4 | 5 | 5 | 4 | 5 | 4 | 4 | 4 |
| Child benefit/OPB | 9 | 12 | 12 | 12 | 12 | 12 | 12 | 12 | 10 | 8 | 11 |
| Disability benefits | 1 | 2 | 1 | 2 | 2 | 2 | 2 | 2 | 2 | 2 | 2 |
| Means-tested benefits | 17 | 10 | 8 | 7 | 5 | 4 | 4 | 4 | 3 | 3 | 7 |
| *Total cash benefits* | 74 | 77 | 80 | 87 | 84 | 90 | 85 | 93 | 78 | 77 | 82 |
| *Gross income* | 180 | 214 | 234 | 262 | 282 | 304 | 320 | 361 | 373 | 496 | 288 |
| Income tax | 16 | 23 | 28 | 34 | 40 | 46 | 51 | 63 | 69 | 109 | 44 |
| NICs | 7 | 9 | 10 | 11 | 13 | 14 | 15 | 17 | 18 | 21 | 13 |
| *Direct taxes* | 22 | 31 | 38 | 45 | 53 | 59 | 66 | 79 | 87 | 130 | 56 |
| *Net income* | 158 | 182 | 196 | 217 | 229 | 245 | 254 | 282 | 286 | 366 | 232 |
| *Equivalent net income* | 166 | 213 | 240 | 265 | 280 | 305 | 326 | 363 | 388 | 483 | 288 |
| Education | 13 | 13 | 13 | 14 | 14 | 14 | 15 | 16 | 16 | 18 | 14 |
| Health | 24 | 23 | 24 | 24 | 23 | 25 | 23 | 25 | 22 | 21 | 24 |
| *Equivalent final income* | 203 | 249 | 277 | 302 | 317 | 345 | 364 | 404 | 427 | 522 | 326 |
| Annualised equivalent net income (£/year) | 2730 | 3530 | 3940 | 4260 | 4560 | 4870 | 5260 | 5750 | 6420 | 8060 | 4690 |
| Women as a percentage of group | 71 | 59 | 51 | 52 | 50 | 52 | 43 | 46 | 41 | 35 | 50 |
| Average age at death | 76.4 | 76.3 | 76.9 | 78.1 | 77.4 | 78.6 | 77.9 | 79.2 | 76.5 | 76.2 | 77.3 |

more to men than women, this is more than offset by the greater value of health services to women.

Looking at the distributions for men and women separately, lifetime retirement pensions rise up to the eighth decile group for both men and women, before dropping back a little (with age at death). For the whole population, these gradients are counteracted by the composition effect of the much greater preponderance of women in the bottom decile groups. This creates the much flatter distribution of the basic retirement pension for the combined population shown in Table 6.2. Additional Pensions for men under the 1985 SERPS rules are 85 per cent of the value of the basic pension; the corresponding figure for women is 76 per cent (in both cases including inherited rights). This results from women's lower earnings when at work. Following the pattern of pensions, total cash benefits have their lowest values for men and women at the *bottom* of the separate distributions. The generally flat picture shown in Table 6.2 results from the greater number of women – who receive greater benefits on average than men – with low lifetime incomes.

## Changes in ranking caused by benefits and direct taxes

The results so far divide the model population according to incomes *after* the effects of cash benefits, direct taxes and family circumstances, and show how the three factors combine to equalise the distribution. However, the tax and benefit system can also change an individual's position in the distribution. In an extreme case, the overall distribution of income could be just as unequal after the effects of the welfare state as before it, with its apparently equalising effects on the basis of the *ex post* ranking in fact reflecting nothing more than a reordering.

To examine this one can compare the LIFEMOD results using the ranking by equivalent *net* incomes (as in Table 6.2) with an alternative ranking with the division into decile groups carried out using annualised equivalent *original* income (also assuming equal sharing and using the McClements equivalence scale).

If one ranks by original incomes, the gain of the bottom group between lifetime equivalent original and net incomes averages £63,000, compared with only £40,000 when ranked by net income. One of the reasons for some people being at the bottom of the net distribution is, after all, the failure of cash benefits to raise their original incomes. Looking at the ranking by original income would thus give an

---

receive 60 per cent of each couple's net equivalent income regardless of to whom it originally accrued – lifetime net equivalent income is 9 per cent higher than net income for women, but 0.5 per cent lower for men.

exaggerated impression of the effect of benefits and taxes in reducing income inequalities.

If the objective was narrowly focused on raising average incomes for the poorest tenth of the distribution, the relevant comparison would be between the original incomes of the lowest group ranked by original income, and the net incomes of the lowest group ranked by net income. In this case the difference is £44,000. The results ranked by original incomes at both stages overstate this rise by almost half. Those using the ranking by net income at both stages are much less affected by this problem, understating the income gain by a tenth.

These movements within the distribution affect men and women in different ways. Overall 44 per cent of individuals stay in the same decile groups moving from the ranking by annualised equivalent original to that by equivalent net incomes, with 27 per cent moving down one or more group and 29 per cent moving up. Most of these movements are by just one group: only 14 per cent move more than one place. However, only 17 per cent of women move down the distribution, with 40 per cent moving up. For men the figures are virtually the mirror image. To the extent that people are being moved up and down the distribution by cash benefits and direct taxes, women are more than twice as likely to be moving up as men.

## Sensitivity analysis

Some of the results presented so far may stem from the assumptions made in estimating equivalent incomes. In particular, we have assumed equal sharing between couples. We have also allowed for the effects of family composition using the McClements equivalence scale, which gives a relatively low weight to young children in affecting living standards.

Table 6.7 suggests that the findings are, in fact, quite robust to changes in those assumptions. The top panel shows some of the key variables from Table 6.2, using the main assumptions. The second shows the same variables, but on the assumption that each member of a couple contributes only 80 per cent of the original income they receive into the equally shared pool. This has two effects. First, it means that couples starting with unequal original incomes (usually with the man receiving more) end up with unequal net incomes. Secondly, less income is pooled, and so less of it benefits from economies of scale in contributing to living standards (which is why average equivalent net income is some 1.7 per cent lower under this assumption than with equal sharing). This changed assumption does make the distribution of annualised equivalent net income more unequal than in the base case, with only the top decile group having its income level raised. However, the scale of the changes is slight.

**Table 6.7**  Lifetime Total Income by Lifetime Income Distribution (1985 system; alternative definitions of equivalent income; £000s)

| | Decile group of individuals by lifetime equivalent income (annualised)[a] | | | | | | | | | | |
|---|---|---|---|---|---|---|---|---|---|---|---|
| | Bottom | 2 | 3 | 4 | 5 | 6 | 7 | 8 | 9 | Top | All |
| **(a) Equal sharing; McClements equivalence scale** | | | | | | | | | | | |
| Original | 117 | 173 | 209 | 230 | 261 | 281 | 327 | 365 | 425 | 592 | 298 |
| Gross | 182 | 236 | 273 | 298 | 327 | 352 | 393 | 436 | 485 | 651 | 363 |
| Net | 157 | 196 | 222 | 241 | 259 | 277 | 304 | 331 | 362 | 468 | 282 |
| Equivalent net | 159 | 204 | 231 | 255 | 269 | 293 | 312 | 347 | 373 | 468 | 291 |
| Equivalent final | 195 | 239 | 266 | 290 | 304 | 329 | 349 | 385 | 410 | 508 | 327 |
| Annualised equivalent net (£/year) | 2750 | 3550 | 3940 | 4260 | 4560 | 4870 | 5260 | 5750 | 6430 | 8060 | 4940 |
| **(b) 80% of net income pooled; McClements equivalence scale** | | | | | | | | | | | |
| Original | 106 | 154 | 193 | 227 | 248 | 286 | 317 | 369 | 438 | 641 | 298 |
| Gross | 172 | 221 | 260 | 296 | 317 | 353 | 383 | 438 | 496 | 697 | 363 |
| Net | 151 | 186 | 213 | 240 | 253 | 277 | 297 | 333 | 370 | 499 | 282 |
| Equivalent net | 158 | 200 | 226 | 249 | 266 | 285 | 306 | 339 | 366 | 467 | 286 |
| Equivalent final | 194 | 235 | 261 | 284 | 302 | 321 | 342 | 378 | 403 | 507 | 323 |
| Annualised equivalent net (£/year) | 2680 | 3440 | 3850 | 4160 | 4460 | 4790 | 5180 | 5660 | 6370 | 8110 | 4870 |
| **(c) Men receive 60% of equivalent net income; McClements equivalence scale** | | | | | | | | | | | |
| Original | 100 | 149 | 182 | 217 | 247 | 284 | 320 | 377 | 455 | 648 | 298 |
| Gross | 168 | 222 | 259 | 290 | 316 | 353 | 383 | 434 | 510 | 699 | 363 |
| Net | 148 | 188 | 212 | 233 | 251 | 277 | 297 | 330 | 381 | 502 | 282 |
| Equivalent net | 152 | 199 | 223 | 246 | 265 | 291 | 313 | 342 | 387 | 493 | 291 |
| Equivalent final | 188 | 235 | 260 | 283 | 300 | 328 | 347 | 378 | 423 | 532 | 327 |
| Annualised equivalent net (£/year) | 2600 | 3320 | 3750 | 4110 | 4470 | 4880 | 5320 | 5860 | 6710 | 8600 | 4960 |
| **(c) Equal sharing; OECD equivalence scale** | | | | | | | | | | | |
| Original | 116 | 173 | 208 | 234 | 260 | 282 | 322 | 364 | 430 | 588 | 298 |
| Gross | 179 | 238 | 272 | 301 | 327 | 353 | 393 | 431 | 493 | 646 | 363 |
| Net | 155 | 198 | 222 | 243 | 260 | 277 | 304 | 327 | 368 | 464 | 282 |
| Equivalent net | 147 | 192 | 215 | 237 | 254 | 276 | 298 | 323 | 358 | 447 | 275 |
| Equivalent final | 182 | 227 | 250 | 272 | 290 | 313 | 336 | 360 | 396 | 486 | 311 |
| Annualised equivalent net (£/year) | 2600 | 3320 | 3690 | 3990 | 4270 | 4580 | 4960 | 5420 | 6090 | 7720 | 4660 |

**Note:**

a   Ranked by annualised equivalent net income under each definition.

Much the same can be said of the results in the third panel. These are based on the assumption that all income within each couple is pooled, but that the man receives 60 per cent of the benefit, and the woman 40 per cent (regardless of which received the original income). This also produces a higher equivalent net income for the top decile group, but it is still only 7 per cent higher than that in the base case.

Finally, the bottom panel shows the effects of using the 'OECD' equivalence scale, which puts more weight on the effects of children than the McClements scale. This reduces the equivalent incomes of families with children and lone parents. Overall, average annualised equivalent net income is 6 per cent lower than in the base case. However, the effects are spread out through the distribution, and there is little difference in the overall degree of inequality.[11]

In summary, the use of different assumptions about sharing within families or of an equivalence scale putting greater weight on children has little effect on the overall shape of the distributions or on the distributional impact of benefits and direct taxes. The findings illustrated above, for instance in Table 6.2, therefore appear to be robust.

## 5.      Who are the Lifetime Rich and Poor?

The demographic characteristics of those in different parts of the lifetime income distribution are summarised in Table 6.8. The top panel shows the results if individuals are ranked by lifetime equivalent *original* income (that is, allowing for family effects, but not for the welfare state). The bottom panel shows the same information for the ranking by lifetime equivalent *net* income (after allowing for cash benefits and direct taxes; both cases assume equal sharing and use the McClements scale).

The most striking gradient is the one we have already commented on above: 81 per cent of the lifetime poorest in terms of equivalent original income are women, and only 30 per cent of the lifetime richest, with a fairly uniform gradient between. Tax and social security moderate this picture a little, but the gender gradient with net income is still steep.

Where re-ranking after allowing for cash benefits and taxation has a larger effect is with average age at death of each decile group. Those poorest in terms of original income (averaged over years of life from 16) live longer than the average, while those in the top two groups have the shortest lives. Long periods of retirement reduce average original income per year of adulthood, particularly for those without an occupational pension. However, the state pension changes this, so that if one looks at

---

11  The Gini coefficient of annualised lifetime equivalent net income using the OECD scale is 0.169, compared with 0.166 using the McClements scale.

**Table 6.8** Selected Characteristics of Model Population by Lifetime Original and Net Incomes (1985 system; equal sharing; McClements equivalence scale)

| | Decile group of individuals by lifetime equivalent income (annualised) | | | | | | | | | | |
|---|---|---|---|---|---|---|---|---|---|---|---|
| | Bottom | 2 | 3 | 4 | 5 | 6 | 7 | 8 | 9 | Top | All |
| (a) *Ranked by equivalent original income (annualised)* | | | | | | | | | | | |
| Age at death | 78.5 | 78.7 | 76.5 | 76.8 | 75.1 | 73.8 | 74.0 | 72.4 | 71.7 | 70.3 | 74.8 |
| Women (%) | 81 | 65 | 59 | 52 | 50 | 43 | 44 | 41 | 37 | 30 | 50 |
| Ever married (%) | 71 | 90 | 91 | 91 | 93 | 91 | 93 | 91 | 89 | 84 | 88 |
| Years married | 17.9 | 32.7 | 32.6 | 34.1 | 35.1 | 34.3 | 35.3 | 34.1 | 33.2 | 29.5 | 31.9 |
| No. of child years | 22.4 | 32.4 | 28.5 | 29.2 | 31.3 | 28.9 | 28.5 | 24.8 | 22.0 | 18.3 | 26.6 |
| Ever divorced (%) | 44 | 38 | 33 | 32 | 36 | 32 | 37 | 36 | 32 | 35 | 35 |
| Ever lone parent (%) | 39 | 29 | 23 | 22 | 20 | 17 | 16 | 13 | 7 | 6 | 19 |
| Years as lone parent | 4.9 | 3.0 | 1.8 | 1.7 | 1.6 | 1.5 | 1.2 | 0.9 | 0.5 | 0.5 | 1.8 |
| Ever in tertiary education (%) | 40 | 39 | 42 | 46 | 48 | 50 | 58 | 66 | 75 | 83 | 55 |
| Total years of unemployment | 4.7 | 4.4 | 4.5 | 4.3 | 3.9 | 3.7 | 3.3 | 3.3 | 3.1 | 2.7 | 4.3 |
| (b) *Ranked by equivalent net income (annualised)* | | | | | | | | | | | |
| Age at death | 72.7 | 73.7 | 74.8 | 75.8 | 74.9 | 76.1 | 75.4 | 76.3 | 74.0 | 74.1 | 74.8 |
| Women (%) | 71 | 59 | 51 | 52 | 50 | 52 | 43 | 46 | 41 | 35 | 50 |
| Ever married (%) | 66 | 88 | 89 | 90 | 93 | 97 | 91 | 92 | 91 | 87 | 88 |
| Years married (%) | 15.4 | 26.2 | 32.6 | 32.6 | 34.7 | 37.1 | 35.2 | 36.0 | 35.7 | 33.3 | 31.9 |
| No. of child years | 20.7 | 28.8 | 29.8 | 28.6 | 30.0 | 30.9 | 26.5 | 27.3 | 23.9 | 19.6 | 26.6 |
| Ever divorced (%) | 39 | 42 | 37 | 34 | 32 | 35 | 35 | 33 | 34 | 33 | 35 |
| Ever lone parent (%) | 32 | 25 | 24 | 25 | 19 | 20 | 16 | 16 | 10 | 8 | 19 |
| Years as lone parent | 4.1 | 2.8 | 1.8 | 2.2 | 1.7 | 1.4 | 1.2 | 1.0 | 0.7 | 0.6 | 1.8 |
| Ever in tertiary education(%) | 36 | 38 | 40 | 46 | 52 | 50 | 60 | 69 | 73 | 83 | 55 |
| Total years of unemployment | 5.1 | 4.8 | 4.4 | 4.3 | 3.7 | 3.5 | 3.4 | 3.2 | 2.9 | 2.6 | 3.8 |

the picture by net income, age at death tends to rise most of the way through the distribution, but falls back at the top. With state pensions neutralising part of the depressing effect of long periods of retirement, the positive association between higher incomes in people's working lives and length of life shows up more strongly. The picture is, however, complicated by gender differences in age at death which are explored below.

A further steep gradient is found when looking at the incidence of lone parenthood. Nearly 40 per cent of those in the bottom group of lifetime original income experience lone parenthood at some point in their lives.[12] This proportion falls steeply, with only 6 per cent of the top

---

12 Within LIFEMOD lone parents are nearly all women. Only men who become widowers while they have children become lone parents. Otherwise when relationships end, it is assumed that the children stay with the woman.

group ever experiencing it. The average number of years of lone parenthood (averaged over the whole group) falls even more steeply: those at the bottom end of the income distribution are not only more likely to have been lone parents, but to have been so for longer (12.5 years for those lone parents at the bottom, compared to 7.5 years for those in the top group). Again, re-ranking after allowing for cash benefits and taxation tends to lessen these gradients a little, but only a little.

Fewer of the lifetime poorest in terms of original income are ever married than for the rest of the population, and the average number of years married (averaged over the whole group) rises up to the middle of the distribution, after which it falls back somewhat. If anything, the pattern becomes stronger, if one looks at the distribution by net income.

There is a pronounced downward gradient in the number of 'child years'[13] experienced by individuals ranked by original income between the second and top decile groups – having more children around for longer pushes people down the distribution. This is moderated if one looks at the picture by net income, with the peak average number of child years coming in the fifth and sixth decile groups, not the second. Benefits and taxes appear to remove part of the impact of looking after children on living standards. None the less, those at the top of the lifetime income distribution have fewer responsibilities for children than any of the other groups, even when viewed on a net income basis.

Finally, as one might expect from lone parenthood, experience of divorce tends to push people down the lifetime distribution, although the gradient is not very pronounced. The very different patterns for men and women which cause this are examined in more detail below.

The table also gives two indicators of economic characteristics. Experience of tertiary education rises, as one would expect, through the distribution – from 36 per cent of those at the bottom of the net income distribution to 83 per cent at the top. There is also a strong downward gradient in years of unemployment experienced.[14]

Comparing the two panels in Table 6.8 it is clear that, however much cash benefits and direct taxes may be compressing the distribution (and leading to some re-ordering of it), they do not have a very marked effect on many of the characteristics of those who are lifetime rich or poor. Being a woman, experiencing lone parenthood, and not having tertiary education are all factors tending to push people down the distribution, and the welfare state seems to make little difference to their effects on the

---

13  The number of child years is the total number of years with a child present in an individual's family, counting each child separately. Thus a husband and wife who have two children in their family, each for 16 years, would both be allocated a total of 32 child years.

14  Total years of unemployment gives the sum of all separate spells of unemployment in years (not the number of years in which some unemployment is experienced).

ranking. Where there is an effect, by contrast, is with the age gradients. As we have already seen, cash benefits are dominated by pensions, and they clearly do have an impact in reducing the effect of having a long life on pulling people down the distribution.

## Looking separately at men and women

The pronounced gender gradient shown in Table 6.8 has a confusing effect on the apparent impact of some of the other characteristics. Women have longer life expectancy than men, for instance, and have shorter periods in the labour force, reducing the number of years in which they can experience unemployment. What is going on becomes a lot clearer if one separates out the characteristics of the men and the women in each part of the income distribution.[15] This is done in Figure 6.3.

First, average **age at death** generally rises as one moves up the distribution, with its maximum in the eighth decile group for both men and women. The gradient at the bottom is particularly pronounced for men. Right at the top, however, the gradient is reversed. As explained above, long periods in retirement tend to reduce lifetime income averaged over all years of adulthood. The general tendency is none the less for those higher up the distribution to have longer lives.

There is a great contrast is the way in which experience of **divorce** affects men and women. Forty-seven per cent of women in the bottom income group are ever-divorced, compared with only 18 per cent in the top group. Conversely the incidence of divorce rises across the income distribution from 19 per cent to 41 per cent for men (and this is after allowing for maintenance payments). All of these differences reflect the inequality between men's and women's original incomes. Being in a couple generally raises the equivalent income of women, but often reduces that of men.

**Children** are, perhaps appropriately, a mixed blessing. For men, the average number of child years peaks for people in the middle of the income distribution, above which it falls. Two effects are going in opposite directions here: children are associated (but not exclusively) with the benefits from sharing within couples (particularly for women). However, they also reduce equivalent incomes. The richest men on a lifetime basis tend to have had the fewest responsibilities for children.

The effects of **lone parenthood** are as already discussed. Nearly half of the women at the bottom of the distribution experience it at some stage in their lives (for an average total of 13 years for those who do so), but

15 The analysis which follows looks at men and women in different parts of the *overall* distribution, not in different decile groups of the separate distribution for men and women. The distribution used is that of annualised equivalent income, assuming equal sharing and using the McClements scale.

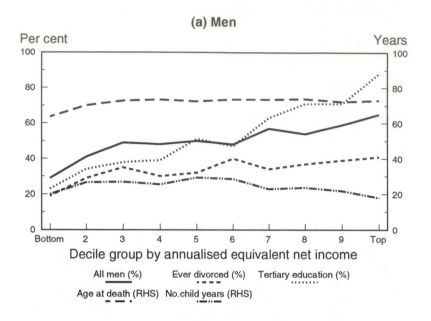

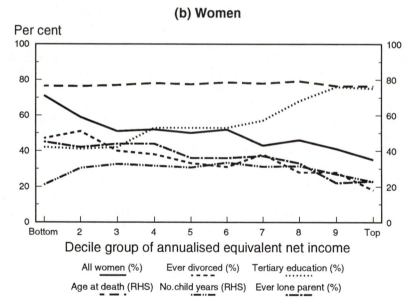

**Notes:**
1985 tax and social security systems; equal sharing; McClements equivalence scale.

**Figure 6.3** Characteristics by Lifetime Income

only a quarter of those women at the top (for an average of 8 years). Given that few men experience lone parenthood, the steeper gradient in Table 6.9 than in the bottom panel of Figure 6.3 reflects the preponderance of men at the top of the distribution.

Roughly the same proportions of men and women experience some **tertiary education**. However, the association with lifetime income is much stronger for men than for women. The proportion of men who are ever in tertiary education rises from 23 per cent at the bottom to 88 per cent at the top. For women the rise is from 42 per cent to 75 per cent. Again, gender inequalities in earnings mean that women's own qualification levels are less important to their position in the distribution than they are for men.[16]

## Sensitivity to sharing assumptions and equivalence scales

Again, these results may reflect the assumptions made about equal sharing and the equivalence scale used. With either version of unequal sharing described above, the gender gradients steepen. With only 80 per cent of net income pooled, the proportion of women in the bottom lifetime income group rises to 81 per cent (from 71 per cent with equal sharing in Table 6.8). This share increases to 88 per cent if men are assumed to end up with 60 per cent of all couples' equivalent incomes. With the first version of unequal sharing, the proportion of women in the top group falls to 24 per cent (from 35 per cent). With the second it falls to only 9 per cent.

In both cases more married people end up being located in the bottom income group, as do more lone parents, and more of those experiencing divorce (there are also more of those experiencing divorce at the top of the distribution, presumably men in this case). The gradients with tertiary education and unemployment become slightly less steep, as the demographic factors gain in relative importance. However, none of the differences from the picture given by Table 6.8 is large.

The main effect of using the OECD equivalence scale rather than the McClements scale is to raise the average number of child-years for those placed in the bottom group, and to reduce it for those placed at the top, doubling the downward gradient between bottom and top by comparison with Table 6.8. There is also a rise in the proportion of those in the bottom group who are lone parents. The differences for other characteristics are slight. As with the limited effects of changing the

---

16 Part of the rise in tertiary education with decile group for women reflects the 'assortative mating' probabilities built into LIFEMOD (that is, that better educated women are more likely to marry better educated men) as well as the effects on women's own original incomes.

sharing assumption, the results discussed above appear to be largely robust to the equivalence scale used.

## 6.   Changes to Tax and Social Security between 1985 and 1991

As explained in Chapter 5 (section 5), we examined the effects of the changes to the British tax and social security system between 1985 and 1991 on the LIFEMOD population. The results of this exercise in terms of the lifetime income distribution can be seen in Table 6.9, which gives the same results for the 1991 system as Table 6.2 does for the 1985 system. The first thing to note is the fall of one-third in the average value for the whole population of gross lifetime cash benefits – from £66,000 under the 1985 rules to £44,000 under those of 1991 (both at 1985 prices). The bulk of this fall is accounted for by a two-thirds reduction in the average value of lifetime receipts of Additional Pensions from the state under SERPS.[17] In addition, the value of Child Benefit and One Parent Benefit is one-third lower, while other benefits lose a sixth of their value (mainly from the falling generosity of price-linked benefits in relation to incomes, but also as a result of some tighter qualification rules).

With most of the change resulting from SERPS, the fall in the aggregate value of cash benefits is least for the bottom two lifetime income decile groups,[18] so the overall distribution of cash benefits becomes less flat and more concentrated at the bottom. Receipts fall almost continuously from the bottom decile group to the top one. In this sense, they have become better 'targeted'. However, the distributional advantage for those at the bottom is outweighed by the fact that the fall in benefits represents a greater proportion of their gross incomes than it does for those at the top. The ratio of gross income between top and bottom groups increases slightly to 3.7 to 1 (from 3.6 to 1 with the 1985 system).

Lifetime direct taxes are 16 per cent lower under the 1991 system, with the absolute gains from this concentrated at the top of the distribution (the proportionate fall is much the same for all income groups). Putting

17  A small part of this fall represents a switch from payments of Additional Pensions to higher payments of Guaranteed Minimum Pensions by occupational schemes (as a result of changes to post-retirement indexation of GMPs). Occupational pensions are also a little higher under the 1991 system because of the reduction to two years from five in the minimum period of membership of private schemes to gain preserved pension rights.

18  The positioning of individuals between decile groups varies slightly between the two tables, as the tax and benefit system has less effect on lifetime net incomes in the 1991 system. The decile groups in the two tables do not thus consist of exactly the same people.

**Table 6.9** Composition of Lifetime Income by Lifetime Income Distribution (1991 system; equal sharing; McClements; £000s)

| | Decile groups of individuals by lifetime equivalent net income (annualised) | | | | | | | | | | |
| | Bottom | 2 | 3 | 4 | 5 | 6 | 7 | 8 | 9 | Top | All |
|---|---|---|---|---|---|---|---|---|---|---|---|
| Earnings | 106 | 157 | 192 | 211 | 237 | 266 | 298 | 327 | 393 | 519 | 271 |
| Maintenance (net) | 0.8 | 0.4 | 0.2 | – | – | -0.2 | -0.1 | -0.3 | -0.4 | -0.4 | – |
| Investment income | 4 | 6 | 6 | 5 | 6 | 8 | 10 | 12 | 15 | 40 | 11 |
| Occupational pensions | 5 | 9 | 12 | 15 | 19 | 19 | 23 | 24 | 31 | 37 | 19 |
| *Total original income* | 115 | 172 | 210 | 232 | 261 | 293 | 331 | 363 | 438 | 595 | 301 |
| | | | | | | | | | | | |
| Student grants | 0.3 | 0.2 | 0.2 | 0.4 | 0.3 | 0.3 | 0.6 | 0.6 | 0.9 | 1.3 | 0.5 |
| Retirement pension | 25 | 24 | 24 | 23 | 23 | 22 | 22 | 23 | 19 | 18 | 22 |
| SERPS (AP) | 4 | 6 | 6 | 6 | 7 | 7 | 7 | 9 | 7 | 7 | 7 |
| Contributory benefits | 3 | 2 | 3 | 3 | 2 | 3 | 2 | 2 | 2 | 2 | 2 |
| Child benefit/OPB | 5 | 5 | 4 | 4 | 4 | 4 | 4 | 4 | 3 | 2 | 4 |
| Disability benefits | 3 | 1 | 2 | 2 | 1 | 3 | 2 | 2 | 3 | 3 | 2 |
| Means-tested benefits | 15 | 8 | 7 | 6 | 6 | 4 | 4 | 4 | 3 | 3 | 6 |
| *Total cash benefits* | 54 | 47 | 46 | 41 | 44 | 43 | 42 | 44 | 38 | 36 | 44 |
| | | | | | | | | | | | |
| *Gross income* | 169 | 220 | 256 | 277 | 306 | 336 | 372 | 407 | 476 | 631 | 345 |
| | | | | | | | | | | | |
| Income tax | 14 | 24 | 30 | 35 | 41 | 48 | 57 | 66 | 84 | 131 | 53 |
| NICs | 6 | 10 | 12 | 13 | 15 | 17 | 18 | 20 | 23 | 25 | 16 |
| *Direct taxes* | 20 | 33 | 42 | 48 | 56 | 65 | 75 | 86 | 106 | 156 | 69 |
| | | | | | | | | | | | |
| *Net income* | 149 | 186 | 214 | 228 | 249 | 271 | 297 | 321 | 370 | 475 | 276 |
| | | | | | | | | | | | |
| *Equivalent net income* | 153 | 199 | 223 | 241 | 264 | 279 | 306 | 340 | 372 | 472 | 285 |
| | | | | | | | | | | | |
| Education | 14 | 13 | 12 | 13 | 14 | 14 | 15 | 16 | 17 | 20 | 15 |
| Health | 24 | 22 | 22 | 22 | 22 | 21 | 21 | 22 | 20 | 19 | 22 |
| *Equivalent final income* | 190 | 234 | 258 | 277 | 300 | 314 | 342 | 378 | 409 | 511 | 321 |
| | | | | | | | | | | | |
| Annualised equivalent net income (£/year) | 2530 | 3360 | 3760 | 4080 | 4420 | 4750 | 5190 | 5720 | 6490 | 8270 | 4860 |
| Average age at death | 74.5 | 75.3 | 75.5 | 75.1 | 75.8 | 74.6 | 74.8 | 75.5 | 73.3 | 73.1 | 74.8 |

the effects of tax and benefit changes together, the result is a fall in lifetime equivalent net income of £6,000 for the bottom group, losses for the next eight groups, and a gain of £4,000 for the top decile group. In annualised terms, the bottom group's income falls by 8 per cent (to £2,530), while the top group's rises by 3 per cent (to £8,270). Looking at the overall shape of the distribution, the Gini coefficients for different definitions of lifetime net and final incomes as shown in Table 6.3 all rise by one percentage point.

## 7.    Summary

- The results from analysing LIFEMOD as if it were a cross-section of individuals of different ages match those drawn from a cross-section of the actual 1985 population in terms both of income inequality and of average incomes.

- The distribution of incomes on a lifetime basis is considerably less unequal than that seen in cross-sections of annual incomes. However, despite the equalising effects of benefits in cash and kind and of direct taxes, there remain substantial differences between individuals in lifetime living standards.

- Those who are observed as poor in any one year may not be poor on a lifetime basis. In particular those in full-time education can be 'temporarily poor', but lifetime rich. On the other hand, lone parenthood is associated with both annual and lifetime poverty.

- Women have lower average lifetime living standards than men, although this difference is much less than it would be without sharing within the family or the intervention of taxes and benefits.

- Moving up through the lifetime income distribution: the proportion of women falls; age-at-death tends to rise (looking at men and women separately); lone parenthood falls; the proportion experiencing divorce falls for women but rises for men; and the proportion undergoing tertiary education rises.

- These findings are robust to different assumptions about the degree of sharing within the family and to the equivalence scale used.

- The changes to the social security and direct tax systems between 1985 and 1991 reduced their lifetime redistributive effects, with the result that equivalent net incomes would, using the later system, be more unequally distributed.

**Chapter Seven**

# Redistribution Between People or Across the Life Cycle?

## Jane Falkingham and John Hills

From the model we can separate receipts of benefits in cash and kind which are 'paid for' at another stage in the same individual's life and those which represent net transfers from others. This tells us – in the 'steady state' world represented by LIFEMOD results – how much of what the welfare state does represents redistribution between people (interpersonal) and how much is intrapersonal redistribution across the life cycle. To do this, we have to decide how to allocate taxes to pay for the benefits, allowing for the fact that aggregate calculated taxes do not necessarily equal the cost of benefits. This is done in two ways:

- Assuming that only *direct* taxes are used to finance benefits, using all of employee National Insurance Contributions and whatever multiple of calculated income tax liabilities is needed to cover the remaining cost of benefits.

- Assuming that a proportion of *both* direct and indirect taxes is used. Indirect taxes are not modelled in LIFEMOD, but in recent years the combined effect of direct and indirect taxes has been close to proportional to gross incomes.[1] The combination of direct and indirect taxes is therefore proxied by assuming financing from the percentage of each individual's gross income required to pay for aggregate benefits.

---

1  For instance, CSO (1993, Appendix 4, Table 2) shows the Gini coefficients of equivalised gross income and equivalised post tax income (i.e. after both direct and indirect taxes) as equal, at 0.32, in 1985.

In other words, the counterfactual assumptions are that, without the welfare state, individuals would pay correspondingly less tax (i) in proportion to their direct tax liabilities or (ii) in proportion to gross incomes.

## 1.    Financing from direct taxes

The first four lines of Table 7.1 show – by lifetime income decile group – total lifetime cash benefit receipts (under the 1985 system), education and health benefits in kind and the total of these. For all individuals in the model the total averages £102,000. This is more than the average £82,000 of lifetime direct taxes paid by model individuals (Table 6.2). The fifth line shows what each group would pay in direct taxes, assuming that benefits were financed by all of employee National Insurance Contributions and that income tax would be raised by 32 per cent proportionately to meet the balance of costs. The rest of the table shows net receipts and payments using these 'allocated' tax payments.

   During each year of life individuals may pay tax, receive benefits or (for perfectly good reasons) both. In the last case, some or all of the benefits they receive in a year will be 'paid for' by their own tax payments that same year. Examples would be: people receiving taxable benefits

**Table 7.1** Lifetime Totals of Net Taxes and Benefits by Lifetime Income Distribution (benefits financed by direct taxes only; 1985 system; equal sharing; McClements; £000s)

| | Decile groups of individuals by equivalent net income (annualised) | | | | | | | | | | |
| | Bottom | 2 | 3 | 4 | 5 | 6 | 7 | 8 | 9 | Top | All |
|---|---|---|---|---|---|---|---|---|---|---|---|
| Cash benefits | 65 | 64 | 65 | 68 | 66 | 71 | 66 | 71 | 60 | 58 | 66 |
| Education | 13 | 13 | 13 | 13 | 14 | 13 | 15 | 16 | 17 | 20 | 15 |
| Health | 22 | 21 | 22 | 22 | 21 | 23 | 22 | 22 | 20 | 20 | 22 |
| *Total benefits* | 101 | 98 | 99 | 104 | 101 | 107 | 103 | 109 | 98 | 98 | 102 |
| *Allocated direct tax*[a] | 30 | 49 | 62 | 71 | 84 | 93 | 111 | 131 | 155 | 232 | 102 |
| Self-financed benefits | 29 | 45 | 55 | 61 | 68 | 74 | 79 | 88 | 85 | 91 | 67 |
| *Lifetime net benefits* | 72 | 53 | 44 | 42 | 33 | 33 | 24 | 21 | 12 | 7 | 34 |
| *Lifetime net tax* | 1 | 4 | 7 | 9 | 16 | 19 | 32 | 43 | 69 | 140 | 34 |
| Average lifetime gain[b] | +71 | +49 | +37 | +33 | +17 | +14 | -8 | -22 | -57 | -134 | - |

**Notes:**
a    All employee NICs and 132 per cent of income tax allocated to pay for benefits.
b    Net lifetime benefits minus net allocated tax averaged over decile group as a whole.

(such as the state pension); people receiving non-taxable benefits but who pay tax on other income (for instance, women with earnings receiving Child Benefit or people in work benefiting from health services); or people receiving benefits because they are out of work for part of a year, but who have earnings and pay tax in the rest of it. They may also pay for their own benefits in *other* years of their lives. Over their whole lives, individuals are either net lifetime taxpayers or net lifetime benefit recipients (or, conceivably, some may exactly break-even).[2]

The table shows the scale of such 'self-financing' of benefits (intrapersonal redistribution), together with the net lifetime taxes or benefits of individuals in excess of self-financed benefits (interpersonal redistribution). Thus, on average, although model individuals receive an average of £102,000 in gross benefits over their lifetimes, £67,000 of this represents benefits which individuals effectively pay for themselves.

Within the bottom decile group nearly all are net lifetime beneficiaries – receiving £72,000 averaged over the whole group – but even here a few are net lifetime taxpayers, with the amounts they pay averaging £1,000 over the whole group. Thus of the £101,000 of average gross benefits received by this bottom group over their lives, £29,000 represents amounts paid by individuals for their own benefits, and £72,000 represents net receipts from others. A small amount of these net receipts comes from others at the bottom of the distribution.

As one moves up the income distribution, the proportion of gross benefits which represents intra- rather than interpersonal redistribution grows rapidly. By the third decile group, the majority of the group's gross receipts are self-financed. For the top group, £91,000 out of their average £98,000 gross receipts is self-financed, and the net taxpayers within the group pay out £140,000 (averaged over the whole decile group).

This pattern is summarised in Figure 7.1. The top panel shows average gross benefits in cash and kind going to each decile group. These benefits are divided between those which are self-financed over individuals' lifetimes, and those which represent the net benefits of

---

2   Algebraically the various measures can be expressed as follows. Let $B_i$ be the gross cash benefits received by individual i over his or her lifetime, and $T_i$ be the gross (allocated) taxes they pay over their lifetime. Then the aggregate gross lifetime cash benefits for the model population are given by:
  $G = \Sigma_i B_i = \Sigma_i T_i$
Self-financed benefits are given by:
  $SFB_i = T_i$ (if $B_i > T_i$)
       $= B_i$ (if $B_i \leq T_i$)
An individual's net lifetime gain is:
  $N_i = B_i - T_i$
Total *inter*personal redistribution is given by:
  $IR = \Sigma_i (N_i \mid N_i > 0)$
Total *intra*personal redistribution is the sum of self-financed benefits:
  $IA = \Sigma_i SFB_i$
(and by construction, $G = IR + IA$).

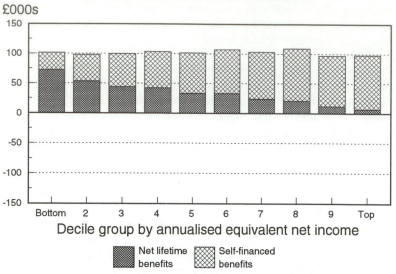

**(a) Gross benefits in cash and kind**

Decile group by annualised equivalent net income

Net lifetime benefits    Self-financed benefits

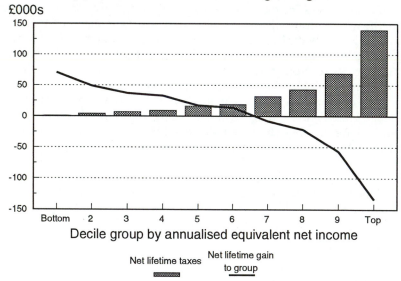

**(b) Net lifetime taxes and average net gain**

Decile group by annualised equivalent net income

Net lifetime taxes    Net lifetime gain to group

**Note:**
1985 tax and social security systems; equal sharing; McClements equivalence scale.

**Figure 7.1** Lifetime Benefits and Taxes by Income Group

'lifetime gainers'. These gains are paid for by the net taxes of 'lifetime losers', shown by the columns in the lower panel. It is these net lifetime taxes and benefits which represent the interpersonal redistribution which is going on. Judged by Robin Hood criteria, this redistribution is clearly progressive, although somewhat approximate, with some net lifetime taxpayers at the bottom and a rather more significant number of net lifetime gainers at the top.

Meanwhile, self-financed benefits in the top panel illustrate the intrapersonal redistribution going on. Of the average £102,000 gross lifetime benefits received by the sample, two-thirds (67 per cent) represents intrapersonal redistribution. Only one-third (33 per cent) represents interpersonal redistribution, where one person gains over their lifetime at the expense of another.

The final line of Table 7.1 and the line in the lower panel of Figure 7.1 show the net redistribution achieved between the decile groups as a whole on these assumptions. The bottom six groups are net gainers, and the top four groups are net losers, particularly the top group.

## 2.    Financing from all Taxes

The results in the previous section are based on the assumption that cash benefits, education and health services are financed by progressive direct taxes (which would require higher direct tax rates than were actually imposed in 1985). Part of the redistribution they show may result from this assumption. Table 7.2 shows the results of making the alternative assumption, that financing comes from a share of all tax revenues, approximated by using a share (28.0 per cent, to be precise) of each individual's gross income. Four features stand out:

- The less progressive financing system means that the proportion of intrapersonal redistribution rises to 75 per cent, and that of interpersonal redistribution falls to 25 per cent.
- The average net gains to the bottom six decile groups are reduced by 36 per cent, while the net loss of the top group falls by 37 per cent.
- The interpersonal redistribution involved, while of a smaller scale than when direct taxes are assumed to be the source of finance, is none the less progressive. The average lifetime gain of £50,000 for the bottom group is still substantial by comparison with their average lifetime original income of £117,000 (Table 6.2).
- Total benefits are relatively flat across lifetime decile groups. It is the *combination* of flat benefits with either a progressive or proportional tax system which has the redistributive effects.

Table 7.2 Lifetime Totals of Net Taxes and Benefits by Lifetime Income
Distribution (benefits financed by percentage of gross income; 1985 system;
equal sharing; McClements; £000s)

| | Decile groups of individuals by equivalent net income (annualised) | | | | | | | | | | |
|---|---|---|---|---|---|---|---|---|---|---|---|
| | Bottom | 2 | 3 | 4 | 5 | 6 | 7 | 8 | 9 | Top | All |
| Total benefits | 101 | 98 | 99 | 104 | 101 | 107 | 103 | 109 | 98 | 98 | 102 |
| Allocated taxation[a] | 51 | 66 | 77 | 84 | 92 | 99 | 110 | 122 | 136 | 182 | 102 |
| Self-financed benefits | 49 | 62 | 68 | 73 | 76 | 81 | 85 | 91 | 87 | 92 | 76 |
| Lifetime net benefits | 51 | 37 | 31 | 30 | 25 | 26 | 19 | 19 | 11 | 6 | 25 |
| Lifetime net tax | 2 | 5 | 8 | 10 | 16 | 17 | 26 | 31 | 49 | 90 | 25 |
| Average lifetime gain[b] | +50 | +32 | +22 | +20 | +9 | +9 | -7 | -13 | -38 | -84 | - |

Notes:
a    28.0 per cent of gross income used as proxy for impact of whole tax system.
b    Net lifetime benefits minus net allocated tax averaged over decile group.


## 3.    Sensitivity to Sharing Assumptions and Equivalence Scales

While the way in which individuals are ranked in the distribution will
not affect conclusions about the balance between inter- and intrapersonal
redistribution, it might affect the conclusions reached about
redistribution between the lifetime rich and poor.

Table 7.3 suggests that this is not the case, however. The first two
panels show the effects of ranking individuals with the two assumptions
about unequal sharing within the family used before, with financing
assumed to come from direct taxes only. Comparing the results with
those in Table 7.1, in both cases the redistribution between income groups
is increased. The net gains of those now placed in the bottom six groups
are larger than before, as are the net losses of those in the top three groups.
Meanwhile, using the OECD instead of the McClements equivalence
scale makes virtually no difference. If one ranks by equivalent original
income, the net gains for the bottom two groups are larger than with the
ranking by net income, as are the net losses for the top two groups. The
overall pattern of redistribution remains much the same.

**Table 7.3** Lifetime Totals of Net Taxes and Benefits by Lifetime Income Distribution: Alternative Rankings (benefits financed by direct taxes only; 1985 system; £000s)

| | Decile groups of individuals by equivalent net or original income (annualised) | | | | | | | | | | |
|---|---|---|---|---|---|---|---|---|---|---|---|
| | Bottom | 2 | 3 | 4 | 5 | 6 | 7 | 8 | 9 | Top | All |
| (a) *Ranked by equivalent net income: 80% of net income pooled; McClements equivalence scale* | | | | | | | | | | | |
| Lifetime net benefits | 76 | 61 | 49 | 42 | 36 | 27 | 24 | 15 | 8 | 2 | 34 |
| Lifetime net tax | - | 2 | 4 | 7 | 11 | 18 | 29 | 39 | 72 | 158 | 34 |
| Average lifetime gain | +76 | +59 | +44 | +34 | +25 | +9 | -5 | -24 | -63 | -156 | - |
| (b) *Ranked by equivalent net income: Men receive 60% of equivalent net income; McClements equivalence scale* | | | | | | | | | | | |
| Lifetime net benefits | 79 | 67 | 57 | 44 | 34 | 26 | 16 | 9 | 5 | 2 | 34 |
| Lifetime net tax | - | 1 | 2 | 5 | 11 | 15 | 25 | 45 | 75 | 161 | 34 |
| Average lifetime gain | +79 | +66 | +55 | +39 | +24 | +11 | -9 | -36 | -70 | -159 | - |
| (c) *Ranked by equivalent net income: Equal sharing; OECD equivalence scale* | | | | | | | | | | | |
| Lifetime net benefits | 70 | 55 | 43 | 42 | 35 | 32 | 27 | 18 | 13 | 6 | 34 |
| Lifetime net tax | 1 | 5 | 7 | 11 | 15 | 19 | 29 | 44 | 69 | 139 | 34 |
| Average lifetime gain | +68 | +50 | +36 | +30 | +20 | +13 | -2 | -26 | -56 | -134 | - |
| (d) *Ranked by equivalent original income: Equal sharing; McClements equivalence scale* | | | | | | | | | | | |
| Lifetime net benefits | 98 | 65 | 50 | 39 | 30 | 19 | 19 | 10 | 7 | 3 | 34 |
| Lifetime net tax | - | 1 | 2 | 6 | 11 | 21 | 30 | 46 | 74 | 151 | 34 |
| Average lifetime gain | +98 | +65 | +48 | +33 | +19 | -2 | -11 | -35 | -67 | -148 | - |

## 4.     Redistribution Between Men and Women

We have already seen that women have much lower lifetime incomes than men, and that the welfare state redistributes between rich and poor. One would, *a priori*, expect from this that women would be generally net lifetime gainers from the welfare state and men generally net losers. Tables 7.4 and 7.5, giving the results on the two alternative bases for financing, show that this is indeed the case. If financing is assumed to come from direct taxes, the net effect of the system is an average lifetime transfer of £50,000 from men to women. If financing is assumed to come from a percentage of gross incomes, the average transfer is £40,000.

Within both of the separate distributions for men and women, the pattern of net gains is progressive, but is very different for the two cases. Even women in the ninth decile group of the overall distribution are net gainers on average with financing in either way. Meanwhile only the men in the bottom three decile groups gain on average, if financing is from direct taxes (or only the bottom two groups, if it comes from all taxes).

Even women near the top of the income distribution (allowing for sharing in their partners' incomes) are generally gainers from the system, whereas some men who certainly could not be described as 'lifetime rich'

**Table 7.4** Lifetime Totals of Net Taxes and Benefits by Lifetime Income Distribution: Men and Women (benefits financed by direct taxes only; 1985 system; £000s)

| | Decile groups of individuals by equivalent net or original income[a] (annualised) | | | | | | | | | | |
|---|---|---|---|---|---|---|---|---|---|---|---|
| | Bottom | 2 | 3 | 4 | 5 | 6 | 7 | 8 | 9 | Top | All |
| *Men* | | | | | | | | | | | |
| Total benefits | 76 | 77 | 80 | 81 | 81 | 83 | 87 | 88 | 84 | 88 | 83 |
| Allocated tax | 37 | 64 | 79 | 88 | 102 | 113 | 134 | 158 | 187 | 268 | 133 |
| Lifetime net benefits | 42 | 21 | 16 | 12 | 8 | 6 | 6 | 2 | 2 | 1 | 10 |
| Lifetime net tax | 3 | 8 | 14 | 18 | 29 | 36 | 52 | 73 | 105 | 181 | 60 |
| Average lifetime gain | +39 | +13 | +2 | -6 | -21 | -30 | -46 | -70 | -102 | -180 | -50 |
| *Women* | | | | | | | | | | | |
| Total benefits | 111 | 113 | 117 | 125 | 121 | 129 | 124 | 134 | 117 | 116 | 120 |
| Allocated tax | 27 | 39 | 47 | 56 | 66 | 74 | 82 | 100 | 110 | 165 | 70 |
| Lifetime net benefits | 84 | 75 | 71 | 70 | 58 | 58 | 47 | 43 | 26 | 17 | 58 |
| Lifetime net tax | - | - | - | 1 | 3 | 3 | 6 | 8 | 18 | 67 | 8 |
| Average lifetime gain | +84 | +74 | +70 | +69 | +55 | +56 | +41 | +35 | +7 | -50 | +50 |

**Note:**
a    Equal sharing; McClements equivalence scale.

**Table 7.5** Lifetime Totals of Net Taxes and Benefits by Lifetime Income Distribution: Men and Women (benefits financed by percentage of gross income; 1985 system; £000s)

| | Decile groups of individuals by equivalent net or original income[a] (annualised) | | | | | | | | | | |
|---|---|---|---|---|---|---|---|---|---|---|---|
| | Bottom | 2 | 3 | 4 | 5 | 6 | 7 | 8 | 9 | Top | All |
| *Men* | | | | | | | | | | | |
| Total benefits | 76 | 77 | 80 | 81 | 81 | 83 | 87 | 88 | 84 | 88 | 83 |
| Allocated tax | 53 | 75 | 88 | 94 | 105 | 113 | 126 | 140 | 158 | 206 | 123 |
| Lifetime net benefits | 28 | 13 | 9 | 7 | 5 | 4 | 4 | 2 | 2 | 1 | 6 |
| Lifetime net tax | 5 | 11 | 16 | 20 | 29 | 34 | 43 | 55 | 76 | 119 | 46 |
| Average lifetime gain | +24 | +2 | -8 | -13 | -24 | -30 | -38 | -53 | -74 | -118 | -40 |
| *Women* | | | | | | | | | | | |
| Total benefits | 111 | 113 | 117 | 125 | 121 | 129 | 124 | 134 | 117 | 116 | 120 |
| Allocated tax | 50 | 60 | 65 | 73 | 79 | 85 | 90 | 101 | 105 | 139 | 81 |
| Lifetime net benefits | 61 | 53 | 52 | 52 | 45 | 47 | 37 | 38 | 23 | 15 | 44 |
| Lifetime net tax | - | - | - | 1 | 2 | 2 | 4 | 4 | 11 | 38 | 5 |
| Average lifetime gain | +61 | +53 | +52 | +51 | +42 | +44 | +34 | +33 | +12 | -24 | +40 |

**Note:**
a    Equal sharing; McClements equivalence scale.

are net losers.[3] As well as being about redistribution within the life cycle, and about redistribution between the lifetime rich and poor, the welfare state is crucially about redistribution between men and women.

## 5.     Effects of Changes to the System by 1991

Table 7.6 summarises the equivalent information to that in the tables above to show the redistribution implied using the 1991 direct tax and social security systems instead of those of 1985 (see Chapter 5 for a discussion of the changes between 1985 and 1991). In the 1991 case, with a smaller fall in direct taxes than in cash benefits, income tax payments only have to be increased by 21 per cent to cover the cost of benefits in the direct tax case. In the alternative case, 23 per cent of gross incomes are required to finance benefits in cash and kind.

As the table shows, both intra- and interpersonal redistributions are less under the 1991 system, although the former falls slightly more (in line with the Government's opposition to what is sometimes pejoratively referred to as 'churning'). As a result, the proportion of gross benefits which fall into the 'Robin Hood' category rises slightly (from 33 to 34 per cent in the direct tax case; from 25 to 26 per cent when a share of gross incomes is used).

Comparing the average lifetime gains for each decile group under the two systems, it is clear that the changes between them reduce the redistribution away from the top decile group. Its net loss falls by £25,000 in the direct tax case, or £12,000 in the alternative.[4] If financing is assumed to come from direct taxes, the net gains of the bottom half of the distribution are reduced from an average of £41,000 to £37,000. However, if financing is from gross incomes, the fall is only from £27,000 to £26,000.

As well as this reduction in the redistributive effect of social security over the lifetime, the changes between 1985 and 1991 also have a major effect on the relative positions of men and women. As women receive greater cash benefits than men, but pay much less tax, the reduction in the two over the period benefits men, while women lose. Under the 1991 systems, the average net gain of women is reduced to £40,000 assuming

---

3   The position is only slightly modified if one allows for unequal sharing within the family. Using the assumption that women only receive 40 per cent of the pooled net equivalent income of couples, women in the bottom eight decile groups are net gainers on average, while those in the top two groups are net losers. Men now placed in the bottom four groups (with financing from direct taxes) or three groups (with all taxes) are net gainers; the other groups are net losers on average.

4   These are larger gains than the £4,000 gain in lifetime equivalent final income for the top group seen by comparing Tables 6.2 and 6.8. This is because this group gains – in the terms being examined here – from the reduction in the scale of taxes needed to finance welfare benefits.

financing from direct taxes, or £32,000 assuming financing from all taxes. The changes in systems between 1985 and 1991 were therefore equivalent to a reduction in the average net lifetime transfer from men to women of £10,000 or £8,000 (depending on the financing assumption), or of 20 per cent (in both cases).

The reductions in redistribution between both rich and poor and between men and women interact. Comparing Tables 7.4 and 7.6, for instance, the main effect of the change to the 1991 system (assuming financing from direct tax) is a reduction in the net losses for men in the top three decile groups of the overall distribution, and a reduction in the net gains for women in the second to eighth decile groups.

**Table 7.6** Lifetime Totals of Net Taxes and Benefits by Lifetime Income Distribution: 1991 Tax and Social Security Systems (£000s)

| | Decile groups of individuals by equivalent net income[a] (annualised) | | | | | | | | | | |
|---|---|---|---|---|---|---|---|---|---|---|---|
| | Bottom | 2 | 3 | 4 | 5 | 6 | 7 | 8 | 9 | Top | All |
| (a) *Benefits financed by direct tax only*[b] | | | | | | | | | | | |
| *All* | | | | | | | | | | | |
| Total benefits | 91 | 82 | 81 | 80 | 80 | 78 | 78 | 82 | 75 | 75 | 80 |
| Allocated tax | 23 | 38 | 49 | 56 | 65 | 75 | 87 | 100 | 124 | 184 | 80 |
| Lifetime net benefits | 68 | 45 | 37 | 31 | 26 | 21 | 16 | 15 | 8 | 5 | 27 |
| Lifetime net tax | - | 1 | 5 | 7 | 11 | 18 | 25 | 33 | 58 | 114 | 27 |
| Average lifetime gain | +68 | +44 | +32 | +24 | +15 | +3 | -9 | -18 | -50 | -109 | - |
| *Men* | | | | | | | | | | | |
| Average lifetime gain | +43 | +14 | +1 | -6 | -15 | -26 | -38 | -54 | -81 | -143 | -40 |
| *Women* | | | | | | | | | | | |
| Average lifetime gain | +77 | +61 | +60 | +50 | +45 | +34 | +31 | +23 | +1 | -42 | +40 |
| (b) *Benefits financed by percentage of gross income*[c] | | | | | | | | | | | |
| *All* | | | | | | | | | | | |
| Total benefits | 91 | 82 | 81 | 80 | 80 | 78 | 78 | 82 | 75 | 75 | 80 |
| Allocated tax | 39 | 51 | 59 | 64 | 71 | 78 | 86 | 94 | 111 | 147 | 80 |
| Lifetime net benefits | 53 | 33 | 27 | 23 | 20 | 16 | 13 | 13 | 7 | 4 | 21 |
| Lifetime net tax | 1 | 1 | 6 | 7 | 11 | 16 | 22 | 25 | 43 | 76 | 21 |
| Average lifetime gain | +52 | +31 | +21 | +16 | +9 | - | -9 | -12 | -36 | -72 | - |
| *Men* | | | | | | | | | | | |
| Average lifetime gain | +32 | +7 | -5 | -10 | -17 | -24 | -33 | -42 | -61 | -97 | -32 |
| *Women* | | | | | | | | | | | |
| Average lifetime gain | +59 | +45 | +45 | +38 | +35 | +26 | +25 | +21 | +4 | -23 | +32 |

**Notes:**
a    Equal sharing; McClements equivalence scale.
b    Benefits financed by all of NICs and 121 per cent of income tax.
c    Benefits financed by 23 per cent of gross income.

## 6.        Redistribution Between 'Risk Groups'

So far in this analysis we have neglected the 'insurance' aspect of the welfare state. Looking back from the grave-side (which is what we have been doing), certain individuals may be net losers from the combination of tax and benefits in cash and kind over their lives. This may, however, simply reflect their good fortune in avoiding the circumstances – such as unemployment or bad health – against which the welfare state protects us all (or their bad fortune in not living long enough to collect much by way of pensions). If they were looking forward from when they were young, knowing the potential risks they faced, but not whether they themselves would actually suffer them, their tax payments might constitute an actuarially fair insurance premium.

Table 7.7 separates out how much of the 'interpersonal' redistribution revealed *ex post* in Table 7.1 can be ascribed to this 'insurance' function of the welfare state. It shows the net gains and losses of the population divided into 28 'risk groups' according to their circumstances at the age of 25. The factors used to separate out the groups are gender, education, marriage and children. In effect, the table divides up the population according to factors which could be identified at the start of their working lives.

For instance, men who leave school at 16 and are married with children by the age of 25 (the second row of the table) are on average net losers (over the whole of their lives) from the combination of welfare benefits and the taxes used to fund them. The amount of their average net loss – between £25,000 and £30,000 depending on whether financing is from direct tax or a share of gross income – represents the amount they are paying for welfare benefits in excess of an actuarially fair valuation of what they could expect to receive from them. For men who go on to higher education, and are neither married nor have children by the time they are 25, the excess is between £97,000 and £147,000.

In looking at the net gains and losses, two factors dominate. First, the higher the level of education (and hence lifetime income), the greater the average net loss for the male risk groups, or smaller the net gain for female risk groups. Second, *all* the female risk groups are net gainers on average; all of the male risk groups are net losers.

The 'non-insurance' interpersonal redistribution achieved by the system is equal to the amounts being transferred between risk groups. As all female risk groups are gainers and all male groups are losers this equals, as it happens, the average net transfer from men to women divided by two (to give an average over the whole population, not just over one gender). Thus only £25,000 (direct tax financing) or £20,000 (financing from gross incomes) of the £102,000 average gross lifetime benefits to model individuals represents *ex ante* interpersonal redistribution from the standpoint of risk groups divided at age 25.

**Table 7.7** Lifetime Redistribution by Risk Groups (1985 system; £000s)

| Risk group[a] | Total benefits | Net gain:[b] Direct tax | Net gain:[b] Gross income | Annualised equivalent net income[c] |
|---|---|---|---|---|
| **Men** | | | | |
| *Leave school at 16* | | | | |
| Married:   no children | 75 | -27 | -30 | 4720 |
| children | 77 | -25 | -30 | 4590 |
| Not married: no children | 81 | -17 | -19 | 4580 |
| children | - | - | - | - |
| *School to 17/18* | | | | |
| Married:   no children | 73 | -53 | -44 | 5320 |
| children | 90 | -44 | -39 | 4930 |
| Not married: no children | 85 | -56 | -43 | 5410 |
| children | - | - | - | - |
| *Further education* | | | | |
| Married:   no children | 88 | -57 | -45 | 5390 |
| children | 82 | -72 | -57 | 5430 |
| Not married: no children | 89 | -69 | -49 | 5700 |
| children | - | - | - | - |
| *Higher education* | | | | |
| Married:   no children | 96 | -147 | -97 | 6970 |
| children | 96 | -144 | -92 | 6560 |
| Not married: no children | 96 | -116 | -73 | 6730 |
| children | - | - | - | - |
| *All* | 83 | -50 | -40 | 5190 |
| **Women** | | | | |
| *Leave school at 16* | | | | |
| Married:   no children | 111 | +60 | +42 | 4550 |
| children | 123 | +71 | +51 | 4620 |
| Not married: no children | 111 | +55 | +41 | 4210 |
| children | 116 | +71 | +48 | 4220 |
| *School to 17/18* | | | | |
| Married:   no children | 111 | +27 | +24 | 5170 |
| children | 122 | +55 | +41 | 4730 |
| Not married: no children | 110 | +38 | +31 | 4590 |
| children | 132 | +70 | +52 | 4320 |
| *Further education* | | | | |
| Married:   no children | 133 | +33 | +33 | 5220 |
| children | 135 | +58 | +48 | 4830 |
| Not married: no children | 127 | +36 | +35 | 4850 |
| children | 134 | +60 | +48 | 4420 |
| *Higher education* | | | | |
| Married:   no children | 140 | +13 | +26 | 5860 |
| children | 137 | +34 | +36 | 5180 |
| Not married: no children | 129 | +10 | +21 | 5620 |
| children | 139 | +36 | +36 | 5330 |
| *All* | 120 | +50 | +40 | 4690 |

**Notes:**
a    Divided by circumstances at age 25.
b    Columns give results with alternative financing assumptions.
c    £ per year; equal sharing; McClements equivalence scale.

To recap, then:

- Model individuals receive an average of £102,000 over their lifetimes in cash benefits (under the 1985 system) and from public spending on education and health.
- Of this, an average of between £67,000 (financing from direct taxes) and £76,000 (gross incomes) is self-financed.
- A further £10,000 (direct taxes) or £6,000 (gross incomes) effectively represents 'insurance' payments made to cover benefits paid in contingencies which only affect some individuals.
- The remaining £25,000 (direct taxes) or £20,000 (gross incomes) represents the *ex ante* interpersonal redistribution over and above the insurance aspect of welfare benefits.

## 7.    Summary

- The British welfare state achieves both inter- and intrapersonal redistribution, but with the latter being on a larger scale.
- As it was structured in 1985, between two-thirds and three-quarters of gross lifetime benefits are effectively self-financed (more or less depending on how benefits are assumed to be financed), that is represented a 'savings bank' function of the welfare state.
- Between one-quarter and one-third of gross benefits consist of lifetime transfers between different individuals, if one looks at the position *ex post*.
- Netting out the 'insurance' aspect of welfare benefits, the amount of *ex ante* interpersonal redistribution falls to between 20 and 25 per cent.
- The lifetime poor are generally the net gainers from the interpersonal redistribution which is occurring, and the lifetime rich the net losers. Overwhelmingly women are net gainers from the system and men net losers.
- The changes to tax and social security between 1985 and 1991 reduced the scale of redistribution, particularly that between men and women. The average net lifetime transfer between men and women falls by 20 per cent (or by between £8,000 and £10,000 at 1985 prices).

**Chapter Eight**

# Education Funding, Equity and the Life Cycle

## Howard Glennerster, Jane Falkingham and Nicholas Barr

Until recently higher education for undergraduates was provided free of charge but access to it was limited. This has resulted in perverse distributional effects with those who benefit from education receiving higher lifetime incomes, yet the cost of this education being spread across the total population. It has also resulted in perverse, but not necessarily irrational, private decisions with those who might be expected to face the highest private rates of return to tertiary education also being the least likely to participate in it. This chapter discusses the benefits received from education and training and examines various options for the funding of higher education – options which result both in a more equitable distributional outcome and which would allow the release of additional resources necessary for the expansion of tertiary education.

## 1.    Education as Investment

Education and training have a number of characteristics that make them unusual. Though partly enjoyed for its own sake education is, to a large extent, undertaken because it increases an individual's future earning capacity. It has all the characteristics of a personal investment (Becker, 1964; Schultz, 1963). The asset is, however, the individual's own human capital, her knowledge and capacity. This cannot, outside a slave society, be used as collateral for a loan. Rich parents *can* act as lenders, relying on their own stock of assets or credit worthiness, but to rely on this alone would lead both to under-investment in human capital and to inequity between potentially equally able people.

Employers also have an interest in a trained and educated labour force but the market fails here too. Any employer who educates an employee or gives her a general training is likely to find that person competed away by an employer who has no training scheme. Big employers who have other long term claims on their staff may think the risk worthwhile but most firms will aim to free-ride on others. The result is that the costs of general training are either borne by the young employee or not undertaken at all (Becker ,1964; Bennett, Glennerster and Nevison, 1992a). The market will again produce too little training and training that is not open to those from lower income families.

Education and training are very costly in relation to income. The costs are of two kinds:

- Learning takes time. Some learning can be done on the job but many skills need to be acquired before a person is worth employing and others can only be learned by devoting exclusive time to the task. Something has to be given up to do this, either paid work and thus earnings or leisure which individuals value. Carers must pay for substitute care. All three kinds of *opportunity cost* may be incurred by a woman returning to education after the birth of a child.

- Formal education is expensive, people-intensive and difficult to automate, especially for young children. In higher education top quality learning best takes place in an environment where those doing the teaching are also researching – an environment of discovery and questioning. Teachers must devote much of their time to that activity as well as instruction.

Taken together, the opportunity cost and the formal tuition costs of staying on beyond 16 to reach a first degree, for example, amounted to about £40,000 in 1985 prices, in our average LIFEMOD case. That is a scale of investment equivalent to the average family buying a house. If the family were trying to invest this sum in two children, let alone improving the education of the husband or wife, education would become by far the most expensive investment decision of its life cycle.

Households' different capacities to move income through time to purchase education have important efficiency and equity effects. The result of leaving educational finances entirely to households would be both inefficient for the wider society as well as inequitable. The state therefore has a critically important role in making widespread educational investment possible and the cost equitably spread.

## 2.    The Case for a Different Kind of Intervention

The state has, in the past century, stepped in to remedy some of the market failures outlined above, but in the process it has created other inefficiencies and inequities. The possible means the state could adopt to finance education include:

- Free provision of state schools and universities paid for out of taxes levied on all people during periods of work.

- Provision of vouchers, financed out of general taxation, to enable parents and students to buy education at any level.

- State guarantees for private loans for educational purposes taken out from a bank or other lender.

- Provision of loans to individuals free of security but backed by the state's capacity to tax that individual later in life. The individual has to repay, whatever her future income, a mortgage type scheme.

- Provision of loans but with repayments linked to the individual's capacity to pay – an income-contingent loan which the individual ceases to repay when the debt is paid off (Blaug, 1966).

- Provision of free education beyond the statutory school-leaving age that carries with it an obligation to pay a higher rate of income tax in perpetuity – a graduate tax addition (Glennerster et al., 1968).

- A subvention on employers to pay for the higher human capital content of their labour force.

In practice, until very recently, the state in the UK has relied on the first of these mechanisms to the exclusion of the rest. Other countries have been more adventurous (Woodhall, 1989; Chapman, 1992; Chapman and Harding, 1993). More recently, much interest has been shown in a variety of schemes to diversify the income of higher education institutions (Barden, Barr and Higginson, 1991; Barnes and Barr, 1988; Barr, 1991, 1993b; Russell, 1993). The results of relying on the present form of tax-based lifetime redistribution of education costs can be illustrated by looking at the experience of the LIFEMOD cohort. A number of features stand out.

### The distribution of education benefits

Spending on education is heavily front-loaded (see Figure 8.1). Like physical assets, human capital depreciates, becomes obsolete, during a lifetime. This is now occurring with greater rapidity than ever before. The opportunity cost of taking time out to restore a person's human capital, however, rises the older the person and the higher her normal earnings. As a result, little educational expenditure in the UK is incident on individuals above the age of 25. In many other European countries employers are required to give their older employees time off to enhance their training and some countries put a levy on employers which is used to finance older workers' education and training (Glennerster, 1982).

The benefits of education are perversely redistributional. As Table 6.2 (p.116) showed, those located the highest lifetime income group in LIFEMOD receive on average 50 per cent more in benefits in kind from

Expenditure £s

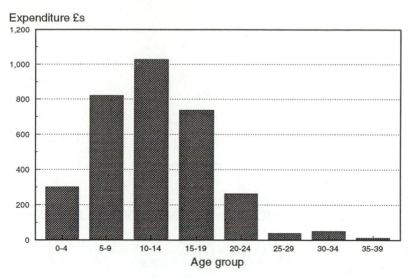

Figure 8.1 Average Per Capita Education Expenditure by Age Group

education than those individuals in the bottom group. The vast majority of this is due to differences in receipt of post-16 education. Figure 8.2 shows that the value of higher education benefits derived by the lifetime richest fifth of the model population is worth more than five times that derived by the poorest fifth. Barriers still exist for those from less fortunate homes, cultural and financial. The most favoured leap those barriers and then gain the much higher in-kind benefits available to those receiving higher education.

The benefits of education are still substantially restricted. Although education is compulsory from the ages of 5–16 in the UK, pre-school education is very limited in access compared to other European countries and so is participation in higher education.

There are two reasons for this low participation. First, higher education has been very expensive for the reasons outlined above. The resource cost of undergraduate university courses has probably been the highest in the world. Pupil–teacher ratios have been low, research treated as an integral part of all university activity, and the Government has paid students' living expenses. This was a uniquely generous settlement on the post-war generation of students. It was, however, incompatible with mass higher education. The generality of taxpayers have not been willing to pay the taxes required to finance such generosity to the younger generation. This has restricted the *supply* of places in higher education.

Second, UK employers have traditionally not rewarded those who stay on to gain qualifications as much as employers in other countries. This has been especially true for lower level further education and

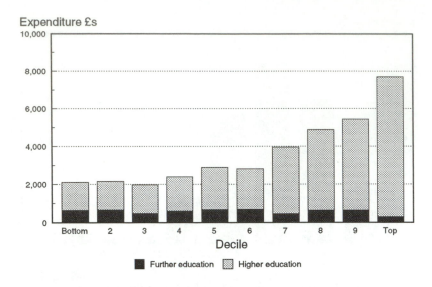

**Figure 8.2** Expenditure on Further and Higher Education by Decile Group of
Annualised Lifetime Net Income

training (Bennett, Glennerster and Nevison, 1992a). This has restricted
the *demand* for higher and further education from individual young
people who see it may not be in their best interests to forego wages in
return for little extra later.

### The private investment decision

Despite the fact that the state has provided free instruction for all
undergraduates in the UK since the early 1960s, and substantial subsidies
on other forms of post-school instruction, the decision to stay on at school
or continue with further education is not costless. A young person
foregoes the earnings that they could have gained if they had entered the
labour market directly. Young people therefore weigh up the immediate
loss they suffer by deciding to continue with their education against the
benefits. Large amongst those benefits will be the expectation of higher
future earnings but it also matters to young people when those higher
earnings will come. Some may prefer to earn quickly and place a
relatively low valuation on high earnings late in their career and thus
apply a high discount rate to their future earnings stream. They may also
see the investment as a risky one or they may lack personal or family
experience of the rewards of higher education or training and be
suspicious of them. Low demand to stay on at school may therefore result
from entirely rational calculations by young people about their life cycle.

Bennett, Glennerster and Nevison (1992a, b) show that, on average, young people might expect a private rate of return on their investment in A levels of 6 per cent for men and 10 per cent for women. For those who stay on into higher education there was an expected additional return of 6 per cent for women and 7 per cent for men (see Table 8.1). However, the rates of return middle class young people might deduce they could earn by staying on were lower than those for working class children. Boys from professional homes would expect a private rate of return of only 4 per cent compared with 7 per cent for all boys. Children from middle class homes will be more acceptable to employers, have better contacts in the labour market and hence be likely to land a good job anyway. Hence, a university course may not increase their opportunities as strikingly as for someone from a working class home.

But although children from working class homes might expect to gain a higher private rate of return for staying on into higher education, evidence from cross-sectional studies shows that they are still less likely to do so than their working class contemporaries (figures from General Household Survey (GHS), 1992). Two plausible explanations can be put forward. One is that those from working class families have different time preferences. If they apply plausibly higher discount rates to their future income streams the decisions we observe at 16 become consistent and rational. The other hypothesis is that the costs of borrowing are higher for children from poorer homes, their access to the capital market is more restricted.

We can, therefore, see how intertwined are the issues of lifetime and 'Robin Hood' income distribution in the case of education. If the state makes it possible for individuals, and the economy, to benefit by helping to finance an individual's investment in education or training but only some members of the population make use of that opportunity, for

Table 8.1  Expected Private Real Rates of Return

| | Father's socio-economic group | | | | |
|---|---|---|---|---|---|
| | Professional employer manager | Intermediate junior non-manual | Skilled, semi-skilled, manual | Unskilled manual | Overall (at sample mean) |
| Males | | | | | |
| A levels | 10.41 | -0.25 | 5.78 | -0.90 | 6.04 |
| Higher education | 4.00 | 7.95 | 6.10 | 25.10 | 7.08 |
| Females | | | | | |
| A levels | 4.85 | 15.32 | 10.59 | 13.49 | 9.80 |
| Higher education | 6.28 | 5.15 | 5.33 | 8.42 | 5.84 |

Source:
Bennett, Glennerster and Nevison, 1992b, Table 2, p.136.

reasons of taste or ignorance, the benefits will accrue unevenly. They may fall most beneficially on those who are already in the highest social or income groups.

Where the state decides to finance education beyond the compulsory school leaving age questions of equity as well as efficiency arise. If only some choose to use this lifetime redistribution facility, should all taxpayers contribute to it? In so far as higher education contributes to all our well-being the answer may be yes, but, in so far as the benefits are captured by those who earn the higher incomes *as a direct result of their fellow citizens' investment in them* the answer is no.

Both efficiency and equity arguments therefore suggest that part of education expenditure that is used to finance individuals' chosen investment in education should be recovered in the form of income-related payments. In the next section we discuss the various means by which this might be done. Because LIFEMOD simulates complete life histories, it is possible to estimate how much of any loan will be repaid and how quickly. Thus both the tempo and the quantum of repayments under alternative loan regimes can be estimated.

## 3.      Principles for Reform

Any reform of higher education should, we argue, have the following characteristics (Barr and Falkingham, 1993; Barr, Falkingham, Glennerster, 1994):

- For reasons of efficiency and equity, costs of extended education should be shared between the general taxpayer, who gains from the side-effects of a highly educated workforce, and the individual student who benefits from enhanced earning potential.

- Any scheme should minimise any deterrent effect on poorer potential students.

- Students should not be asked to repay more than the cost of their own loan. Any redistribution or subsidy to poorer students should be organised explicitly through direct grants, the cost of which should be borne by taxpayers generally.

- Repayment should be made in such a way as to minimise default both on grounds of equity for those who do pay and to maximise revenue.

- Repayment should be spread over an extended period. First, it eases the burden of repayment, reducing the deterrent effect for students with a high discount rate and high earnings late in life. The early repayments of mortgage-type loans like the current Government scheme fall most heavily and riskily upon those with little parental support. Second, since human capital is a lifetime asset, it is efficient if repayments are spread over a longer period.

- Any scheme should maximise access to post-school education. One of the main restrictions on university and other further education expansion has been the cost to the exchequer. Therefore, loans should be organised in such a way that they do not count towards public expenditure, otherwise the public expenditure saving will be lost. The scheme should be capable of being privatised even if part of the risk is guaranteed by the state. If the state takes on the collection role as part of the tax system, that risk should be minimal.

These basic principles lead on to a second set of derived principles of administration:

- Repayments must be income-related or income-contingent in the jargon of student loans. This reduces the potential barrier for those who may not believe they will earn enough to repay. Income-contingent loans in other countries have not reduced access from poorer social groups. Fully income-related schemes also enable them to tax back contributions from those with lower incomes. Schemes like the present UK student loan scheme are only partially income-related (Department of Education and Science (DES), 1988, 1993). They ask nothing of those below an earnings limit and full repayment above that figure. This proves inefficient in terms of recovery, as we shall see.
- The repayment system best adapted to achieving low default, at present in the UK, is the National Insurance system. A student wishing to take out a loan to help pay for higher education would have an addition made to her National Insurance number and for the rest of working life, up to the point when the debt was repaid, a 1 per cent addition, for example, could be made on the NI contribution. In Australia the general income tax system is used for this purpose and such a mechanism would be perfectly practicable in any reformed tax–benefit system in the UK.

In what follows we test such a scheme on our LIFEMOD population. We also compare it to the present UK Government's student loan scheme and to a full 'graduate tax' as well as an employer user charge.

## 4.    Alternative Schemes Investigated

### Loans

We look at loans for full-time and part-time students in higher education and advanced further education on the assumption that each borrows

£1,000 (in 1985 prices) for each year of her studies.[1] The sum borrowed could be used for maintenance, for tuition fees (as in Australia), or for both. Two schemes are investigated.

*Scheme 1* is the current UK Government scheme for higher education. Students borrow £1,000 which they repay in ten equal annual instalments at a zero real interest rate,[2] except that repayment is suspended in any year in which the individual's earnings fall below 85 per cent of the national average for full-time male employees.

*Scheme 2* is an income-contingent loan (ICL) in which students borrow £1,000, with repayment in the form of an additional 1 per cent on their National Insurance contributions (NICs).[3] Repayment stops once the loan, plus any interest, has been repaid. The income-contingent scheme would be operated alongside National Insurance contributions, with repayments withheld at source in parallel with the main NIC.

The two schemes are investigated under different assumptions. Four ICL repayment regimes are considered: where loans pay a zero real interest rate (like the Government scheme), and where they pay a real interest rate of 1, 2 or 3 per cent. The results are estimated assuming that graduate earnings (i) do not grow at all in real terms, (ii) grow annually at 1½ per cent, or (iii) grow annually at 3 per cent.[4] This growth is in *addition* to the endogenous 'seniority earnings pattern' implicit in LIFEMOD. We assume that all full-time students and 50 per cent of part-time students take out a loan.

No loan scheme will have 100 per cent compliance. NICs have a default rate of 1 to 1½ per cent. The rate is low partly because most NICs are deducted at source by employers. In addition, there is little *incentive* to evade contributions, since evasion generally has a cost in present or future benefit, in particular pensions. Furthermore, the administrative cost of such repayments will be small because collection is 'piggy-backed' onto an existing, well-functioning system. Mortgage loans have none of the desirable built-in incentives of NICs. In the USA the default rate on the Federal Government loan scheme is about 13 per cent (DES, 1988, para. 94; Reischauer, 1989). In addition, and separately, mortgage loans

---

1   This figure was chosen because it is easy to rescale. Note, however, that £1,000 was somewhat over 10 per cent of average earnings in 1985. Thus a three-year undergraduate leaves with debts of about 30 per cent of average male earnings, in today's (1994) terms an amount just over £4,500.

2   The real interest rate is the excess of the rate of interest over the rate of inflation. With a zero interest rate, the loan is indexed to changes in the price level, but no interest is charged (an equivalent formulation is that the interest rate is equal to the inflation rate).

3   The repayment is 1 per cent of income below the upper earnings limit for National Insurance contributions, for individuals whose earnings exceed the lower earnings limit.

4   The government costings presented in the White Paper on student loans (Department of Education and Science, 1988) assumed 3 per cent real earnings growth.

have high administrative costs, especially when (as in the UK) the administration of student loans is on a stand-alone basis. The estimates below assume a default rate of $1\frac{1}{2}$ per cent for the income-contingent scheme and 10 per cent for the Government scheme. We use the latter figure because that is the assumption underlying the calculations in the student loans White Paper (DES, 1988). Although it is too early for quantitative analysis, early outcomes give grounds for believing that this estimate is distinctly optimistic.

## Graduate tax

The income contingent loan scheme just described should be clearly distinguished from a graduate tax. With a loan, repayment is 'switched off' once the loan plus interest has been repaid, so that no one repays more than she has borrowed. With a graduate tax, in contrast, repayment continues until some specified time, e.g. the age of retirement, with the result that high-earning graduates repay more than they have borrowed. Here we investigate a graduate tax of 1 per cent of taxable income below the National Insurance upper earnings limit for all persons who have attended at least two years of post-18 education. The default rate, once more, is assumed to be $1\frac{1}{2}$ per cent.

## Employer user charges

Students are one set of beneficiaries of education and training. Employers are another. One way of increasing industry's contribution and avoiding the incentive to free-ride (referred to above) is through a user charge on employers of trained men and women, the resources thereby derived being channelled back into the education/training of the next generation of young people. Under such an arrangement, employers would not contribute to the costs of training their competitors' workforces; they would pay only for those workers whom they deemed it worthwhile to employ, and only for as long as they employed them. Such user charges get round the disincentive to provide training.

The specific scheme investigated here is a user charge of 1 per cent added to the employer NIC for all employees with at least two years of post-18 education. Unlike the graduate tax it is payable on *all* gross income, i.e. it is not limited to earnings below the NIC upper earnings limit. A default rate of $1\frac{1}{2}$ per cent is assumed.

## 5.    How the Different Schemes Performed[5]

The results for the different loan schemes are shown in Tables 8.2 and 8.3 for men and women respectively, for full- and part-time students in advanced further and higher education. The tables show the amount of loan repaid by individuals in the LIFEMOD cohort (i) for different loan schemes, (ii) for different assumptions about the interest rate paid on student loans, and (iii) for different assumptions about the rate with which graduates' earnings will grow.

Table 8.2  Loans: Advanced Further and Higher Education, Full-time and Part-time: Men

|  | Proportion of borrowers who repay in full | Proportion of loan repaid | Mean repayment period (years) | Repayment as per cent of annual earnings |
|---|---|---|---|---|
| **Zero earnings growth** | | | | |
| Government scheme | 83.9 | 87.2 | 16.0 | 1.90 |
| Income-contingent scheme | 73.1 | 91.5 | 25.7 | 0.88 |
| Income-contingent scheme (1%i) | 57.4 | 85.8 | 27.1 | 0.88 |
| Income-contingent scheme (2%i) | 39.7 | 74.6 | 27.3 | 0.88 |
| Income-contingent scheme (3%i) | 22.6 | 58.1 | 23.4 | 0.88 |
| **1½ per cent earnings growth** | | | | |
| Government scheme | 83.9 | 87.1 | 16.0 | 1.64 |
| Income-contingent scheme | 78.9 | 94.0 | 22.3 | 0.88 |
| Income-contingent scheme (1%i) | 75.3 | 91.3 | 24.3 | 0.88 |
| Income-contingent scheme (2%i) | 65.9 | 86.6 | 26.5 | 0.88 |
| Income-contingent scheme (3%i) | 49.1 | 76.5 | 27.5 | 0.88 |
| **3 per cent earnings growth** | | | | |
| Government scheme | 83.9 | 87.1 | 16.0 | 1.44 |
| Income-contingent scheme | 82.9 | 95.3 | 19.8 | 0.88 |
| Income-contingent scheme (1%i) | 80.5 | 93.7 | 21.4 | 0.88 |
| Income-contingent scheme (2%i) | 76.9 | 91.0 | 23.3 | 0.88 |
| Income-contingent scheme (3%i) | 73.1 | 86.7 | 26.0 | 0.88 |

Source: LIFEMOD.

---

5    These results are drawn from Barr and Falkingham (1993), which also contains results for loans and employer user charges for the 16–19 age group.

**Table 8.3** Loans: Advanced Further and Higher Education, Full-time and Part-time: Women

| | Proportion of borrowers who repay in full | Proportion of loan repaid | Mean repayment period (years) | Repayment as per cent of annual earnings |
|---|---|---|---|---|
| **Zero earnings growth** | | | | |
| Government scheme | 44.9 | 64.3 | 22.2 | 2.20 |
| Income-contingent scheme | 27.2 | 67.3 | 24.8 | 0.96 |
| Income-contingent scheme (1%i) | 18.5 | 53.4 | 23.6 | 0.96 |
| Income-contingent scheme (2%i) | 13.6 | 39.5 | 22.5 | 0.96 |
| Income-contingent scheme (3%i) | 10.6 | 27.8 | 23.4 | 0.96 |
| **1½ per cent earnings growth** | | | | |
| Government scheme | 45.1 | 63.7 | 22.2 | 1.80 |
| Income-contingent scheme | 45.5 | 77.4 | 25.8 | 0.96 |
| Income-contingent scheme (1%i) | 34.3 | 66.1 | 25.9 | 0.96 |
| Income-contingent scheme (2%i) | 22.3 | 51.9 | 24.0 | 0.96 |
| Income-contingent scheme (3%i) | 15.3 | 38.0 | 22.5 | 0.96 |
| **3 per cent earnings growth** | | | | |
| Government scheme | 45.1 | 63.0 | 22.2 | 1.50 |
| Income-contingent scheme | 61.9 | 83.9 | 25.1 | 0.96 |
| Income-contingent scheme (1%i) | 51.7 | 76.2 | 25.8 | 0.96 |
| Income-contingent scheme (2%i) | 39.8 | 65.0 | 25.9 | 0.96 |
| Income-contingent scheme (3%i) | 27.0 | 51.1 | 24.7 | 0.96 |

**Source:** LIFEMOD.

Four performance indicators are considered. The first column shows the proportion of *debtors* who repay in full by retirement (at which stage any outstanding loan is assumed to be written off); likewise the Government absorbs the outstanding loan of people who die before statutory pensionable age. Thus, with zero earnings growth, 83.9 per cent of male borrowers repay in full under the Government scheme, 73.1 per cent under the comparable income contingent scheme.

The second column shows the proportion of the total *debt* the cohort as a whole repays; thus with zero earnings growth, 87.2 per cent of total lending is repaid under the Government scheme, 91.5 per cent under the comparable income-contingent scheme. The third column shows the average repayment period for individuals who repay in full whilst the fourth column gives the burden of loan repayments as a percentage of the graduate's subsequent earnings.

## Zero earnings growth

With zero real earnings growth, more men repay in full under the Government scheme, 84 per cent, compared with 73 per cent under the income-contingent scheme. The picture is reversed, however, if we look at the fraction of total borrowing which is repaid – 87 per cent under the Government scheme and over 91 per cent under the income-contingent scheme. Thus under the income-contingent scheme, men would be seen by lenders as good risks. A 10 per cent guarantee would cover the shortfall, if the world continued as assumed by LIFEMOD.

This result merits explanation. Under the Government scheme, repayment is zero for people with incomes below 85 per cent of the national average; otherwise it is 10 per cent of the loan. In contrast, the income-contingent loan, precisely because it *is* income-contingent, makes it possible to impose some repayment on people on lower incomes. Thus it is possible to collect repayments (albeit often small) on earnings above the lower earnings limit for NICs (currently about £54 per week), whereas the Government scheme collects only from people whose earnings exceed 85 per cent of the national average (currently about £200 per week). Thus two effects are operating: (i) repayments under the income-contingent scheme are often smaller than those under the Government scheme, but (ii) at least some repayment is possible in the £54 – £200 range, where repayment under the Government scheme is zero. As a practical matter, the effect of (ii) is stronger than (i), and therefore the income-contingent scheme ends up collecting more than the Government scheme.

The average repayment period for men who *do* repay is sixteen years for the Government scheme, given the provision that repayment is suspended for people earning less than 85 per cent of the national average. Under the income-contingent scheme it takes about twenty-six years to repay. As suggested earlier, the longer repayment duration under the income-contingent scheme is a point in its *favour*. It is efficient if repayment of a loan can be spread over the life of the asset. Thus repayment should be spread over three years for new car; for a university degree they should be distributed over the entire duration of labour market activity.

Because the Government scheme is spread over a shorter period, repayments constitute a much higher proportion of income than under the income-contingent scheme (1.9 per cent compared with 0.9 per cent). Like any conventional mortgage loan, the scheme involves 'front-loading' of repayments, i.e. requiring high repayments at a time when income is lower than in future.

Differences between men and women are significant. About 45 per cent of women repay in full under the Government scheme, but only 27 per cent under the income-contingent scheme. Looking at the fraction of borrowing repaid, however, we find again that women's total repayments are slightly more under the income-contingent scheme (67 per cent) than under the Government scheme (64 per cent). As discussed shortly, the picture for women improves considerably with a positive real earnings growth.

## The effect of earnings growth

The effect of earnings growth depends on which scheme is examined. Repayments under a mortgage-type scheme depend little, if at all, on earnings. Thus repayments are higher and/or faster under the government scheme only to the extent that more people creep over the 85 per cent threshold. In contrast, repayments under the income-contingent scheme depend very directly on earnings, and so earnings growth considerably improves repayment prospects.

Figure 8.3 illustrates the effect of real earnings growth on repayment patterns, showing the fraction of *total borrowing* which is repaid. For men the Government scheme performs better in the early years but in later years repayments under the income-contingent scheme catch up and eventually overtake the Government scheme. With real earnings growth of 1½ per cent, men's repayments under the income-contingent scheme increase to 94 per cent of total loans, compared with 87 per cent for the Government scheme, and the proportion of men who repay in full rises from 73 per cent to 79 per cent. Given the high proportion of men who repay fully, the effect of earnings growth is more to speed up repayment than to increase the number of men repaying. For women, in contrast, the introduction of real earnings growth substantially increases the proportion who can repay their income-contingent loan in full (from 27 per cent to 46 per cent); and women repay a larger share of total borrowing under the income-contingent scheme (77½ per cent of total lending is repaid) than under the Government scheme (64 per cent).

With 3 per cent real earnings growth the income-contingent scheme repays 95 per cent of lending for men, significantly more than the Government scheme. In principle, the income-contingent scheme for men and women combined, would require only a 10 per cent guarantee. Such loans could pay a real interest rate of 2 per cent and still yield slightly more repayments than the Government scheme (which charges no real interest).

## Graduate taxes and employer user charges

We have analysed loans in order to compare income-contingent arrangements with the existing scheme. We now briefly discuss two additional, but separate, options. Graduate taxes could be used *instead* of

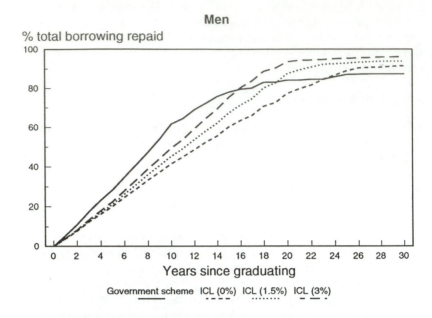

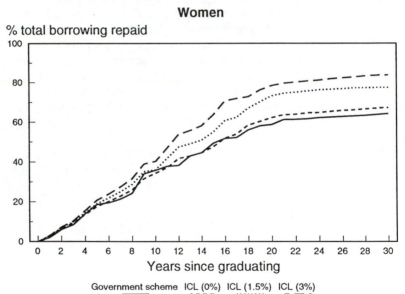

**Note:**
Three variants of Income-Contingent Loans (ICL) are shown. Figures in brackets give
assumed real earnings growth.

**Figure 8.3** Cumulative Proportion of Total Borrowing Repaid Higher
Education (full- and part-time)

a loan scheme; employer user charges could be used *in addition* to either a loan scheme or a graduate tax.

The yield of such alternatives is substantial. Table 8.4 shows that a **graduate tax** of 1 per cent would repay 132.5 per cent of total borrowing compared with around 80 per cent if repayment ceased once the loan was repaid. Thus with a graduate tax, assuming zero earnings growth, richer graduates repay 50 per cent more than they would under a loan. The yield increases to over 180 per cent of the cohort's borrowing with earnings growth of 1½ per cent, and to nearly two and a half times total lending with 3 per cent earnings growth. **Employer user charges,** in the case of full-time and part-time students, yield over 1½ times as much as an equivalent loan at zero earnings growth, rising to 3 times total lending if real earnings grow at 3 per cent. A possible implication is a user charge at a lower rate, say ½ per cent.

Although a graduate tax appears to hold out the possibility of raising more revenue than an ICL it is less attractive on equity grounds. In contrast with an ICL a graduate tax repayment continues after the loan has been repaid in full, with the result that high-earning graduates repay more than they have borrowed. They contribute to the cost of educating poorer graduates. We do not see the justice in that. If there is a case for helping poorer graduates, the cost should fall upon taxpayers generally, like any other redistributive measure. In the case of employer user charges, we wish merely to point out the possibility that they might be used further to increase the resources available for higher education; alternatively, they might be used as a funding mechanism for other parts of the education and training system.

**Table 8.4** Graduate Tax and Employer User Charge as Per Cent of Total Loan Liability: Advanced Further and Higher Education: Full-time and Part-time

|  | Yield of Graduate Tax | Yield of Employer User Charge |
|---|---|---|
| **Men and Women** | | |
| Zero earnings growth | 132.5 | 156.4 |
| 1½ per cent earnings growth | 181.4 | 215.4 |
| 3 per cent earnings growth | 253.3 | 302.0 |
| **Men** | | |
| Zero earnings growth | 167.1 | 204.0 |
| 1½ per cent earnings growth | 231.2 | 283.7 |
| 3 per cent earnings growth | 326.4 | 401.7 |
| **Women** | | |
| Zero earnings growth | 87.3 | 94.5 |
| 1½ per cent earnings growth | 116.1 | 125.9 |
| 3 per cent earnings growth | 157.0 | 170.7 |

**Source:** LIFEMOD.

## 6.     Conclusion

We have suggested that the current loan scheme for higher education should be reformed (i) by collecting repayments alongside National Insurance contributions, and (ii) by largely privatising student loans. This makes it possible to improve quality and increase equity at minimal cost in public expenditure. Bennett, Glennerster and Nevison (1992a, b) suggested that the *average* rate of return to education for middle class children has been fairly low. Is it desirable in those circumstances to follow the policies suggested in this chapter? There are several reasons why the present policies are not in conflict with the earlier findings. First, Bennett, Glennerster and Nevison (1992b) found that the rate of return is higher for children from non-professional backgrounds, i.e. the very people for whom access is most important. Second, we know that if entry gates are narrow, middle class applicants 'crowd out' other students; supply-side expansion widens the gates, to the particular benefit of applicants from poorer backgrounds. Third, figures for the later 1980s suggest an upward trend in rates of return to at least some types of education and training.

The point, however, highlights the need to design policy with considerable care, precisely to avoid deterring both potential applicants and their subsequent employers. The main conclusion is the effectiveness of the income-contingent mechanism in achieving this, through (a) its high repayment yield, despite (b) the low burden it places on individuals. The mechanism makes it possible to achieve a number of desirable objectives simultaneously.

*   It raises substantial additional resources for education and training without major reliance on additional tax funding (a desirable result if only because major public expenditure increases on education and training are clearly not on offer).

*   The cost would fall on those who benefit most from the expenditure.

*   It minimises the deterrent to young people to pursue education or training. Moreover, the introduction of loans raises resources which can be used *inter alia* to give the greatest help to those who need it most, e.g. by giving 100 per cent vouchers to groups whom one wants particularly to help.

*   Even if all the savings were used to reduce government borrowing, there would still be significant gains: the tax burden of financing higher education would be fairer; it would be possible to raise the ceiling on student borrowing, thereby increasing the amount students have to live on; it would be possible to make loans available to students returning to higher education whose grant entitlement has been exhausted; and it would be possible to extend the loans available to graduate students.

**Chapter Nine**

UK
J16
J12
J13
D31

# Gender, Lone-parenthood and Lifetime Income

## Maria Evandrou and Jane Falkingham

### 1.    Introduction

From previous chapters gender emerges as a key variable in determining an individual's position in the lifetime income distribution. Lifetime earnings for women are, on average, only half those of men. Women have been found to have lower average living standards than men, even though lifetime cash benefits are worth two-thirds more for women than for men. Seventy-one per cent of the poorest lifetime income decile group[1] are women, whereas they constitute only 35 per cent of the richest group (Table 6.8, Chapter 6). However, it is not just being a woman that is important. Other factors also play a major role in determining lifetime earnings and income. In particular, experience of an episode of lone parenthood has been identified as a important predictor of low lifetime income. The impact of lone parenthood on lifetime income patterns is not unique, but varies according to the *type* of lone parenthood, its *duration* and the *stage of the life cycle* at which it occurs. In this chapter we examine variation in income across the life cycle by type of lone parent and assess the performance of the social security system in protecting their living standards and other disadvantaged groups.

As previous chapters have shown, results from LIFEMOD can be used in a number of ways. In this chapter different sources and types of income are viewed both *across* the life cycle, that is allowing us to look at how income varies with age, and are also summed at the *end* of the life

---

1    Measured by equivalent net income.

167

cycle to give lifetime totals – the latter method providing a summary of the end result of the former.


## 2.    Lifetime Income and Gender

### The position of women and men

Table 9.1 summarises the differences in lifetime income between men and women found in LIFEMOD. Women experience lower lifetime earnings than men. The reason for this is two-fold: firstly, the *'gender gap'* between men and women's earnings when in work; and secondly, the higher proportion of 'working years of life' spent out of the labour force by women due to childbirth and other caring responsibilities. This has been referred to as the *'family gap'* (Waldfogel, 1993).

As we have seen in Chapter 5, women's earnings are, on average, 10 per cent lower than men's below age 25. This gap increases with age, as more women are employed in part-time positions. However, even amongst women who are continuously employed in full-time jobs throughout their working lives a gender differential in pay persists. This combined with women's shorter working lives means that total lifetime earnings for all women are only half those for men.

The lower lifetime earnings of women are reflected in lower lifetime occupational pensions in their own right, but this is offset by greater receipts from pensions inherited from their spouses. Labour market interruptions result in disadvantage which is extended into retirement. Cross-sectional analysis has also shown the impact of labour market experience upon pension entitlement and level received (Joshi and Davies, 1991; Bone *et al.*, 1992; Ginn and Arber, 1994). Thus, prior to the intervention of the welfare state, men's lifetime income is, on average, nearly twice that of women. If it were not for the fact that women live on average more than five years longer than men and so have longer to accumulate income, the ratio would have been much higher.

**Table 9.1** Lifetime Income Components by Men and Women (£000s)

|                                             | Men   | Women | Ratio M:W |
|---------------------------------------------|-------|-------|-----------|
| Lifetime earnings                           | 363   | 178   | 2.04      |
| Occupational pension and investment income  | 28    | 27    | 1.04      |
| Maintenance                                 | -0.8  | 0.9   | 0.90      |
| Original income                             | 390   | 206   | 1.89      |
| Cash benefits                               | 49    | 82    | 0.60      |
| Gross income                                | 439   | 288   | 1.52      |
| Net income                                  | 332   | 232   | 1.44      |
| Equivalent net income                       | 294   | 288   | 1.02      |
| Final income                                | 367   | 270   | 1.35      |
| Annualised equivalent net income            | 5,190 | 4,690 | 1.11      |

The social security system acts to reduce the differences in lifetime resources between the sexes. Cash benefits, dominated by pensions and in particular payments under SERPS, reduce the ratio between men's and women's gross lifetime income to 1.5. With their greater original incomes, men pay more tax over their lifetimes than women and after tax the differential between men and women has been reduced to a factor of 1.4.

The family also acts to redistribute income; the effect of allowing for family circumstances is to increase women's net lifetime incomes by a quarter but to reduce that of men by a tenth. At this point, on average, men's and women's lifetime incomes appear to be almost equal. However, this crucially depends upon the assumption of *equal sharing of income within the family* unit which, as work by Pahl and others (Pahl, 1989, 1990) has demonstrated, may be an unrealistic one in a significant number of cases.[2] Even if we accept this heroic assumption, as noted above, women live longer than men. Annualising equivalent net income has the effect of widening the differential between genders. On average, men have equivalent net incomes over 10 per cent higher than women's for *each year* of their adult lives, even after the equalising effect of the social security system and the family have been taken into account.

All of these figures are based on averages which disguise variation in the life experiences of different men and women. Although women are, on average, worse off over the lifetime than men, not all are – 35 per cent of the top lifetime income group are women. Table 9.2 examines some of the characteristics that are related to whether a particular man or woman finds him- or herself at the top or bottom of the distribution of lifetime living standards. As in common with other chapters, we use annualised equivalent net income as a measure of relative *living standards*.

Demographic factors are particularly important for women. Getting married and staying married is virtually essential for a woman to reach the top part of the LIFEMOD income distribution, although there are some never-married women in the top quintile group. For men, the proportion who are ever married peaks in the middle of the distribution. Alongside this, the number of years married rises throughout the distribution for women, but falls through the top half of the distribution for men.

The experience of divorce also impacts upon men and women in very different ways. Forty-nine per cent of women in the bottom income group are ever divorced, compared to only 24 per cent in the top group. Conversely the incidence of divorce rises across the income distribution from 25 per cent to 40 per cent for men. Thus, divorce generally has a positive effect on men's lifetime living standard but a negative effect on

---

2  Relaxing the assumption of equal sharing reduces the redistributive impact of the family between men and women. Sensitivity analysis is presented in Chapter 6.

**Table 9.2** Selected Demographic and Economic Characteristics by Lifetime Income Quintile Group

|  | Bottom | 2 | 3 | 4 | Top | All |
|---|---|---|---|---|---|---|
| **Men** | | | | | | |
| **(a) Demographic characteristics** | | | | | | |
| Age at death | 67.3 | 72.9 | 72.9 | 73.6 | 72.6 | 72.2 |
| Ever married (%) | 73.6 | 84.8 | 92.6 | 86.1 | 84.7 | 85.0 |
| Years married | 23.9 | 32.1 | 35.7 | 33.5 | 31.8 | 31.9 |
| Ever with children | 64.3 | 77.1 | 83.1 | 71.3 | 68.0 | 73.0 |
| Number of child years (all) | 23.8 | 26.2 | 28.9 | 23.3 | 19.8 | 32.2 |
| Ever divorced | 24.6 | 32.3 | 35.8 | 35.5 | 39.8 | 34.0 |
| Years as lone parent | - | 0.2 | - | - | - | 0.1 |
| **(b) Economic characteristics** | | | | | | |
| Ever in tertiary education (%) | 30.0 | 38.5 | 48.0 | 68.0 | 82.0 | 56.0 |
| Years of tertiary education | 0.5 | 0.6 | 0.9 | 1.4 | 2.0 | 1.1 |
| Total years in which unemployed | 12.4 | 9.6 | 8.0 | 6.9 | 5.3 | 8.0 |
| Ever receiving occupational pension | 35.3 | 43.3 | 49.9 | 50.6 | 51.8 | 47.0 |
| **Women** | | | | | | |
| **(a) Demographic characteristics** | | | | | | |
| Age at death | 76.3 | 77.5 | 78.0 | 78.6 | 76.4 | 77.3 |
| Ever married (%) | 79.1 | 94.8 | 97.0 | 98.3 | 96.1 | 92.0 |
| Years married | 19.1 | 33.0 | 36.1 | 38.1 | 38.8 | 31.9 |
| Ever with children | 67.4 | 81.4 | 79.8 | 80.7 | 69.3 | 75.0 |
| Number of child years (all) | 25.2 | 32.1 | 32.0 | 31.3 | 25.0 | 29.1 |
| Ever divorced | 48.6 | 38.7 | 31.5 | 32.7 | 23.9 | 36.0 |
| Years as lone parent | 5.3 | 3.7 | 2.9 | 2.5 | 1.6 | 3.4 |
| **(b) Economic characteristics** | | | | | | |
| Ever in tertiary education | 41.2 | 47.3 | 53.2 | 62.6 | 75.4 | 54.0 |
| Years of tertiary education | 0.8 | 0.9 | 2.5 | 1.3 | 1.5 | 1.1 |
| Total years in which unemployed | 6.3 | 5.0 | 4.3 | 4.0 | 3.8 | 5.0 |
| Ever received occupational pension | 31.5 | 35.5 | 38.9 | 42.7 | 48.3 | 38.0 |

those of women. This finding is confirmed by other research (Burkhauser *et al.*, 1991; Hoffman and Duncan, 1988; Hauser and Fischer, 1990).

Looking at economic characteristics, men with a high incidence of unemployment are more likely to be in the bottom income group, whereas for women it is not as important. Experience of tertiary education rises from the bottom to the top income group, as we would expect, however the gradient (30 to 82 per cent) for men is steeper than that for women (41 to 75 per cent) – indicating that it has a greater impact upon lifetime income for men than for women.

Thus the route to a high lifetime standard of living appears to be very different for men and women. For men, the labour market is of prime importance whereas for women the route to lifetime economic security still lies in the marriage market, with marriage mitigating the inequality in original incomes between men and women. This has important implications for the lifetime welfare of women who do not enter the marriage market or for whom this market 'fails'.

Nearly half of the women at the bottom of the distribution have experienced at least one episode of lone parenthood[3] at some stage in their lives (for an average total of 13 years for those who do so), but only a quarter of those women at the top (for an average of 8 years). Few men experience lone parenthood, only 1 per cent, but for those who do, they are disproportionately concentrated at the lower end of the income distribution.

In summary, marriage, divorce, children and lone parenthood all appear to influence relative lifetime living standards. Looking how these differentials are built up *across the life cycle* helps us to assess their impact.

### The impact of divorce, children and lone parenthood across the life cycle

If we stood at the grave-side and looked back over the lifetimes of women with different life histories, we would find different patterns of income for different groups. Figure 9.1 illustrates how relative living standards for women with different histories vary with age. It is important to bear in mind when interpreting these, and other figures detailing movement across the life cycle, that (i) the figures are averages for the group as a whole at a given age, and (ii) that the women at any given moment are not necessarily in the state that describes them *throughout* their lifetime. For example, the mean income at age 30 for women who are 'ever a lone parent' reflects the income of women who are currently lone mothers, women who have been lone mothers but are not now, and women who are not now but will become lone mothers at some stage in the future.

From the top panel in Figure 9.1 the 'gains' from marrying for women are clear. Women who never marry, and never have children (the solid line) experience a fairly constant standard of living until their mid-40s when average income begins to drop. This is due to a combination of increasing part-time employment, unemployment and early retirement. After age 60 their income is very low. A similar pattern of income is seen in the bottom panel for those women who never marry but do have children. Again there is particular disadvantage in later life.

Children act to reduce living standards for those that marry, delaying somewhat the rise in living standards. The 'cost' of children can be thought of as the shaded area between the two lines. The cost of children to women, in terms of relative living standards is low compared with the effect of divorce. This is represented by the shaded area between the solid and dashed line in the lower panel, that is income for ever married

---

3   Note that in LIFEMOD cohabiting unions of three or more years are treated as 'married' and women with children living in such unions are not defined as lone parents for our purposes.

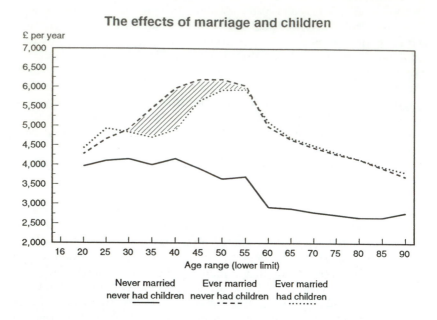

The effects of marriage and children

£ per year

Never married
never had children

Ever married
never had children

Ever married
had children

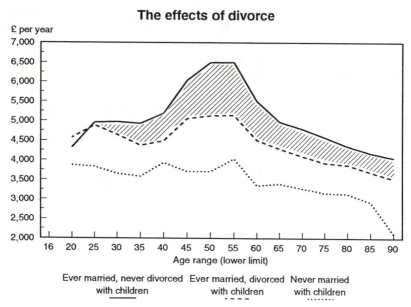

The effects of divorce

£ per year

Ever married, never divorced
with children

Ever married, divorced
with children

Never married
with children

**Figure 9.1**  Women's Equivalent Net Income Across the Lifetime by Life
Course Events

women with children who never divorce and those married women with children who do. The effect of divorce is to depress living standards, particularly in middle age – the years where children will also be present in the home. However, the effect of divorce continues beyond the 'empty-nest' stage and women continue to experience lower living standards later in life. The impact of divorce and the costs of childbearing has been documented with survey data and simulations (Kiernan and Wicks, 1990; Joshi, 1990).

Although divorce is the main route to lone parenthood, it is not the only one. Below we go on to look at how different experiences of lone parenthood impact upon lifetime living standards.

## 3.     Lone Parenthood and Income over the Life Cycle

Lone parenthood amongst the LIFEMOD population is almost exclusively a female experience. Only 1.5 per cent of men experience an episode of lone parenthood compared with 37 per cent of women. There are several pathways into lone parent status – extra-marital conception, or through marital breakdown either from a divorce or via widowhood. The results presented below demonstrate that the type of lone motherhood experienced has a differential impact on lifetime income.

Thirteen per cent of women ever experience being a single lone mother, 24 per cent become a lone mother at some stage in their life cycle through divorce and a further 3 per cent from being widowed.[4] This compares with cross-sectional data from the 1985 General Household Survey (OPCS, 1988) which shows that in that 9 per cent of all adults are lone parents. Obviously the proportion over the lifetime is much higher as this is just a snapshot in time and does not include persons who have been a lone parent but who are no longer, or persons who have yet to become lone parents.

### Characteristics of lone mothers

Before going on to look at how experience of lone motherhood impacts upon relative lifetime living standards, it is useful to look at how other lifetime characteristics vary according to whether a woman has ever been a lone mother (Table 9.3).

---

4    This sums to more than 37 per cent as 16 per cent of single lone mothers go on to experience a further episode of lone parenthood through divorce.

**Table 9.3** Characteristics of LIFEMOD Women, by Lifetime Lone Parenthood (LP) Status

| | All | Never LP no child | Never LP child | Ever LP | Single LP | Divorced LP | Single and divorded LP | Widowed LP |
|---|---|---|---|---|---|---|---|---|
| Proportion of all women | 100 | 24.7 | 38.1 | 37.2 | 10.7 | 21.5 | 2.1 | 3.1 |
| Age at death | 77.2 | 74.0 | 77.9 | 78.0 | 77.9 | 77.7 | 80.5 | 78.3 |
| Ever in tertiary education (%) | 54.0 | 54.0 | 53.0 | 54.0 | 47.0 | 58.0 | 49.0 | 51.0 |
| Years where spell of unemployment | 4.8 | 5.8 | 4.1 | 4.9 | 5.0 | 4.7 | 5.4 | 4.8 |
| Total time unemployed (yrs) | 2.3 | 2.8 | 1.9 | 2.3 | 2.3 | 2.2 | 2.5 | 2.2 |
| Ever receiving occupational pension | 38.4 | 32.9 | 39.3 | 41.0 | 39.4 | 41.7 | 36.6 | 44.3 |
| Ever married (%) | 91.8 | 74.9 | 100 | 94.5 | 80.8 | 100 | 100 | 100 |
| Age married (if married only) | 26 | 33 | 24 | 25 | 31 | 22 | 26 | 23 |
| Years married | 31.8 | 19.8 | 43.8 | 27.4 | 29.8 | 26.8 | 23.6 | 26.2 |
| Ever divorced | 36.4 | 27.3 | 12.2 | 67.1 | 9.4 | 100 | 100 | 14.8 |
| Years divorced | 8.7 | 7.4 | 2.4 | 16.1 | 2.1 | 24.2 | 23.8 | 2.2 |
| Years a lone parent | 3.4 | 0 | 0 | 9.2 | 10.4 | 8.5 | 12.2 | 7.4 |
| Annualised lifetime equivalent income | 4690 | 4595 | 4997 | 4441 | 4560 | 4373 | 4170 | 4686 |

Lone mothers, are on average, as likely to have attended a tertiary education institution as all women, although women who are ever a single lone mother are less likely to have any tertiary education than other women. Lone mothers are also as prone to unemployment as on average. Again there are differences between the types of lone mothers with women who have experienced at least two episodes of lone motherhood, one as a single mother and a subsequent period as a divorced mother, suffering a higher incidence and duration of unemployment than on average.

Receipt of an occupational pension also varies, with women who have been both single and divorced lone mothers having a lower probability of receipt. This group are also married for fewer years than on average and hence have spent a shorter period of their life 'benefiting' from shared income with a spouse. These differences are reflected in their lower lifetime annualised equivalent net income. They experience an income of over £500 less than women on average *for each year of their adult lives.* Ever divorced lone mothers are similarly disadvantaged by over £300 a year. If we compare these levels to women with children who have never divorced then the relative disadvantage doubles to £600 a year of adult life.

## Total lifetime income – standard of living

Figure 9.2 shows how relative living standards as measured by equivalent net income vary *across the life cycle* for these different lifetime lone mother types. From the top panel we can see that the level of equivalent net income of lone parent mothers is lower than that of women who never experienced lone motherhood – particularly between the ages of 20 and 55 years. This is the period of the life cycle during which women will be experiencing lone motherhood. However, even after the majority have left that state, women who are ever lone mothers continue to experience a lower standard of living.

The bottom panel shows the time path of equivalent net income for the different types of lone mothers. The different patterns with age reflect the timing of the experience of lone motherhood. **Single** lone mothers have a much lower level of income at younger ages, but after age 35 their income rises and from 55 onwards mirrors those women who never experience lone motherhood over their lifetime. The income of ever **divorced** lone mothers is lowest when they are in their mid-thirties. It begins to fall early on in the lifecycle and only starts to rise again between 40 and 55 years. The crossing over of these two income curves reflects (i) the higher likelihood of single lone mothers marrying as age increases and (ii) the increased likelihood of divorce between age 30 and 40. This pattern is reflected in the living standards for women who are **both single and then later divorced** lone mothers. Although their income begins to rise during their early twenties, it falls dramatically in their late twenties as they begin to divorce. They never recover their position and experience lower living standards throughout their life until very late old age.[5]

Much of these differences in relative living standards is due to not benefiting from shared income from a spouse for extended periods. As we have seen from Figure 9.1, the absence of the family as an informal redistributive mechanism can depress lifetime living standards. However, there are also inequalities in receipt of income from both the labour market and the State by type of lone parent. The top panel of Figure 9.3 shows how market income from earnings and, after retirement, from occupational pensions varies with age for the different types of lone mothers, whilst the bottom panel presents analogous information for income from the social security system. After retirement, by far the largest components of cash benefits are the basic state pension and entitlements under SERPS.

Lone mothers in general are in receipt of lower average annual earnings than other women. Women who are ever widowed lone

---

5   The number of observations at ages above 80 is low, and little weight should be given to trends at this stage of the life cycle.

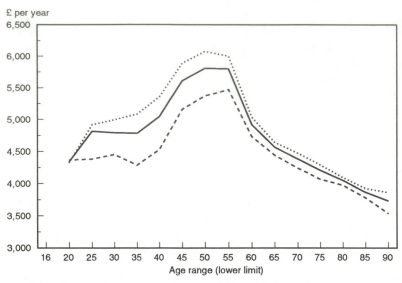

All women  Ever a lone parent  Never a lone parent

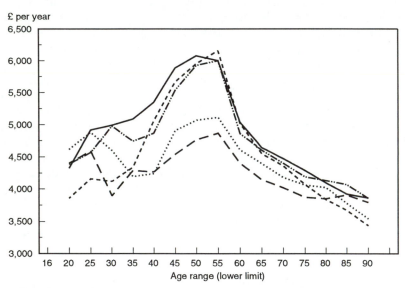

Ever Single LP  Ever Divorced LP  Ever Single and Div LP  Ever Widowed LP  Never LP

**Figure 9.2** Women's Equivalent Net Income Across the Lifetime by Ever Lone Parent Status

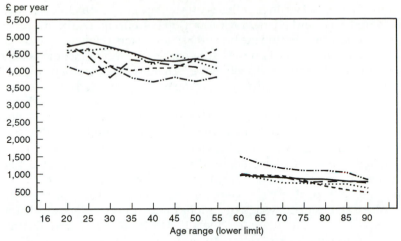

Annual average market income; earnings and occupational pension by ever lone parent status

Ever Single LP   Ever Divorced LP   Ever Single and Div LP   Ever Widowed LP   Never LP

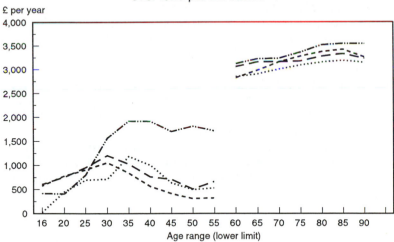

Annual average cash benefits received by ever lone parent status

Ever Single LP   Ever Divorced LP   Ever Single and Div LP   Ever Widowed LP

**Figure 9.3** Income over the Life Cycle by Ever Lone Parent Status

mothers experience particularly low earnings as do single lone mothers. This is a function of their lower labour force participation. When they do work, single lone mothers are more likely to work full-time than other groups (comparable cross-sectional patterns are found in the GHS figures; OPCS, 1993c). In part this is due to the age of their children (who will be older as they had them at a younger age), but can also be attributed to the disincentives within the tax and benefit system (Holtermann, 1993). That is, with increasing earnings, the combined effect of income tax and the withdrawal of social security benefits results in fewer financial gains from employment for lone parents, compared to a married or cohabiting parent.

Prior to retirement, widowed lone mothers have relatively low market incomes. After retirement the reverse is true, with widowed lone mothers receiving levels of occupational pensions on average £300 per year higher than other women and nearly £500 per year higher than divorced lone mothers, reflecting both higher absolute levels of benefit and a higher probability of receipt (as discussed in Table 9.3).

The social security system treats lone mothers very differently. Before retirement, all lone mothers receive a higher level of cash benefits than non lone mothers. Receipt rises with age to the mid-thirties and then falls, reflecting the presence of children. The most striking feature is the *entirely* different pattern for widowed lone mothers. They receive cash benefits on average three times as much as other groups and there is little fall with age. After retirement widows continue to do better than average, whilst divorced mothers fare worse. This reflects implicit bias of the current system, with 'deserving' and 'undeserving' recipients. The welfare state as designed by Beveridge did not take into account the contingency of divorce (Baldwin and Falkingham, 1994; Millar, 1994).

These differential patterns of income by age translate into lower overall lifetime living standards for lone mothers (as shown in Table 9.3). Table 9.4 presents lifetime totals for the different components of income of lone parent groups. A woman who has never been a lone mother receives on average £294,000 of equivalent net income over her lifetime, compared with £275,000 for women who spend some period of their life as a lone mother. The effect on lifetime income depends on type of lone motherhood; women who have been single mothers at some stage accumulate £279,000 whilst women who have become lone mothers through divorce receive on average £10,000 less at £269,000. Widowed lone mothers, however, experience lifetime living standards of the same level as women who have never been lone mothers – £293,000. This latter group receive on average over a third as much more in cash benefits over their lifetimes than other lone mothers, £122,000 compared with £90,000 for all lone mothers.

**Table 9.4** Lifetime Income Components by Different Lone Parent Groups
(£000s)

|                      | Never LP | Ever LP | Ever SLP | Ever DLP | Ever S/DLP | Ever WLP |
|----------------------|----------|---------|----------|----------|------------|----------|
| Lifetime earnings    | 179      | 176     | 175      | 179      | 175        | 158      |
| Maintenance          | 0.2      | 2.2     | 2.7      | 3.6      | 3.1        | 0.2      |
| Occupational pension | 17       | 18      | 16       | 15       | 20         | 4        |
| Original income      | 204      | 207     | 199      | 210      | 208        | 210      |
| Cash benefits        | 77       | 90      | 85       | 87       | 101        | 122      |
| Gross income         | 281      | 297     | 285      | 296      | 309        | 332      |
| Net income           | 225      | 241     | 23       | 241      | 254        | 269      |
| Equivalent net income | 294     | 275     | 281      | 270      | 269        | 293      |

## Duration and timing of lone motherhood and lifetime income

The **duration** of lone motherhood affects lifetime living standards. As a group LIFEMOD lone mothers spent on average 9.1 years in a lone state. Using the Women and Employment Survey data, Ermisch (1992) found the median duration of lone parenthood to be much lower; that is, nearly five years for women who had been previously married and just under three years for never married lone mothers.

The LIFEMOD average duration varies according to type of lone parent, with single lone mothers experiencing the longest average duration, 10.4 years (range 1–34). Divorced lone mothers spend an average of 8.5 years (range 1–31); women with two spells spend an average of 5 years as a single mother (1–16) and a further 7.2 years as a divorced lone mother (1–17); whilst women who are widowed spent the shortest average time as a lone mother, 6.3 years (range 1–28). There is considerable variation around these mean figures and as Figure 9.4 shows those spending *longer* than average have lower lifetime living standards.

The **timing** of lone motherhood is also influential in determining income levels. Over a third of single lone mothers are teenage lone mothers, entering this family status before age 20, and over 80 per cent do so before age 25. Few young women become lone mothers through divorce, with only 9 per cent of all ever divorced lone mothers entering this state prior to their twenty-fifth birthday. Table 9.5 shows that these young entrants are more disadvantaged in terms of the labour market and lifetime earnings than other groups. It may be that having children at a young age is the disadvantaging factor rather than the lone motherhood *per se*. However, these teenage lone parents do not catch up their relative position later on. They also receive fewer cash benefits over their lifetime. Generally, the later the age of entry into single lone motherhood, the higher are lifetime earnings and other income measures.

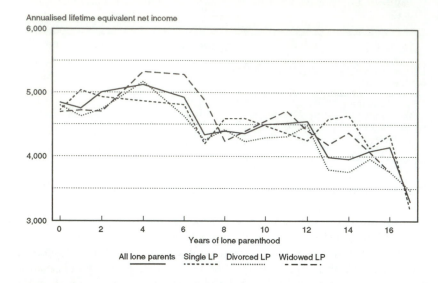

**Figure 9.4** Lifetime Living Standards by Duration of Lone Parenthood

**Table 9.5** Lifetime Income Components of Lone Mothers by Age of Entry into Lone Parenthood (£000s)

|  | Ever single lone mother | | | Ever divorced lone mother | | |
|---|---|---|---|---|---|---|
| Age at entry into lone parenthood | Under 20 | 20–24 | Over 25 | Under 25 | 25–34 | Over 35 |
| Lifetime earnings | 150 | 188 | 190 | 149 | 179 | 179 |
| Original income | 173 | 220 | 211 | 175 | 206 | 221 |
| Cash benefits | 85 | 92 | 89 | 90 | 91 | 93 |
| Gross income | 257 | 313 | 300 | 265 | 298 | 313 |
| Net income | 214 | 254 | 243 | 224 | 242 | 253 |
| Equivalent net income | 271 | 292 | 269 | 267 | 271 | 276 |
| Ever married (%) | 92 | 87 | 67 | - | - | - |
| Ever divorced (%) | 23 | 32 | 12 | - | - | - |
| Years divorced (%) | 4 | 8 | 3 | 20 | 22 | 22 |
| Years as lone parent | 10.3 | 10.9 | 11.2 | 8.9 | 9.9 | 7.3 |

Looking at the timing of entry into lone motherhood through **divorce**, *a priori* it is not clear in which direction lifetime living standards would be affected. Getting divorced at a later age may reduce the chances of remarriage and so depress lifetime living standards. However, any children would also be older and so possibilities for participation in the labour market are increased. Overall, older divorced mothers have higher lifetime living standards than women who became divorced lone mothers at a younger age. This is primarily due to their higher original income, which offsets the relatively lower gains from adjusting for family circumstances (that is, equivalising). Access to the labour market can therefore mitigate the absence of a partner, emphasising the importance of future labour market policies and practices and the potential created for altering lifetime income position.

## 4.     Other Women

Although we have focused on lone motherhood as a correlate of low lifetime living standards, as we saw in Table 9.2 other life course experiences are also related to being located at the lower end of the lifetime income distribution. This is further illustrated in Table 9.6 with groups of individuals who experienced labour market interruptions due to unemployment or due to caring for prolonged periods for incapacitated family members, and also those leaving school at particular ages.

Women with caring responsibilities for five or more years, that is, for a sick, disabled or frail adult or child, have lower lifetime earnings compared with all women. However, because 40 per cent receive an occupational pension, lifetime original income is similar to that of women who leave school at 18 years. Taking family circumstances into account

**Table 9.6**  Lifetime Income (£000s) and Other Socio-economic Characteristics of Other Female Groups

|  | All women | Left school at 16 | Left school at 18 | Unemployed in 10 or more years | Carer for 5 or more years |
|---|---|---|---|---|---|
| **(a) Income** | | | | | |
| Lifetime earnings | 178 | 145 | 181 | 140 | 165 |
| Original income | 205 | 167 | 210 | 159 | 192 |
| Cash benfits | 82 | 80 | 82 | 85 | 101 |
| Gross income | 287 | 247 | 292 | 243 | 294 |
| Net income | 231 | 206 | 233 | 201 | 234 |
| Equivalent net income | 287 | 269 | 289 | 252 | 283 |
| **(b) Demographic characteristics** | | | | | |
| % of all women | 100.0 | 41.0 | 18.4 | 12.2 | 6.9 |
| Age at death | 77.2 | 77.3 | 77.0 | 79.4 | 83.4 |
| Ever married (%) | 91.2 | 91.7 | 92.5 | 84.5 | 91.2 |
| Years married | 31.8 | 32.6 | 30.0 | 24.9 | 32.7 |
| Ever divorced | 36.3 | 35.6 | 38.9 | 36.3 | 40.1 |
| Ever with children | 75.2 | 76.6 | 70.3 | 59.2 | 78.8 |
| Number of child years (all) | 29.0 | 29.9 | 26.1 | 20.4 | 30.4 |
| Years as lone parent | 3.4 | 3.2 | 3.7 | 3.5 | 3.1 |
| **(c) Economic characteristics** | | | | | |
| Ever in tertiary education (%) | 53.9 | n/a | 75.2 | 52.6 | 49.5 |
| Years of tertiary education | 1.1 | n/a | 1.2 | 0.9 | 1.1 |
| Years of unemployment | 4.8 | 5.1 | 4.6 | 12.4 | 4.8 |
| Ever receiving occupational pension | 38.2 | 37.6 | 39.4 | 37.0 | 40.1 |

by equivalising income has the effect of increasing lifetime net income of all women by 24 per cent. For carers lifetime income rises by a smaller amount (21 per cent).

Studies investigating the employment and economic impact of caring for sick or elderly dependants using GHS data have found full-time participation rates of carers to be depressed, compared with those without such caring responsibilities; a greater likelihood of part-time employment amongst female carers than non-carers; and lower average earnings amongst employed carers than that of employed persons who are not carers (Evandrou, forthcoming; Parker and Lawton, 1990, 1994).

Further examination of the findings in Table 9.2 indicate that early withdrawal from school, such as at 16 years, depresses lifetime earnings for women, compared with leaving at 18 years. It is clear that labour market interruptions due to high incidence of unemployment has a particularly marked effect upon lifetime earnings, which is not significantly raised through state benefits. It is also the case that although the state benefit system helps it does not fully redress the position of carers in order to protect their lifetime living standards.

## 6.    Summary

- Men's lifetime original income is almost twice that of women's. The tax and social security system reduces the ratio between men's and women's net income to 1.4. The family acts to further reduce this gender inequality.

- The route to a high lifetime standard of living is different for men and women – for men the labour market is of prime importance whereas for women it remains the marriage market. This has important consequences for women and for policy makers.

- Women who experience some time as a lone mother have lower lifetime living standards than other mothers, receiving on average £500 less than other women for each year of their adult life. The *most* disadvantaged are women who experience both single and divorced lone motherhood with lifetime incomes of almost 20 per cent less than women who are never a lone parent.

- Both the timing and duration of lone motherhood affect lifetime living standards. The longer the duration, the lower lifetime income. The relationship with age is less clear. Mothers who divorce at an older age are more likely to be in employment and the negative impact on lifetime income is less severe. Access to the labour market can mitigate the absence of a partner.

- Labour market policies can play a critical role in reducing the impact of lone parenthood on lifetime living standards by (i) reducing the knock on effect of interrupted work histories later in life and (ii) by encouraging greater access to employment either through direct provision of childcare or indirect assistance via subsidised fees, childcare disregards in benefits and tax allowances. Future social security policy, particularly for lone mothers, cannot progress if developed in isolation of labour market and childcare policies and practices.

Chapter Ten

# For Richer, for Poorer, in Sickness and in Health: The Lifetime Distribution of NHS Health Care

## Carol Propper

UK

$I11$ $H40$
$I12$ $HS1$
$I18$ $H22$

This chapter uses LIFEMOD to investigate the distribution of health care over the lifetime. It focuses on two specific questions: first, how is the need for health care, the receipt of health care and payment through taxation for this health care distributed over the life cycle? and second, how would policy change which affected the financing of health care alter this distribution?

The distribution of health care in the UK has been the subject of considerable debate and research interest. In an influential article, Le Grand (1978) argued that this distribution favoured the middle classes. More recent analyses have concluded that the distribution of finance for NHS care is progressive, but the distribution of NHS care received, standardized for need, tends to be relatively neutral across income groups (O'Donnell and Propper, 1991). The finding that the distribution of finance is progressive is perhaps not surprising, as the main source of finance for health care in the UK is taxation and general taxation is mildly progressive (CSO, 1993). More surprising is the neutrality of the delivery side. The distribution of NHS care is not flat; those who have lower incomes receive more health care than those with higher incomes. However, those who are poorer also have poorer health. When the distribution of health care is standardised for need, as proxied by morbidity, the ensuing standardised distribution is fairly flat across income groups. This suggests that on a cross-sectional basis, the NHS delivers equal care for equal need.

These findings emerge from analyses of cross-sectional data analysed by income groups – snapshots of a population at a single point. However, the pattern over individuals' lifetimes may be rather different. If those who are relative gainers in early years of their lives are also relative gainers later on in their lives, then the lifetime pattern may be one of

184

considerable departure from horizontal equity. Alternatively, some groups may receive more health care while they live, but they may die earlier, so receiving less in old age than their contemporaries. It is not possible to examine this issue using existing data sets. Panel data of sufficient length for the UK do not, and will not, exist for several years. The course adopted here is to use simulated data from LIFEMOD.

Section 1 of the chapter briefly outlines how health status and health care are modelled in LIFEMOD. Section 2 examines the distribution of morbidity and health care receipts, and section 3 examines the distribution of finance. In section 4 finance and delivery are examined together to provide a picture of the net incidence of the current arrangements. Section 5 examines the effects of a policy change on the finance side – the introduction of compulsory private finance for those in the top three income decile groups.

## 1.     Simulating Health and Health Care

The single cohort simulated in LIFEMOD can be analysed in three different ways, each way providing answers to different questions. First, the data can be used to examine patterns in the lifetime levels of key variables. So, for example, annual health care receipts and payment for this care through taxation can be summed over each individual's lifetime to calculate lifetime distributions. LIFEMOD thus allows investigation of relative gains and losses across different groups. Second, LIFEMOD data can be used to examine patterns over the life cycle. So, for example, it can be used to examine whether certain groups gain early but lose later, or whether early gainers are the same persons as late gainers. Finally, the data can be treated as a single cross-section, and used to examine policy change.

Within LIFEMOD the distribution of two measures of health status are simulated. These are chronic and acute morbidity. While there is a wide number of measures of morbidity, the measures used in LIFEMOD (a) had to be available in large scale data sets and (b) had to be available in a data set which contained information on health care utilisation and a variety of socio-economic characteristics, including gender and income. The only data set which met these criteria was the General Household Survey (GHS). All data used in LIFEMOD are therefore from the 1985 GHS.

The LIFEMOD simulation has the following form. For each observation in LIFEMOD, for each year of life, two measures of self-assessed morbidity (the incidence of acute and chronic illness), and a single measure of the value of health care received, annual NHS expenditure, are simulated.

More formally, the simulation process first calculates:

$$pr(m_{ijt}=1) \qquad\qquad =f(x_{it}),\, j=1,2 \qquad\qquad\qquad (1)$$

where $m_{ijt}$     =1 if morbidity $j$ occurs,
                    0 otherwise
       $x_{it}$     =vector of variables including age, work status,
                    socio-economic status

$i$ indexes the individual, $t$ the year, $j$ the type of morbidity.

A Monte Carlo process is used to assign a value of 1 or 0 to the two health status indicator variables. Conditional on the realisations of these two events, the level of NHS expenditure for observation $i$ in year $t$ is determined by

$$E(exp_{it}) \qquad =pr(exp_{it}>0 \mid z_{it}) \times E(exp_{it} \mid exp_{it}>0) \qquad (2)$$

where $exp_{it}$     =total NHS expenditure person $i$ year $t$
      $z_{it}$       =vector of variables including age, work status,
                     socio-economic status and predicted morbidity

The first term in (2) is the estimated probability that individual $i$ will use the NHS in year $t$. This probability depends on a set of variables which include predicted health status from equation (1), demographics and individual socio-economic characteristics. A Monte Carlo process is used to determine the realisation of this event. If this event is realised, the level of NHS expenditure is determined by the second term in (2). This realisation of this second term is deterministic and depends only on age and gender (further details are given in Propper and Upward, 1993).

The functional forms of equations (1) and (2) are based on econometric estimates of the incidence of acute and chronic morbidity and of the probability of incurring NHS expenditure in a given year. These estimates are derived from the 1985 GHS. Thus (as for the rest of LIFEMOD) the incidence of an event is modelled as the 1985 incidence. The nature of LIFEMOD (and any simulation model) means vectors $x_{it}$ and $z_{it}$ can contain only those variables whose incidence is simulated elsewhere in LIFEMOD. As there is no health care supply side in LIFEMOD, the vector $z_{it}$ contains no measures of health care supply. However, as only the first term of equation (2) – the probability of use of the NHS – is modelled as a function of individual behaviour in LIFEMOD, and as initial contact with the medical care providers is generally argued to be the result of demand side factors, the omission of supply side variables does not seem inappropriate.

Perhaps more serious is the limited relationship between health status, income and employment that could be modelled in LIFEMOD. Health status in year $t$ is modelled as a function of employment status and income in year $t$. But wage income and employment status are not modelled as dependent on health. Finally, as in the rest of LIFEMOD, behavioural responses to policy change is assumed to be zero. Incorporation of behavioural response to policy or tax change is problematic for LIFEMOD purposes, both because econometric studies designed to estimate such responses give widely differing results and because these estimates are typically derived from cross-section data or short panel data. If individual behaviour in the long run differs from short run behaviour, this will not be captured in the model. Thus the health simulations are derived, as the rest of LIFEMOD, on the basis of a cohort which lives in a 1985 steady state world.

## 2.      The Distribution of Morbidity and Receipts of NHS Health Care

Cross-sectional analyses of the equity of health care delivery systems have concluded that in many European health care systems, health care standardised for need is relatively equally distributed across income groups (Rutten *et al.*, 1993). These studies measure need by self-assessed morbidity and treatment by the value of health care received. LIFEMOD can be used to simulate the extent to which these results would be replicated were it possible to examine individuals over their lifetimes.

### The unstandardised distribution of morbidity and expenditure

The simulated incidence of acute and chronic morbidity in LIFEMOD is similar to the pattern found in the 1985 GHS. Table 10.1 compares the average cross-sectional incidence of morbidity predicted by LIFEMOD with that from the 1985 GHS.

Within these totals, in LIFEMOD women have a higher incidence of both acute and chronic sickness than men across all age groups. Individuals in LIFEMOD have longer duration of life than those in current cross-sectional data. Morbidity is positively associated with age. Therefore the mean incidence of morbidity in LIFEMOD is slightly higher than in the cross-sectional data; the average incidence of chronic morbidity in LIFEMOD among adult men being 35 per cent and among adult women being 40 per cent whereas the proportions in the 1985 GHS are 35 and 38 per cent respectively. The average incidence for adult men and women of acute sickness in LIFEMOD is 11 per cent for men and 15 per cent for women. The GHS figures are 10 and 14 per cent respectively.

Various lifetime totals can be calculated for each observation in the model. For health care receipt and morbidity, lifetime totals are derived by summing over the length of life. A lifetime average for an individual can be derived by dividing the relevant lifetime total by the number of years of life of that individual. These annualised values can then be averaged across income groups, income being defined in a number of different ways depending on the purpose of the analysis.

Table 10.1 Incidence of Morbidity by Age, LIFEMOD and 1985 GHS (percentages)

|  | Age | | | | |
|---|---|---|---|---|---|
|  | 0–15 | 16–44 | 45–64 | 65–74 | 75+ |
| Acute morbidity |  |  |  |  |  |
| GHS | 12 | 11 | 12 | 16 | 21 |
| LIFEMOD | 11 | 12 | 12 | 16 | 19 |
| Chronic morbidity |  |  |  |  |  |
| GHS | 13 | 22 | 43 | 56 | 63 |
| LIFEMOD | 12 | 25 | 43 | 54 | 59 |

N=234,707.

Table 10.2 presents the simulated distribution of the average lifetime incidence of morbidity and health care receipt (all variables adjusted for length of life) across individuals ranked by lifetime income. The measure of lifetime income used here is annualised lifetime gross equivalent income, which allows for income sharing within households and for changes in household structure over the life cycle of the observation. Gross income is used in the present analysis as this measure was used in earlier examinations of the distribution of health care in the UK (O'Donnell and Propper, 1991).[1,2] The table indicates that the distributions of both morbidity and health care receipts are weakly pro-poor: that is, over a lifetime the poor are both sicker and receive a higher share of NHS health care expenditure. The lower percentage share of NHS expenditure received by the top income decile group reflects, in part, the higher proportion of private health care consumed by it. As the focus of interest of LIFEMOD was the allocation of benefits from and payments to the welfare state, private health care utilisation was not included in the simulations (though assumptions about utilisation of private health care are made in the policy change analysis presented in section 5).

---

1   Individuals with zero recorded lifetime income are omitted from all the analysis presented here (individuals who died before reaching 16 years). The remaining sample is 3,983 individuals.

2   Analysis using net equivalised income show similar patterns to those reported here, both on the finance and delivery side.

**Table 10.2** Distribution of Lifetime Annualised Morbidity and NHS Expenditure (individuals ranked by annualised equivalent gross income)

| Annualised lifetime income decile group | Percentage share chronic morbidity | Percentage share acute morbidity | Percentage share NHS expenditure |
|---|---|---|---|
| Bottom | 10.67 | 11.27 | 10.43 |
| 2 | 10.56 | 10.49 | 10.40 |
| 3 | 10.31 | 10.19 | 10.40 |
| 4 | 10.27 | 9.90 | 10.37 |
| 5 | 10.15 | 10.13 | 10.02 |
| 6 | 9.72 | 9.94 | 10.15 |
| 7 | 9.73 | 9.52 | 9.66 |
| 8 | 9.74 | 9.85 | 9.97 |
| 9 | 9.46 | 9.37 | 9.63 |
| Top | 9.27 | 9.27 | 8.97 |

$N$=3,983 (excludes those who die before age 16).

**Table 10.3** Cross-sectional Distribution of Morbidity and NHS Expenditure (individuals ranked by annual equivalent gross income)

| Annual income decile | Percentage share chronic morbidity | Percentage share acute morbidity | Percentage share NHS expenditure |
|---|---|---|---|
| Bottom | 8.90 | 10.43 | 5.91 |
| 2nd | 12.00 | 11.94 | 10.56 |
| 3rd | 11.59 | 11.07 | 13.36 |
| 4th | 11.94 | 11.03 | 16.32 |
| 5th | 11.21 | 10.83 | 13.66 |
| 6th | 10.37 | 10.20 | 11.36 |
| 7th | 9.65 | 9.45 | 8.95 |
| 8th | 9.37 | 8.67 | 7.31 |
| 9th | 8.14 | 8.21 | 6.52 |
| Top | 7.83 | 8.15 | 6.05 |

$N$=234,123 (excludes those under 16).

To examine differences between the lifetime and cross-section distributions, the LIFEMOD cross-section can be compared with the LIFEMOD lifetime distributions. The LIFEMOD cross-sectional distribution is given in Table 10.3. Comparison of Table 10.3 with Table 10.2 indicates that over the lifetime the distribution of both morbidity and expenditure is less unequal than indicated by a cross-sectional snapshot. In the cross-sectional data, the low morbidity within the bottom decile group is due to the young age of the bottom annual income group in LIFEMOD. (This is not a feature of actual cross-sectional data in which a higher proportion of older people fall in the lowest two groups than in LIFEMOD[3]). Interestingly the pattern in the LIFEMOD cross-section is

---

3   Older people in LIFEMOD are richer than those in the present population as people in current retired age groups have labour force participation patterns determined up to 30 years ago. Observations which are retired in LIFEMOD have age–gender specific

similar to that in certain European countries with younger populations (for example, Ireland). Table 10.2 indicates that over the lifetime, the differences between individuals are smoothed out. Those who are older, particularly those over 75, have a higher incidence of morbidity, health care use and lower income, which means lifetime distributions are more even than those suggested by a cross-sectional snapshot.

### Distribution of standardised health care expenditure

Previous empirical research has examined the distribution of health care standardised for need (Le Grand, 1978; Collins and Klein, 1980; O'Donnell *et al.*, 1993). Table 10.4 presents the analogous results for LIFEMOD data. The method of standardisation used on the LIFEMOD data is equivalent to indirect standardisation as used in the construction of standardised mortality ratios (van Vliet and van de Ven, 1985). The standardising variables are morbidity and gender.[4] The results indicate a distribution that is more or less flat. This distribution is in fact very similar to that derived from analyses of cross-sectional data between the mid-1970s and the late 1980s in the UK (Propper and Upward, 1992).

**Table 10.4** Percentage Shares of Annualised Lifetime Health Care Expenditure Standardised for Need (individuals ranked by annualised equivalent gross income)

| Annualised lifetime income decile group | Standardised by both acute and chronic morbidity | Standardised by chronic morbidity only |
|---|---|---|
| Bottom | 9.62 | 9.68 |
| 2 | 9.89 | 9.93 |
| 3 | 10.03 | 10.04 |
| 4 | 9.97 | 9.80 |
| 5 | 9.93 | 9.92 |
| 6 | 10.23 | 10.12 |
| 7 | 10.08 | 10.07 |
| 8 | 9.99 | 9.99 |
| 9 | 10.48 | 10.45 |
| Top | 9.98 | 10.00 |

$N$=3,983 (excludes seventeen observations who died before age 16).

---

labour force participation rates of 1985, and also benefit here from SERPS under 1985 rules.

4   For standardisation purposes, continuous variables need to be grouped into discrete variables. The distribution of each of the two lifetime morbidity measures was segmented into quartiles. From these quartiles dummy variables were defined.

## 3.        The Distribution of Finance for NHS Care

Health care in the UK is primarily funded (95 per cent) from general taxation. Thus the distribution of finance for health care is basically the distribution of general taxation. In LIFEMOD, direct taxes (income tax and National Insurance) are allocated to each individual in each year of life, but indirect and corporate taxation are not modelled. The assumption made to derive the data presented here is that all health care expenditure is financed from direct taxation. Neither user charges for health care nor private insurance premiums were modelled, as cross-sectional analysis has shown that while the distribution of such payments differs from that of direct taxation, inclusion of these charges little alters the overall distribution of finance per health care (basically because charges and private insurance account for only a small part of UK health care finance; O'Donnell *et al.*, 1993).

### Lifetime averages

In examining income and taxation, the data can be presented in terms of either annualised lifetime or total lifetime values. Table 10.5 shows the distribution of annualised lifetime income, income tax and National Insurance contributions by each lifetime income decile. Summary indices are presented at the bottom of each column. The Gini coefficients indicate a departure from equality in annualised lifetime income and the two types of tax. The Suits index is a measure of the departure from proportionality in tax payments relative to income. It gives greater weight to departures from proportionality which occur within higher income groups than those which occur within lower income groups. A positive sign for the index indicates a progressive tax, a negative sign a regressive tax.[5]

The net effect, as shown by the Suits index, is that lifetime payment of income tax is progressive while lifetime payment of National Insurance is neutral. Annualisation appears to make little difference to the results, as the distribution of the relevant lifetime totals (i.e. not adjusted for length of life) is very similar to that of Table 10.5.

Table 10.6 presents the distribution of annual payments in the LIFEMOD cross-section.[6] Comparison of Tables 10.5 and 10.6 indicates that the lifetime distribution of income is less unequal than the cross-sectional distribution. As tax is a function of income, the lifetime

---

5    For further discussion of this measure see van Doorslaer and Wagstaff (1993).

6    The distribution is similar to those in the 1985 FES or GHS, except that the bottom quintile of persons in LIFEMOD accounts for less income than in either the FES or GHS. See Chapter 6, section 1 for further discussion.

distribution of taxes is also less unequal. The net effect on the progressivity of income tax payments is similar in both the cross-sectional and the lifetime analyses, as shown by the Suits indices. However, the lifetime distribution of National Insurance is less progressive than the cross-sectional distribution. Taking income tax and National Insurance together, the Suits index for the lifetime distribution is mildly less progressive (0.10) than for the annual distribution (0.17).

**Table 10.5** The Distribution of Annualised Lifetime Income and Payments (individuals ranked by annualised equivalent gross income)

| Annualised lifetime income decile | Percentage share income | Percentage share income tax | Percentage share National Insurance |
|---|---|---|---|
| Bottom | 4.91 | 2.23 | 3.55 |
| 2 | 6.51 | 4.20 | 5.99 |
| 3 | 7.28 | 5.21 | 6.96 |
| 4 | 8.33 | 6.84 | 8.46 |
| 5 | 8.86 | 7.78 | 9.18 |
| 6 | 9.42 | 8.66 | 10.01 |
| 7 | 10.60 | 10.63 | 11.37 |
| 8 | 11.71 | 12.52 | 12.61 |
| 9 | 13.53 | 15.70 | 14.33 |
| Top | 18.85 | 26.21 | 17.54 |
| Gini coefficient | 0.204 | 0.35 | 0.23 |
| Suits Index | | 0.14 | 0.01 |

$N = 3,983$.

**Table 10.6** The Distribution of Annual Gross Equivalent Income, Income Tax and National Insurance Payments (individuals ranked by annual gross equivalent income decile)

| Annual income decile group | Percentage share income | Percentage share income tax | Percentage share National Insurance |
|---|---|---|---|
| Bottom | 1.65 | 0.10 | 0.16 |
| 2nd | 3.71 | 0.40 | 1.90 |
| 3rd | 5.54 | 2.20 | 3.74 |
| 4th | 6.86 | 4.13 | 4.17 |
| 5th | 8.02 | 6.06 | 6.32 |
| 6th | 9.37 | 8.55 | 8.91 |
| 7th | 10.99 | 11.27 | 12.08 |
| 8th | 13.01 | 14.42 | 16.00 |
| 9th | 16.29 | 19.30 | 20.46 |
| Top | 24.47 | 33.91 | 22.60 |
| Gini | 0.34 | 0.53 | 0.46 |
| Suits Index | | 0.19 | 0.11 |

$N = 234,123$.

## 4.    Net Incidence

### Distribution across income groups

LIFEMOD can be used to examine net incidence of NHS payments and receipts over the lifetime. Net incidence is defined as the difference between what individuals receive and what they pay. Under the NHS arrangements individuals can receive health care expenditure and pay taxes during the same time period. Maintaining the assumption that health care is financed purely from direct taxation, the amount of direct tax paid by each observation was scaled down so that the average lifetime payment for health care equalled the value of health care received. The average net gain is thus set to zero. The distribution of net gains under this assumption is given in Table 10.7. This shows that individuals in the bottom six decile groups of lifetime income are net gainers, whilst those in the top four groups are net losers. Given the relatively flat distribution of health expenditure, the main determinant of this lifetime redistribution from poor to rich is the income tax system. (Note that the health care received is not adjusted for need in this analysis.)

If observations are ranked by annual income and the data set is treated as a single cross-section, the distribution becomes more extreme (column (1), Table 10.9 below). Thus, as for the distribution of expenditure, analysis of lifetime net receipts by lifetime income shows that some of the inequality observed in the cross-sectional distribution disappears.

Figures 10.1 and 10.2 show this distribution of gains and loses over the life cycle. Figure 10.1 presents the average *annual* gain in each quintile group, where the groups are defined in terms of annualised gross equivalent lifetime income. All groups are gainers before the age of 15. Once income is earned and taxes are paid, annual net gains tend towards zero. Richer individuals remain net payers until retirement, a function of

**Table 10.7** Net Incidence of Average Annual Health Care Transfers by Lifetime Annualised Income (individuals ranked by annualised equivalent gross income)

| Annualised lifetime income decile group | Average net incidence (£ per year rounded) |
|---|---|
| Bottom | 214 |
| 2 | 147 |
| 3 | 109 |
| 4 | 95 |
| 5 | 55 |
| 6 | 21 |
| 7 | -23 |
| 8 | -68 |
| 9 | -166 |
| Top | -383 |

*N*=3,983.

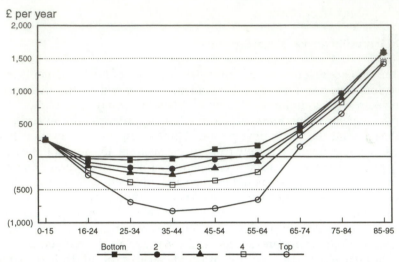

**Note:**
Health care assumed financed from all direct tax.

**Figure 10.1**  Annual Average Health Care Transfers (individuals by
annualised lifetime income quintile groups)

**Note:**

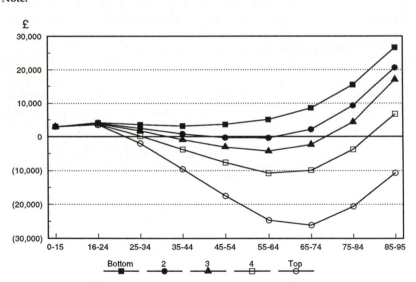

Health care assumed financed from all direct tax.

**Figure 10.2**  Cumulative Average Transfers for Health Care (individuals by
annualised lifetime income quintile groups)

their higher than average taxes and marginally lower than average health care expenditure. Net gains for the lowest quintile group are close to zero for the duration of working life. On retirement, net gains for all groups become positive, as predicted health care expenditure rises and direct taxes fall. Post-retirement, only the richest group pays significant amounts of tax, and their average health care receipts remain lower than those of the other four groups,[7] so their net gains remain below those of individuals in the other groups. Figure 10.2 shows the cumulative incidence of average net gains over the life cycle for survivors (the cumulative counterpart of Figure 10.1). Individuals are again grouped into lifetime annualised equivalent income quintile groups. Data are per person averages. The figure shows that all groups begin as gainers. By their thirties, individuals in the top three quintile groups become losers. Only after age 65 do annual health care receipts begin to exceed taxes paid, and for those surviving to age 95 all but those in the top quintile are net gainers from the system. When viewed over the whole lifetime, only individuals in the top quintile on average contribute more than they receive.

## Distribution by gender

Analysis of LIFEMOD data by gender indicates women have both lower lifetime and cross-sectional income. Consequently they pay less tax, both cross-sectionally and over the lifetime. Over the lifetime, total direct tax paid per man is £107,000 and by women is £56,000 (see Tables 6.5 and 6.6). In terms of morbidity, women experience on average higher incidence of both acute and chronic morbidity, in part a consequence of their higher longevity. As a consequence, total lifetime health care expenditure is higher for women than for men. Average lifetime total health care expenditure is £19,500 for men and £23,500 for women.

Figures 10.3 and 10.4 show the life cycle distribution underlying these lifetime totals. Figure 10.3 shows the distribution of average annual gains over the life cycle. Both genders are net gainers until the age of 15. Between 16 and 44 both genders are net losers. Thereafter men remain net losers until after retirement, when they become net gainers.

Figure 10.4 shows average cumulative gains for those who are alive and shows what those who survive until a certain age will on average receive. The average female is a cumulative gainer for all her life. In contrast the average man is never a net gainer.

---

7   This is due to their higher use of private services as well as their marginally better health.

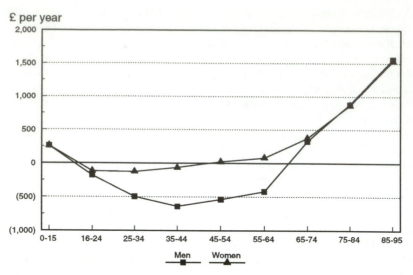

**Figure 10.3** Annual Average Health Care Transfers by Gender

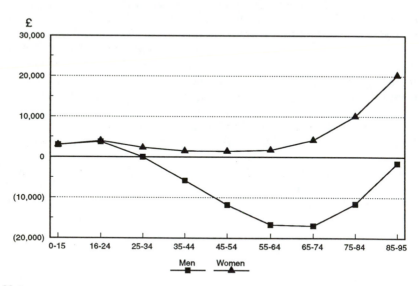

**Figure 10.4** Average Cumulative Annual Health Care Transfers by Gender

### Intrapersonal versus interpersonal redistribution

A similar analysis to that of chapter 7 can be undertaken to determine the extent of intrapersonal versus interpersonal redistribution of NHS health care expenditure. It is assumed that health care is paid for by taxes allocated across individuals on the same basis as the distribution of income tax plus national insurance. Given this, Table 10.8 shows the distribution of net health care benefits.

The first line of the table shows total lifetime health care benefits received per person in each decile group. The last column shows the average across all groups. From the table it is clear that receipts in each decile group are similar across all the groups. Thus the average amount received by those in the lowest decile group over their lifetime is £23,000, and the average amount received by all persons is £22,000 (rounding masks some variation).[8] The next line of the table gives total lifetime allocated tax payments per person in the group. Under the balanced budget assumption the average allocated tax is £22,000. The average lifetime allocated tax paid by members of the bottom group is £5,000, the average for the top group is £52,000.

Table 10.8 Lifetime Total of Payments for, and Benefits from, NHS by Lifetime Income (£000s)

| | Decile group of annualised equivalent gross income | | | | | | | | | | |
| | 1 | 2 | 3 | 4 | 5 | 6 | 7 | 8 | 9 | 10 | All |
|---|---|---|---|---|---|---|---|---|---|---|---|
| Total benefits | 23 | 22 | 22 | 23 | 22 | 22 | 22 | 22 | 20 | 19 | 22 |
| Allocated tax[a] | 5 | 9 | 13 | 14 | 17 | 20 | 24 | 28 | 33 | 52 | 22 |
| Intrapersonal redistribution | | | | | | | | | | | |
| Annual | 1 | 2 | 3 | 3 | 4 | 4 | 5 | 5 | 6 | 7 | 4 |
| Lifetime | 4 | 7 | 9 | 10 | 11 | 12 | 13 | 13 | 12 | 11 | 11 |
| Lifetime net benefits | 17 | 13 | 10 | 9 | 7 | 6 | 4 | 3 | 2 | 1 | 7 |
| Lifetime net taxes | 0 | 0 | 1 | 1 | 2 | 4 | 6 | 9 | 15 | 34 | 7 |
| Average lifetime gain | 17 | 13 | 9 | 8 | 5 | 2 | -2 | -6 | -13 | -33 | 0 |

*N*=3,983.
**Note:**
a    Funded by income tax and National Insurance

8    The distribution between groups is slightly different from that shown, for instance, in Table 6.2 as the classification here is by gross, not net, incomes.

The rest of the table shows net receipts and payments using these allocated taxes. During each year of life individuals may pay tax, receive health care or both. If they both pay and receive, some of the benefits received will have been 'paid for' by their own tax contribution in that year. The third line of the table shows the average amount of health care benefit which was paid for by each person in the same year as health care was used. This is annual intrapersonal transfer. On average £4,000 of the £22,000 health care benefits received by individuals over their lifetime is paid for and received in the same year. The size of this sum varies across decile group being lowest in the lowest group, a reflection of the fact that the lowest group pays least tax.

The next line of the table shows the amount of health care expenditure which is taken in one year but 'paid for' by tax contributions in other years of the same individual's life. Thus a further £11,000 of the £22,000 total health care expenditure represents intrapersonal transfer. Again, there is considerable variation in this sum across decile groups. For the lowest group, £4,000 of taxes represent lifetime intrapersonal transfer. For the highest income group, this sum is £11,000. The sum of these two rows gives total intrapersonal redistribution. On average around 70 per cent (£15,000 out of £22,000) of total health care expenditure in the LIFEMOD cohort is intrapersonal redistribution. Given that the receipt of health care does not depend on income (in that it is not means-tested) and the life cycle nature of health care receipt, the relatively high proportion of health care benefit which is paid for at another stage of the life cycle is unsurprising.

Over the lifetime individuals can be either net gainers or net payers. The next two lines gives the average amount received or contributed by these two categories of persons over their lifetime. The average amount received by net gainers is £7,000, balanced by the average amount paid by net payers. The number of net gainers and the amount gained falls as income rises. The number of net payers and the amount paid rises as income rises. In the bottom three groups there are very few people who are net lifetime taxpayers and the amounts they contribute are under £500 on average. As we move up the income distribution the number and amount of tax paid by net payers increases. The final line of the table shows average lifetime gain for each group. Over the whole cohort lifetime gain is zero by construction. Between groups net gain is a negative function of income. The large contribution of the top group relative to all other groups is clear.[9]

---

9   The same analysis was repeated under the assumption that health care is financed in proportion to income rather than from income tax (as in the 'finance from all taxes' results in Chapter 7). This results in a less extreme distribution of average lifetime gain.

## 5.    The Introduction of Private Finance

LIFEMOD can be used to simulate policy change in the method of financing health care. One possible policy change is to allow public finance only for individuals below a certain income. Those above this income would have to purchase health insurance to finance their health care expenditure.

Simply requiring individuals above a certain income to purchase private health insurance whilst maintaining taxes at the same level would, in a static analysis, result in a distribution which benefits lower income groups more than the current system. The policy change analysed here removes the entitlement to NHS care for those above a certain income level but in return gives all individuals in this group a tax credit. The same individuals are also required to purchase private health insurance to cover the costs of their health care. (This policy is not dissimilar to the finance arrangements in operation in the Netherlands prior to recent reforms.)

In more detail, the policy analysed is as follows. Using LIFEMOD as a cross-sectional data set, all individuals in the top 30 per cent of the income distribution (income defined as gross equivalent annual income) are no longer entitled to NHS care, are given a tax credit, and are required to pay a compulsory premium to a private health insurance scheme. The tax credit is set equal to the average health care expenditure for the whole population. Initially, it is assumed the premiums for the private health insurance are set on the basis of age–gender specific expenditure for the whole population. So, for example, a woman aged 50 whose income fell into one of the top three decile groups of the income distribution would pay a premium equal to the average health care expenditure of all females aged between 45 and 54. Individuals with incomes in the bottom seven groups remain entitled to NHS treatment and do not receive any tax credit.

It is assumed that NHS health expenditure is raised from all direct tax (i.e. income and National Insurance). However, under the policy change, the reduction in taxes paid by those in the top three decile groups will not automatically equal the reduction in NHS expenditure resulting from their loss of entitlement to NHS care. To permit comparison with the distribution of net incidence under 1985 arrangements, total taxes were scaled down to ensure a balanced budget for health care.

Two comparisons can be made with 1985 arrangements. The first is to compare the distribution of annual net health care expenditure under the present system and the policy change. In this comparison, some assumption has to be made about the level and cost of the health care the top three decile groups get from their private insurance. The second is to compare net state transfers, i.e. excluding payments for and benefits from private health care.

More formally, the 1985 arrangements give individual i net benefits, where

$$\text{net benefit}_i \qquad = NHSexp_i - a^* taxes_i \qquad\qquad (3)$$

where $a$      = the scaling factor required to balance the budget under present NHS arrangements.

Under the policy change, net benefits for health care from the NHS for those in the bottom 70 per cent of the income distribution are:

$$\text{net NHS benefit}_i \qquad = NHSexp_i - b^* taxes_i \qquad\qquad (4)$$

Net benefits for health care from the NHS for those in the top 30 per cent of the income distribution are:

$$\text{net NHS benefit}_{i\ in\ top\ 3} \quad = TC - b^* taxes_i \qquad\qquad (5)$$

where $b$            = scaling factor to ensure a balanced budget across all individuals

TC           = tax credit (= average per person NHS health care expenditure)

Net total health care benefits (i.e. from both public and private finance and delivery) for these in the bottom 70 per cent are the same as welfare state net benefits, i.e. as equation (4). Under the assumption that the costs of health care provided under insurance are the same as those provided by the NHS, net total health care benefits for those in the top 30 per cent of the income distribution are:

$$\text{net total benefits}_{i\ in\ top\ 3} \quad = NHSexp_i + TC - b^* taxes_i - premium_i \qquad (6)$$

where $a$      $= \Sigma_i NHSexp_i / \Sigma_i taxes_i$

$b$         $= (\Sigma_i NHSexp_i - \Sigma_{i\ in\ top\ 3}(NHSexp_i - TC)) / \Sigma_i taxes_i$

TC      $= \Sigma_i NHSexp_i / N$

$premium_i$    = premium paid for private insurance

Table 10.9 presents the cross-sectional distribution, by annual equivalent gross income, of the net incidence of the present system (column 1), the net incidence of the insurance system including payment for and receipt of private care (column 2) and the net incidence of welfare state transfers (i.e. excluding payments for and receipt of private health care for those in the top three decile groups)(column 3). Comparison of columns 1 and 2 indicates that the introduction of an insurance scheme would redistribute gains to individuals in groups 8 and 9 from the rest of the population. The largest changes occur in the middle of the income distribution: those in the six and seventh group would lose most and those in the eight and ninth deciles would gain most.

**Table 10.9** Comparison of Transfers under Current Arrangements and Insurance Schemes (average annual transfer, £)

| Annual income decile group | Current system | Policy option: All health expenditure | Policy option: State transfers only | Policy option: Insurance premiums set to usage of insured group |
|---|---|---|---|---|
| | (1) | (2) | (3) | (4) |
| Bottom | 171 | 171 | 171 | 171 |
| 2 | 278 | 275 | 275 | 275 |
| 3 | 347 | 339 | 339 | 339 |
| 4 | 358 | 346 | 346 | 346 |
| 5 | 210 | 192 | 192 | 192 |
| 6 | 75 | 49 | 49 | 49 |
| 7 | -78 | -108 | -108 | -108 |
| 8 | -228 | -201 | -188 | -187 |
| 9 | -386 | -354 | -341 | -340 |
| Top | -751 | -754 | -736 | -751 |

$N$=234,071.

The results are similar whether the net incidence is calculated to include private health care benefits and payments or on the basis of welfare state transfers only (comparison of columns 2 and 3). Net incidence without the inclusion of net private health benefits is slightly more pro-rich, the reason being that the average health care received by these groups is below the premiums that they pay.

The results in column 2 are based on the assumption that the health care expenditure, and so the insurance premiums, of those in the top 30 per cent is equal to the population average expenditure within the relevant age–gender category. In fact, the health care expenditure of individuals in these decile groups is lower than the relevant age–gender category population average. If health insurance premiums were introduced, it is likely that they would be a function of the expected expenditure of the insured group rather than the expected expenditure of the whole population. Maintaining the assumption of community rating, but defining the community to be only those who are insured, the distribution of net health care payments and receipts would be as in column 4. Comparison of columns 2 and 4 show the absolute losses would be smaller for the eighth and ninth groups if premiums were age–gender–income group adjusted than under premiums adjusted only for age and gender. However, regardless of the way private premiums were set, total tax receipts and NHS payments would remain unchanged, so that this change would not affect the net gains of those in the bottom 70 per cent.

The policy analysed here assumes that health care is financed from taxes levied in proportion to the distribution of direct taxation (i.e. income tax plus National Insurance). However, the results are robust to changes in assumption about the source of tax: a similar redistribution, in magnitude and direction, would occur if health care was financed from only income tax under both the current and the insurance systems.[10]

## 6.    Summary

This chapter has used simulated data from LIFEMOD to examine the lifetime distribution of the current arrangements for financing and allocating health care in the UK. Previous research indicated that the cross-sectional distribution of finance was mildly pro-poor, the distribution of health care standardised for need neutral. Results from LIFEMOD indicate that the shift from a cross-sectional to a lifetime analysis results in more equal distributions of income and morbidity, but the distributions of health care finance relative to income and of health care receipt relative to need are relatively unchanged by this move in perspective. The reason is these latter distributions are functions of two distributions, both of which are flatter across the lifetime than in the cross-section. The reduction in inequality in the distribution of income in the move from a cross-sectional to a lifetime perspective is also accompanied by a reduction in the inequality in the distribution of taxes paid. This means that the distribution of payments for health care, relative to income, is very similar whether a cross-sectional or a lifetime analysis is adopted. Similarly, the distribution of health care is a function of the distribution of morbidity. So while the distribution of the receipt of health care is more equal across lifetimes than in a cross-sectional snapshot, the distribution of health care standardised for need is similar whether a cross-sectional or lifetime perspective is adopted.

The chapter analyses net receipt (benefits minus payments) of the health care system over the lifetime. Under the assumptions made here about taxation, net receipts are a decreasing monotonic function of lifetime income. The gainers are those in the lowest six decile groups and women, the losers are those in the top four decile groups and men. There is also a clear life cycle pattern in this distribution, a result of the strong life cycle patterns in labour market participation and in need for health care. The lifetime perspective taken here also allows a distinction between intrapersonal (within individuals across their lifetime) and interpersonal (across individuals) redistribution. For the health sector of the welfare state, using 1985 financing arrangements (assuming direct taxes are the source) and the steady state assumptions implicit in

---

10  If health care is assumed to be financed only through income tax, the distribution of net gains is more strongly decreasing in income. This is because income tax is more progressive than National Insurance.

LIFEMOD, approximately 70 per cent of the redistribution which occurs is intrapersonal. This is a result of the non-means-tested nature of health care received under the NHS and the age profile of morbidity.

Finally, this chapter has examined one possible policy change to the financing arrangements for health care. The policy examined here removes entitlement to NHS health care for those in the top three income decile groups, in return for a tax credit equal to average health care received. In this form, a move to finance health care through private insurance would benefit those at the top of the income distribution at the expenses of those in the middle, so reducing the extent to which the distribution of net gains from the NHS favours the poor.

Chapter Eleven

# Funding Pensions over the Life Cycle

UK
H55
H23

## Jane Falkingham and Paul Johnson

LIFEMOD is a particularly useful tool for examining pensions policy as pension entitlements are accumulated across the life cycle. Provision of an adequate income in later life was one of the cornerstones of the Beveridge's welfare state. Elsewhere we have argued why the current system of state pension provision is inadequate (Johnson and Falkingham, 1994). In this chapter we use LIFEMOD to estimate the costs and distributional outcomes of a radically different type of pension scheme – we call it a unified funded pension scheme or UFPS – which is designed to combine earnings-related funded pensions with tax-financed minimum pension provision in a single, simple system. The scheme provides minimum pensions at double the current level of the NI pension, targets tax-financed assistance to the lifetime poor without use of a traditional means test and gives pensioners complete control of their pension assets.

The first section of the chapter examines the distribution of pension income within the LIFEMOD population and briefly explores the extent of intra- and interpersonal redistribution implicit in the current system. The next section outlines the basic principles of the proposed UFPS and develops some administrative refinements relevant to the British case. In section 3 results from LIFEMOD are used to estimate the cost of a mature UFPS in Britain. The final section reviews the advantages of a UFPS over the existing pension options in Britain.

## 1.    The Distribution of Pension Income

Pension income accounts for the majority of cash transfers over the lifetime, constituting on average 70 per cent of all such transfers; and for many people this, with the exception of Child Benefit, may be the only direct cash transfer they receive. Figure 11.1 shows the lifetime distribution of pension income from LIFEMOD under 1985 SERPS rules. The amount of flat rate retirement pension is roughly constant across income groups, although in relative terms it is progressive, providing a greater proportion of income to those at the bottom of the lifetime income distribution. Benefits from SERPS are concentrated on those in the middle of the distribution whilst those at the top receive income from occupational pensions schemes amounting to over eight times that received by those at the bottom.

What patterns of redistribution across the life cycle and across individuals are implicit in this? The original objective of Beveridge was to ensure that the flat-rate contributions paid by workers into the National Insurance scheme during their working life were set so as to provide an adequate actuarially assessed income sufficient to cover five-sixths of pension payments (one-sixth was to come from general tax revenue). This was supposed to provide a mechanism for *intra*personal redistribution across the life-course overcoming some of the market failures discussed in Chapter 2; the flat-rate nature of both contributions and benefits meant that *inter*personal redistribution was limited to that brought about by differential mortality and length of time employed.

However, the distributional outcomes of public pension schemes in Britain have fundamentally diverged from Beveridge's design; with the intra- and interpersonal redistribution having become confused. The flat-rate principle has been eroded over time and since 1975 contributions

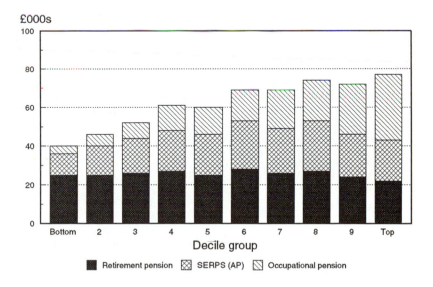

£000s

**Figure 11.1** Receipt of Pension Income by Annualised Lifetime Net Income

have been related to earnings for all income between the lower and upper NI contribution thresholds. This change to earnings-related contributions tied to a primarily flat-rate benefit has automatically brought about an interpersonal redistribution from higher to lower earners.

Using a similar methodology to that employed in Chapter 7 we can identify what proportion of pension benefits are paid for at another stage in an individual's own life cycle and what represent a transfer from other individuals.[1] Over their whole lives, individuals are either net lifetime taxpayers or net lifetime benefit recipients. Table 11.1 shows the total amount of pension benefit (both from the basic state pension and the additional pension from SERPS) received by each decile as well as the scale of such 'self-financing' of benefits from direct taxes (intrapersonal redistribution), together with the net lifetime taxes or benefits of individuals in excess of self-financed benefits (interpersonal redistribution). Thus, on average, although model individuals receive an average of £46,000 in pension benefits over their lifetimes, £28,000 of this represents benefits which individuals effectively pay for themselves, i.e. 61 per cent. However within the bottom decile group of the £36,000 of pension benefits received on average by individuals over their lives, only one-third (£12,000) represents amounts paid by individuals for their own benefits.

As one moves up the income distribution, the proportion of gross benefits which represent intra- rather than interpersonal redistribution grows rapidly and by the third decile group, the majority of the group's (i.e. 68 per cent) gross pension receipts are self-financed. Of pension benefits received by individuals in the top group, 91 per cent are self-financed.

**Table 11.1** Lifetime Pension Benefits and Taxes (1985 system; equal sharing; McClements; £000s)

| | Decile group of individuals by equivalent net income (annualised) | | | | | | | | | | |
|---|---|---|---|---|---|---|---|---|---|---|---|
| | Bottom | 2 | 3 | 4 | 5 | 6 | 7 | 8 | 9 | Top | All |
| Total pension benefits (basic pension + SERPS (AP) | 36 | 40 | 44 | 48 | 47 | 52 | 48 | 54 | 45 | 43 | 46 |
| Self-financed | 12 | 18 | 22 | 25 | 27 | 31 | 33 | 38 | 37 | 39 | 28 |
| Lifetime net benefit | 24 | 23 | 22 | 23 | 19 | 21 | 15 | 16 | 9 | 4 | 18 |
| Lifetime net taxes | 3 | 6 | 8 | 9 | 12 | 12 | 17 | 20 | 32 | 60 | 18 |
| Average lifetime gain | +21 | +16 | +14 | +14 | +7 | +9 | -2 | -5 | -23 | -56 | 0 |

---

1   See footnote 2 in Chapter 7 for an algebraic definition of these measures.

In recent years there has been concern over the cost of the present pension system, and there have been renewed calls for reform. It was fears about the sustainability of present system that led to many of the changes in tax and social security system in the late 1980s. As discussed in chapter 6, these have resulted in a two-thirds reduction in the average value of the amount of SERPS accumulated. The last two years in particular have spored a variety of schemes.

The right wing 'No-turning Back' Group of Conservative MPs (1993) has proposed that higher earners should be encouraged to opt out of NIC but lose entitlement to basic state pension. Their rationale is that the state pension does not contribute very much to the overall retirement income of higher income individuals. Allowing such people to opt out and accumulate all pension income privately would relieve the burden on state. However, in fact the reverse could result. As we can see from Table 11.1 above, the current system incorporates large scale transfers from those at the top end to those at the bottom of income distribution. Allowing those at the top to opt out from the hypothecated tax, NIC, will necessarily result in increased general taxation. This will not be just a temporary blip, with fewer contributors in 'pay as you go' system – but would remove in perpetuity transfers within a cohort between rich and poor.

If an individual can determine at an early stage in their life-course their position in overall lifetime income distribution (and from Chapter 6, section 5 we know that for male graduates this will be relatively transparent!) it will be a rational decision for all individuals in the top quintile group of the lifetime income distribution to opt out. If we leave the issue of SERPS to one side and concentrate only on the basic state pension, the allocated taxes 'lost' to the exchequer would amount to £42,000 per person whilst the savings in terms of state pension payments forgone would be £23,000, i.e. a net loss to the social security system of £19,000 for every opt-outee. This would be a very expensive option for any government, exacerbating rather than reducing the long term pension financing problem.

Researchers at the Institute for Fiscal Studies have proposed an alternative reform to the existing NI pension system which involves the gradual addition of a means-tested supplement to the basic state pension (Dilnot and Johnson, 1992). They argue that this is the only way of containing the cost of the NI pension while also ensuring that an adequate income is provided to the poorest of the elderly. Any move in this direction would involve all the well-known problems and costs of operating a means test, and would do nothing to unravel the distributional complexity of the existing NI system.

A rather different way of providing better incomes for the poor elderly is by means of a Citizen's Income (or basic income) which would be provided tax free to all people every month, with this financed by the abolition of existing income tax relief and by the payment of tax on earned income (Citizens Income, 1993). This proposal also does nothing to clarify the extent to which the system involves intrapersonal, interpersonal and intergenerational transfers, and also introduces potentially important labour supply disincentives. We propose a quite different pension system which explicitly unifies basic and supplementary pension provision, which efficiently targets government financed transfers to the lifetime poor without an explicit means test and which ensures that the intergenerational, intrapersonal and interpersonal transfers are all separately identifiable and independently resourced (Falkingham and Johnson, 1993; Johnson and Falkingham, 1994). This is examined in greater detail below.

## 2.      Principles of a UFPS

The unified funded pension scheme (UFPS) is designed to replace the existing NI basic pension and the majority of state, occupational and personal earnings-related pension schemes with a single pension which combines minimum pension guarantees with earnings-related provision. The scheme is based on the principle of every individual building-up a personal retirement fund (PRF) over her adult life which is used to purchase a pension annuity. Combined with this is a system of annual tax-financed capital transfers to people with low incomes or not in the labour market, together with investment insurance designed to spread portfolio risk across people of different generations.

In the UFPS a set percentage of the gross earnings of each adult would be paid into a personal retirement fund (PRF) which is a long-term savings account designed to facilitate intrapersonal income transfers over the life cycle. These PRFs would be managed by competing retirement trust funds, and individuals would have the right of periodic free transfer of their PRF between funds. Annual statements of contributions and expected future pension benefits would be issued to all contributors. The percentage contribution rate would be fixed so that an individual in receipt of average age-specific income across the earning life-span would have accumulated by some age (say 65) a PRF sufficient to purchase an index-linked annuity equal to some fixed amount (say 50 per cent) of average earnings. Individuals or employers would be entitled to raise their percentage contribution rate to up to twice the statutory level if they wished to raise their ultimate pension replacement rate.

What happens to people who receive less than average lifetime earnings, or who receive no earnings at all because of illness, disability, unemployment or non-waged caring responsibilities? To ensure that people in these categories have access to a minimum acceptable pension at age 65, they will require direct capital transfers into their PRF for each and every year in which their contribution into the PRF is inadequate to maintain the required path of PRF capital growth. This capital transfer will be financed from taxes on current income, and so will be a direct interpersonal tax transfer. This will ensure a guaranteed minimum income for all elderly people irrespective of their past labour market history or marital status, but to preserve savings incentives and a sense of equity this guaranteed pension should be set at a level below the 50 per cent replacement rate accumulated by a worker with an average lifetime earnings trajectory. A replacement rate of 33 per cent of average male earnings might be an acceptable minimum level. This means that for any individual whose income consistently falls significantly below the average age-specific income, then her PRF will consistently receive a capital top-up sufficient to maintain a fund that will buy an index-linked annuity at age 65 equal to 33 per cent of average income. If, however, an individual is sometimes in the labour force in a well-paid job but sometimes in a low-paid job or out of the labour force, her PRF capital top-up would be paid only at the point when the PRF falls below the required minimum age-specific amount.

There are two obvious sources of uncertainty about ultimate pension income within this model of a UFPS. First, the long run real rate of return on PRF assets and the rate of real income growth may not correspond with expectations, and secondly short-term fluctuations in asset values may impose windfall PRF gains or losses at the point of retirement, thereby unexpectedly enhancing or undermining long term saving plans. The first problem is, to some extent, automatically corrected by the minimum pension rule. If the growth rate of real earnings significantly exceeds its expected value but the real rate of return maintains its expected growth rate, then the replacement rate of the annuity purchasable with any PRF will fall over time. To the extent to which this invokes additional PRF top-ups it brings about an interpersonal transfer from prime-age workers (who benefit most from the high real income growth) to lower-paid workers close to retirement. Even so, long-run inadequacy of financing cannot be resolved in this manner, so we would propose that the required pension contribution rate be subject to change by not more than one percentage point each year, and that such a change should be automatically imposed if age-specific PRFs fall below the level required for a 50 per cent replacement rate for a person on average income.

The second problem is more tricky. One of the weaknesses of funded personal pensions is that with each cohort reliant on its own savings it is difficult to insure against risks such as abrupt movements in asset values that affect any particular generation. Within a UFPS several methods can be adopted to spread this risk across cohorts. First, retirement trust funds responsible for managing PRFs could be required to value PRFs on, say, a three-year moving-average basis. The cost of this, either in terms of insurance premiums or charges in the options/futures market would be part of the overall management cost and so would be spread across all birth cohorts. Secondly, more overt insurance protection can be provided by levying an extraordinary capital gains tax on PRF asset growth in times of very high and unanticipated capital appreciation which can be used to build up an asset protection reserve fund to provide, in a period of declining asset values, capital top-ups to the PRFs of people within, say, 5 years of retirement. Some combination of these strategies is probably optimal; although such a system could not give an absolute guarantee of ultimate pension value to someone in mid-career, it would provide greater security than existing pension schemes.

The combination of PRF contributions and tax-financed capital top-ups means that the UFPS is a hybrid pension scheme, incorporating both funded and Pay As You Go principles and combining in one unified administrative structure the safety-net function of a basic public pension and the income replacement function of an earnings-related supplementary pension. This unified structure prevents gaps in coverage (holes in the safety net) and removes the need for individuals to make complex assessments of the expected outcomes of a mixture of different pension schemes. However, in order to assess the potential performance and costs of a UFPS we need to develop some operational parameters.

**Age thresholds**

The current NI system is premised upon the employability of all people from age 16 but rates of economic activity among teenagers in Britain are low and are expected to decline further as tertiary education is expanded. We therefore propose that PRF contributions should begin at age 21, by which age most people will have completed their full-time education.

There would be no requirement to retire at 65. Individuals could defer retirement or the purchase of an annuity if this suited their circumstances, in which case the PRF capital value would continue to grow through the accumulation of interest. The only restriction necessary would be that nobody over the standard age of retirement would be eligible for any means-tested support or assistance in cash or kind unless they were drawing a pension from their past PRF accumulations.

Perhaps more important than the case of deferred retirement is the case of early retirement. Since the UFPS has an income-replacement goal as well as a minimum pension goal, we think that some disincentive to early retirement on minimum pension incomes might be built into UFPS rules to prevent premature labour force exit. A rule which allows early retirement at that point where the PRF will buy an annuity pension equal to 50 per cent of average male earnings might be appropriate. In the simulations presented below we estimate costs for a standard retirement age of 65.

**Capital top-ups**

Capital top-ups for people with inadequate PRF contributions would be relatively straightforward if it were true that all people currently with low incomes also have low lifetime incomes, but as Chapter 6 makes clear this is not always the case. The most obvious example is students who are often poor in their early twenties and so likely to qualify for a PRF capital top-up. But it is inefficient to provide tax-financed capital transfers into the PRFs of students whose short term self-selected poverty will be compensated for by subsequent labour market income.

Such difficulties can be accommodated with a *claw-back system* in which the government reclaims previous capital transfers if subsequent income proves to be high. Each individual PRF operates as a savings account with assets (the individual contributions) and liabilities (the tax-financed capital top-ups). If at the end of each year the PRF was less than the capital sum required to keep it on the required growth path there would be a capital top-up in the form of a loan to the PRF. If an individual reaches the standard retirement age with loans to the PRF still outstanding, these are written off, and the PRF is used to purchase a minimum pension annuity. If, on the other hand, income in later working life is very high, so PRF contributions are in excess of those required to provide a minimum pension, then the excess contributions are used to repay the prior loan.

This system prevents undue transfers to the lifetime wealthy, but it has the advantage of doing so without imposing the labour-market disincentives common in most systems of means-testing. All contributors pay the same statutory percentage contribution rate into their PRF, so the means test and claw-back occur entirely within the PRF account, and do not affect take-home pay. The means test here is on income *across the entire working life*, resulting in more effective targeting of government cash transfers. In order to ensure that additional voluntary contributions to the PRF are not discouraged, these should be accounted for separately and be exempt from any claw-back mechanism.

**Individual or joint contributions during married life?**

A key principle of the UFPS is that pension entitlements are vested in the individual, and based upon individual contributions. This ensures that adequate pensions are secured for all women in their own right, regardless of their past labour market experience. It does, however, mean that the non-working spouse of a high earner would receive PRF capital top-ups despite the high level of *household* income. If it can be assumed that women in these households enjoy the benefits of the high level of income it can be argued that capital top-ups to these women are as unwarranted as those to students and the self-employed. However, there is much debate about the division of income within the household.

In the simulations using the LIFEMOD population we present results on the basis of two different contribution rules – that of individual contributions and that of joint contributions under which an earnings-sharing rule is be applied to the PRF contributions of married couples. For the duration of a union the PRF contributions are split between both partners' PRF accounts. With a contribution rate designed to achieve a 50 per cent replacement rate, and a minimum pension level of 33 per cent of average male earnings, this earnings-sharing rule means that both partners would receive PRF top-ups if household income was below 132 per cent of average adult male earnings, but that the non-working spouse of a partner earning more than this amount does not receive any top-up.

Sharing of contributions automatically ensures equal division of pension entitlements if the partners separate or divorce, and so overcomes some of the adverse pension consequences for women of divorce (Joshi and Davies, 1991). It has the advantage over a non-joint contribution basis; non-working married women are not limited to accumulating a PRF designed to allow only a minimum pension, but can benefit from higher contributions during married life. This earnings-sharing rule means that husbands in effect provide a deferred income for the unwaged reproductive and caring work of their wives, and provides a modest step towards achieving greater income equality within the household between men and women.

**Minimum and maximum contribution thresholds**

A lower earnings limit equivalent to the NI lower earnings limit is incorporated in our UFPS simulations and we assume that contributions are paid on all labour market income above the lower earnings limit, but no contributions are paid from social security benefit income. Some low earners, however, may be in receipt of substantial unearned income. No contributions would normally be levied on unearned income *unless* the individual is in receipt of capital top-ups, in which case contributions could be levied on total income. An upper earnings limit on compulsory contributions could be set at three times median earnings. With a target replacement rate of 50 per cent, this upper earnings limit would provide high earners with a pension income that places them in the upper quartile of the overall income distribution, and so meets the basic income replacement functions of a UFPS.

**Premature death**

The individual nature of the UFPS means that it does not have to deal with survivors' or spouses' benefits. If an individual dies before the standard retirement age, the contributions paid into her PRF, together with accumulated interest, form part of the person's bequeathable estate. Any outstanding loans made to the PRF, on the other hand, should be repaid to the government since the function of PRF capital top-ups is to assist lifetime low earners rather than their surviving beneficiaries. Allowing past pension contributions to be inherited by the beneficiaries of people who die before retirement is a significant improvement on the existing NI and SERPS schemes which allow pension entitlements to be transferred only if the deceased is survived by a spouse or dependant. Because of pre-retirement class differentials in mortality, with people of lower socio-economic class on average dying younger, existing state pension rules have the effect of transferring resources from lower-paid to higher-paid groups. The proposed UFPS would prevent this perverse transfer. On the other hand, class differentials in post-retirement mortality would continue to effect a transfer from the lower to the higher paid through the workings of the annuity market.

## 3.    UFPS Simulations

In this section we present the results of a modelling exercise which replaces the current NI scheme with a simple version of a UFPS. Estimates are derived of the numbers of LIFEMOD men and women who, over their contribution life cycle (ages 21–64) have an income too low to allow the accumulation of a PRF which, at any age, is on a growth path sufficient to buy an annuity equal to at least one-third of average male income at the point of retirement. This is the population that will need PRF capital top-ups, and the cost of these top-ups is calculated. The overall cost of these top-ups is then grossed-up for the UK in 1991 and the TAXMOD tax–benefit model is used to assess the implications of replacing the NI pension with a UFPS.

In the simulations reported below we have included a lower earnings limit and used a PRF contribution rate of 18 per cent. In order to mimic the existing NI system we impose a 10 per cent contribution on employees and 8 per cent on employers.[2] Table 11.2 shows the proportion of people who fail to accumulate a PRF capable of providing an indexed pension

---

2   The required contribution rate for a fully employed male on average earnings was estimated on the basis of various rates of real income growth and real returns on assets. Its derivation is detailed in Falkingham and Johnson (1993).

**Table 11.2** Percentage of LIFEMOD Population who can Purchase Pensions at 33 per cent and 50 per cent Replacement Rates at Age 65

|                                          | All  | Men  | Women |
|------------------------------------------|------|------|-------|
| Own contribution 33 per cent replacement | 50.9 | 79.1 | 25.7  |
| Own contribution 50 per cent replacement | 25.6 | 45.1 | 8.2   |
| Joint contribution 33 per cent replacement | 56.5 | 62.5 | 51.2  |
| Joint contribution 50 per cent replacement | 22.1 | 26.4 | 18.2  |

for target replacement rates of both 33 per cent and 50 per cent of average full-time male LIFEMOD earnings for the two variants of the contribution rules.

The low lifetime incomes of women are reflected in this table; only 25 per cent reach the lower replacement rate target on the basis of their own contributions. Moving from an own contribution to a joint contribution basis fundamentally changes the outcomes, giving women much better, but men significantly worse, results. Nevertheless, even with joint contributions it is clear that many people fail to reach the minimum PRF target and so will require some capital top-up.

Some of those whose PRF falls short of the 33 per cent replacement rate level will only just miss this target, while others (e.g. long-term unemployed) will contribute very little to their own PRF. Summing these across the LIFEMOD population allows us to calculate the mean per capita value of lifetime net capital top-ups for individual and joint contributions, for the entire LIFEMOD population, and for men and women separately, in 1991 prices – this is shown in Table 11.3. Not surprisingly, it is women who receive the majority of the capital top-ups – almost 90 per cent on the basis of individual contributions, and two-thirds of top-ups on the basis of joint contributions.

The estimates in Table 11.3 show the average capital top-up received by each person by age 65; by multiplying these estimates by 564,000, the number of UK citizens who reached age 65 in 1991, we can determine the cost of capital top-ups in 1991 had they been paid only as a lump-sum at retirement age. In practice the PRF clawback system means loans to and repayments from PRFs can occur from ages 21 to 65, but the annual cost of these loans and clawbacks for people of all ages will necessarily equal the annual cost of loans if they are deferred to age 65 and paid as lump sums to that proportion of the population reaching age 65 who have deficient PRFs. For a funded pension system based on individual contributions of 15 per cent of earnings and a minimum pension target

**Table 11.3** Mean Per Capita Amount of Lifetime Capital Top-ups Received by LIFEMOD Population by Age 65 with Minimum Pension Replacement Target of 33 per cent of Male Full-time Earnings

|  |  | Mean (£) |
|---|---|---|
| All LIFEMOD | Own contributions | 14446 |
|  | Joint contributions | 8071 |
| Men | Own contributions | 3046 |
|  | Joint contributions | 5613 |
| Women | Own contributions | 24638 |
|  | Joint contributions | 10269 |

of 33 per cent of average male full-time earnings, the cost is £8.4 billion, and for joint contributions the cost is £4.5 billion.

The tax cost could be compensated for by the abolition of the current NI pension (£25.8 billion in 1991) and associated means-tested benefits to the elderly (around £6.2 billion). In addition, if tax thresholds are kept at their present level, the higher income of pensioners would generate an additional £3.7 billion in income tax revenue, so the combined saving would be £35.7 billion.[3] The abolition of the NI pension would necessarily require a reduction of NI contributions. In 1991 employee NI contributions produced a revenue of £12.1 billion with employers contributing about £19 billion. The non-retirement pension element of NI expenditure amounted to around £8 billion, and this would need to be continued in some form. We assume this continues to be borne by employers whose total NI contributions are reduced to £8 billion, while employee NI contributions are abolished. Table 11.4 shows the balance of exchequer gains and losses.

**Table 11.4** Balance of Exchequer Gains and Losses in Mature UFPS

|  | Revenue gain (£ billion) | Revenue loss (£ billion |
|---|---|---|
| UFPS capital top-ups | - | 4.5 |
| Abolition of retirement pension | 25.8 | - |
| Reduction of existing means-tested pensioner benefits | 6.2 | - |
| Abolition of employee NI contributions | - | 12.1 |
| Abolition of part of employer NI contributions | - | 11.0 |
| Additional tax revenue | 3.7 | - |
| SUM | 35.7 | 27.6 |
| Overall exchequer saving | 8.1 | - |

---

3   Calculated using TAXMOD (Atkinson and Sutherland, 1988).

216 per cent of male average earnings

The fiscal implications of the replacement of the existing NI system with a mature UFPS are as follows: a UFPS contribution of 18 per cent (10 per cent employees and 8 per cent employers) plus employer payments of about 4 per cent for non-retirement NI benefits would replace current NI contributions of just over 20 per cent (10 per cent employees, 10.4 per cent employers). There would, in addition, be an exchequer gain of £8.1 billion per annum, but as we note below, this would need to be used to cover some of the costs of pension system transition. The long run steady state contribution rate would be 2 per cent higher than at present, but this is 4 per cent below the NI contribution rate projected by the Government Actuary (1990) for 2031 if the basic pension continues to be uprated in line with earnings. Furthermore, in the long run the UFPS would provide a minimum pension of 33 per cent of male average earnings, as against 15 per cent for the existing NI system. This outcome is achieved by targeting all the tax-financed capital top-ups on the lifetime poor – the 37 per cent of men and 49 per cent of women (Table 11.3) who would not be able to purchase a minimum 33 per cent replacement pension on the basis of accumulated PRF assets. This targeting would occur entirely through the accumulation and claw-back principle of each PRF, so individuals would never face a conventional pension means test either during their working years or in retirement.

This may seem too good to be true. We believe that the cost estimates are plausible, but we should stress that the comparisons we make are between a *mature* NI system and a *mature* UFPS. New pension systems cannot be implemented overnight – they become mature only when all retirees have pension entitlements based on full contribution histories, and it takes well over half a century to reach this position. A comparison of mature systems, therefore, ignores the fifty years or more of transition between systems, and the costs involved in the transition process. Transition costs are the key issue in pension system reform, particularly where the transition is from a Pay As You Go to a funded system. The costs will be broadly similar whatever the new system – whether it be UFPS, personal pensions or occupational pensions – since the costs are determined primarily by the level of pension entitlements or expectations accumulated under the old system.

In other work we have estimated the cost of pension system transition and indicate how the very large costs might be met without undue tax burdens being placed on any one transitional generation (Falkingham and Johnson, 1993).

## 4.    Summary and Conclusion

In this chapter we have presented outline proposals and cost estimates for a new type of funded pension scheme which incorporates tax-financed capital top-ups for the lifetime poor, and which guarantees basic pensions for all and earnings-related pensions for people with adequate lifetime earnings histories. The UFPS has, we believe, some clear advantages over both the current mix of pension systems and alternative reform proposals such as more purely private pensions or more means-testing of public pensions. We would emphasise five main advantages of the UFPS:

- The basic pension in a mature UFPS is paid at twice the current NI pension level, and is paid on an individual basis, so married couples would receive a minimum pension of two-thirds average male earnings.

- Tax-financed assistance is restricted, through the system of capital top-ups and claw-back, to low lifetime earners which results in more efficient targeting than cross-sectional means tests. This implicit means-test is conducted entirely within each individual's PRF during working life, so there are no means-tests on pension income after retirement. Furthermore, since the system of claw-back does not affect current take-home pay (all contributions are at 18 per cent), the effect on current earnings incentives is likely to be small.

- The annualised nature of the capital top-ups prevents governments making pension promises today while deferring the cost to future generations (as happened with the introduction of SERPS in 1975). In a funded system with annual top-ups for low earners any increase in future pensions involves immediate costs, and so imposes responsible intertemporal decision-making on governments.

- The earnings-sharing rule for PRF contributions of married couples allows married non-earning women to share in the pension accrual of their husbands, and permits fair division of pension entitlements in the event of divorce.

- The full vesting of pension savings in the individual removes the power of employers to determine pension saving plans and retirement decisions.

# References

Aaron, H. J. (1982), *Economic Effects of Social Security*, Washington, DC: The Brookings Institution.

Abel-Smith, B. (1964), *The Hospitals 1800–1948*, London: Heinemann.

Anderson, M. (1990), 'The social implications of demographic change', in Thompson (ed.), Vol. 2 (1990).

Atkinson, A. B. (1991), 'Social insurance', *Geneva Papers on Risk and Social Insurance Theory*, **16**, 2, pp. 113–31.

Atkinson, A. B. (1983), *The Economics of Inequality* (2nd edition), Oxford: Clarendon Press.

Atkinson, A. B. and Bourguignon, F. (1983), 'The comparison of multi-dimensioned distributions of economic status', in *Social Justice and Public Policy*, Atkinson, A. B., Hemel Hempstead: Harvester-Wheatsheaf.

Atkinson, A. B., Bourguignon, F. and Morrisson, C. (1992), *Empirical Studies of Earnings Mobility*, Chur (Switzerland): Harwood Academic Publishers.

Atkinson, A. B. and Sutherland, H. (eds.) (1988), *Tax Benefit Models*, STICERD Occasional Paper 10, London: London School of Economics.

Baldwin, S. and Falkingham, J. (eds) (1994), *Social Security and Social Change: New challenges to the Beveridge Model*, Hemel Hempstead: Harvester Wheatsheaf.

Barden, L., Barr, N. and Higginson, G. (1991), 'An analysis of student loan options', CVCP/CDP Occasional Paper, London: Committee of Vice-Chancellors and Principals and Committee of Directors of Polytechnics.

Barnes, J. and Barr, N., (1988), 'Strategies for higher education: The alternative White Paper', Aberdeen University Press for the David Hume Institute, Edinburgh, and STICERD, London School of Economics.

Barr, N. (1991), 'Income-contingent student loans: An idea whose time has come', in *Economics, Culture and Education: Essays in Honour of Mark Blaug*, Shaw, G. K. (ed.), Aldershot, Hants: Edward Elgar.

Barr, N. (1993a), *The Economics of the Welfare State* (2nd edition), London: Weidenfeld and Nicolson and Stamford, CA: Stamford University Press.

Barr, N. (1993b), 'Alternative funding resources for higher education', *Economic Journal*, **103**, 418, pp. 718–728.

Barr, N. and Falkingham, J. (1993), 'Paying for learning', STICERD Welfare State Programme Discussion Paper WSP/94, London: London School of Economics.

Barr, N., Falkingham, J. and Glennerster, H. (1994), *Funding Higher Education*, Poole: BP Educational Service.

Barro, R. (1974), 'Are government bonds net wealth?', *Journal of Political Economy*, **82**, pp. 1095–117.

Becker, G. (1964), *Human Capital*, New York: NBER Columbia University Press.

Bennett, R., Glennerster, H. and Nevison, D. (1992a), 'Investing in skill: Expected returns to vocational studies', STICERD Welfare State Programme Discussion Paper WSP/83, London: London School of Economics.

Bennett, R., Glennerster, H. and Nevison, D. (1992b), 'Investing in skill: To stay on or not to stay on?', *Oxford Review of Economic Policy*, **8**, 2, pp. 130–158.

Bennett, R., Glennerster, H. and Nevison, D. (1992c), *Learning Should Pay*, London: BP Education Services.

Beveridge, W. H. (1942), *Social Insurance and Allied Services*, Cmnd 6404, London: HMSO.

Beveridge, W. H. (1943), *The Pillars of Security*, London: Allen and Unwin.

Blanchard, O. J. and Fischer, S. (1989), *Lectures on Macroeconomics*, Cambridge, Massachusetts: MIT Press.

Blaug, M. (1966), 'Loans for students', *New Society*, 6 October, pp. 538–9.

Blinder, A. (1974), *Towards an Economic Theory of Income Distribution*, Cambridge, Massachusetts: MIT Press.

Blinder, A., Gordon, R. H. and Wise, D. (1982), 'Social security, bequests and the life cycle theory of savings: Cross-sectional tests', in *The Determinants of National Saving and Wealth: Proceedings of a conference held by the International Economic Association*, Modigliani, F. and Hemming, R. (eds), New York: St Martin's Press.

Blomquist, N. S. (1976), 'The distribution of lifetime income: A case study of Sweden', Ph.D. dissertation, Department of Economics, Princeton University.

Booth, C. (1892), *Pauperism, a Picture; and the Endowment of Old Age, an Argument*, London: Macmillan.

Bone, M., Gregory, J., Gill, B. and Lader, D. (1992), *Retirement and Retirement Plans*, London: HMSO.

Bosanquet, N. and Townsend, P. (1972), *Labour and Inequality*, London: Fabian Society.

Broome, J. (1985), 'The welfare economics of the future: A review of *Reasons and Persons* by Derek Parfit', *Social Change and Welfare*, **2**, pp. 221–234.

Brown, J. (1992), *A Policy Vacuum: Social security for the self-employed*, York: Joseph Rowntree Foundation.

Bryman, A., Bytheway, B., Allat, P. and Keil, T. (eds.) (1987), *Rethinking the Life Cycle*, London: Macmillan.

Burkhauser, R. V., Duncan, G. J., Hauser, R. and Berntsen, R. (1991), 'Wife or frau, women do worse: A comparison of men and women in the United States and Germany after marital dissolution', *Demography*, **28**, 3, pp. 353–374.

Burtless, G. (1990), *A Future of Lousy Jobs?*, Washington, DC: The Brookings Institution.

CSO (1986), 'The effects of tax and benefits on household income, 1985', *Economic Trends*, November, pp. 96–109.

CSO (1987), 'The effects of tax and benefits on household income, 1985', *Economic Trends*, July, pp. 101–17.

CSO (1993), 'The effects of taxes and benefits on household income, 1990', *Economic Trends*, January, pp. 147–187.

Chapman, B. (1992), 'Austudy: Towards a more flexible approach, mimeo, Canberra: Australian National University.

Chapman, B. and Harding, A. (1993), 'Australian student loans', mimeo, Canberra: Australian National University.

Citizens Income (1993), 'Citizens income and elderly people', Aspects of Citizens Income No. 9, London: Citizens Income.

Clark, C. (1938), *National Income and Outlay*, London: Macmillan.

Collins, E. and Klein, R. (1980), 'Equity and the NHS: Self-reported morbidity, access and primary care', *British Medical Journal*, **281**, pp. 111–15.

Coulter, F., Cowell, F. and Jenkins, S. (1992), 'Differences in needs and assessment of income distributions', *Bulletin of Economic Research*, **44**, pp. 77-124.

Department of Education and Science (1988), *Top-Up Loans for Students*, Cmnd. 520, London: HMSO.

Department of Education and Science (1989), *Aspects of Higher Education in the United States of America: A commentary by Her Majesty's Inspectorate*, London: HMSO.

Department of Education and Science (1993), *DES Expenditure Plans 1993–4 to 1995–6*, Cmnd. 2210, London: HMSO.

Department of Health and Social Security (DHSS) (1985), *Reform of Social Security: Programme for Action*, Cmnd. 9691, London: HMSO.

Department of Social Security (DSS) (1991), *Social Security Statistics 1990*, London: HMSO.

Dilnot, A. and Johnson, P. (1992), 'What pension should the State provide?', *Fiscal Studies*, **13**, 4, pp. 1–20..

Dyhouse, C. (1989), *Feminism and the Family in England*, Oxford: Blackwell.

Ermisch, J. (1990), *Fewer Babies, Longer Lives*, York: Joseph Rowntree Foundation.

Ermisch, J. (1992), *Lone Parenthood: An economic analysis*, Cambridge: Cambridge University Press.

Evandrou, M. (forthcoming), 'Paid and unpaid work: The socio-economic position of informal carers in Britain', in *Working Carers and Older People*, Phillips, J. (ed.), Aldershot: Avebury.

Evandrou, M., Falkingham, J., Hills, J. and Le Grand, J. (1993) 'Welfare benefits in kind and income distribution', *Fiscal Studies*, **14**, 1, pp. 57–76.

Evans, M. and Glennerster, H. (1993), 'Squaring the Circle? The inconsistencies and constraints of Beveridge's Plan', STICERD Welfare State Programme Discussion Paper WSP/86, London: London School of Economics.

Falkingham, J., Hills, J. and Lessof, C. (1993), 'William Beveridge versus Robin Hood: Social security and redistribution over the life-cycle', STICERD Welfare State Programme Discussion Paper WSP/88, London: London School of Economics.

Falkingham, J. and Johnson, P. (1993), 'A Unified Funded Pension Scheme (UFPS) for Britain', STICERD Welfare State Programme Discussion Paper WSP/90. London: London School of Economics.

Falkingham, J. and Lessof, C. (1991), 'LIFEMOD – The formative years', STICERD Welfare State Programme Research Note WSP/RN/24, London: London School of Economics.

Falkingham, J. and Lessof, C. (1992), 'Playing God or LIFEMOD – The construction of a dynamic microsimulation model' in *Microsimulation Models for Public Policy Analysis: New Frontiers*, R. Hancock and H. Sutherland (eds.), STICERD Occasional Paper No. 17, London: London School of Economics.

Feldstein, M. (1974), 'Social security, induced retirement and aggregate capital accumulation', *Journal of Political Economy*, **82**, 5, pp. 905–26.

Feldstein, M. (1985), 'The optimal level of social security benefits', *The Quarterly Journal of Economics*, **C**, 2, pp. 305–20.

Floud, J. E., Halsey, A. H. and Martin, F. M. (1956), *Social Class and Educational Opportunity*, London: Heinemann.

Fullerton, D. and Rogers, D. L. (1993), *Who Bears the Lifetime Tax Burden?*, Washington DC: Brookings.

Galler, H. P. and Wagner, G. (1986), 'The microsimulation model of the SFB3 for the analysis of economic and social policies', in *Microanalytic Simulation Models to Support Social and Financial Policy*, Orcutt, G. H., Merz, J. and Quinke, H. (eds.), Amsterdam: North-Holland.

Ghez, G. R. and Becker, G. S. (1975), *The Allocation of Time and Goods over the Life Cycle*, New York: Columbia University Press.

Ginn, J. and Arber, S. (1994), 'Heading for hardship: How the British pension system has failed women', in Baldwin and Falkingham (eds.) (1994).

Glennerster, H. (1982), 'The role of the state in financing recurrent education', *Public Choice*, **36**, pp. 551–71.

Glennerster, H., Merrett, S. and Wilson, G. (1968), 'A Graduate Tax', *Higher Education Review*, **1**, p. 1.

Gordon, C. (1988), 'The myth of family care? The elderly in the 1930s', STICERD Welfare State Programme Discussion Paper WSP/29, London: London School of Economics.

Government Actuary (1990), *National Insurance Fund: Long term financial estimates* (Second Quinquennial Review), HC(89–90)582, London: HMSO.

Hain, W. and Helberger, C. (1986), 'Longitudinal microsimulation of lifetime income', in *Microanalytic Simulation Models to Support Social and Financial Policy*, Merz, J. and Quinke, H. (eds), New York: North-Holland.

Hancock, R., Mallendar, J. and Pudney S. (1992), 'Constructing a computer model for simulating the future distribution of pensioners' incomes for Great Britain', in *Microsimulation Models for Public Policy Analysis: New frontiers*, Hancock, R. and Sutherland, H. (eds.), STICERD Occasional Paper No. 17, London: London School of Economics.

Harding, A. (1990), 'Dynamic microsimulation models: Problems and prospects', STICERD Welfare State Programme Discussion Paper WSP/48, London: London School of Economics.

Harding, A. (1993), *Lifetime Income Distribution and Redistribution in Australia: Applications of a microsimulation model*, Amsterdam: North-Holland.

Harrod, R. (1948), *Towards a Dynamic Economics*, London: Macmillan.

Hauser, R. and Fisher, I. (1990), 'Economic well-being among one-parent families', in Smeeding, O'Higgins and Rainwater (eds.) (1990).

Hewitt, P. (1993), *About Time: The revolution in work and family life*, London: Institute of Public Policy Research.

Hills, J. (1989), 'Counting the family silver: The public sector's balance sheet 1957 to 1987', *Fiscal Studies*, **10**, 2, pp. 66–85.

Hills, J. (ed.) (1990), *The State of Welfare: The welfare state in Britain since 1974*, Oxford: Clarendon Press.

Hills, J. (1991), *Unravelling Housing Finance: Subsidies, benefits and taxation*, Oxford: Clarendon Press.

Hills, J. (1992), 'Does Britain have a welfare generation? An empirical analysis of intergenerational equity', STICERD Welfare State Programme Discussion Paper WSP/76, London: London School of Economics.

Hills, J. (1993), *The Future of Welfare: A guide to the debate*, York: Joseph Rowntree Foundation.

Hills, J. and Lessof, C. (1993), 'Modelling direct tax and social security over the lifetime', STICERD Welfare State Programme Research Note WSP/RN/25, London: London School of Economics.

HM Treasury (1993), *Public Expenditure Analyses to 1995–96* (Statistical Supplement to the 1992 Autumn Statement), Cmnd. 2219, London: HMSO.

Hoffman, S. D. and Duncan, G. J. (1988), 'What are the economic consequences of divorce?', *Demography*, **25**, pp. 641–645.

Holtermann, S. (1993), *Becoming a Breadwinner: Policies to assist lone parents with childcare*, London: Daycare Trust.

Jallade, J.-P. (ed.) (1988), *The Crisis of Redistribution in European Welfare States*, Stoke-on-Trent: Trentham Books.

Jenkins, S. and Cowell, F. (1993), 'Dwarfs and giants in the 1980s: The UK income distribution and how it changed', Economics Department Discussion Paper 93–03, Swansea: Swansea University of Wales.

Johnson, P. and Falkingham, J. (1988), 'Intergenerational transfers and public expenditure on the elderly in modern Britain', *Ageing and Society*, **8**, pp. 129–146.

Johnson, P. and Falkingham, J. (1992), *Ageing and Economic Welfare*, London: Sage.

Johnson, P. and Falkingham, J. (1994), 'Is there a Future for the Beveridge Pension Scheme?', in *Social Security and Social Change: New challenges to the Beveridge model*, Baldwin, S. and Falkingham, J. (eds.), Hemel Hempstead: Harvester Wheatsheaf.

Johnson, P., Conrad, C. and Thomson, D. (eds.) (1989), *Workers versus Pensioners: Intergenerational justice in an ageing world*, Manchester: Manchester University Press.

Johnson, P., Stark, G. and Webb, S. (1990), 'TAXBEN: The new IFS tax benefit model' Working Paper No. 90/5, London: Institute for Fiscal Studies.

Joshi, H. (1990), 'The cash opportunity costs of childbearing: An approach to estimation using British data', *Population Studies*, **44**, pp. 41–60.

Joshi, H. and Davies, H. (1991), 'Pension splitting and divorce', *Fiscal Studies*, **12**, November, pp. 69–91.

Kessler, D. (1989), 'But why is there social security?', in Johnson *et al.* (eds.) (1989).

Kiernan, K. and Wicks, M. (1990), *Family Changes and Future Policy*, York: Joseph Rowntree Foundation.

Kotlikoff, L. J. (1992), *Generational Accounting: Knowing who pays, and when, for what we spend*, New York: Free Press.

Kotlikoff, L. J. and Spivak, A. (1981), 'The family as an incomplete annuities market', *Journal of Political Economy*, **89**, 2, pp. 372–91.

Laslett, P. (1983), *The World We Have Lost*, London: Methuen.

Lazear, E. P. (1981), 'Agency, earnings profiles, productivity and hours restrictions', *American Economic Review*, **71**, pp. 606–620.

Lazear, E. P. (1982), 'Pensions as severance pay', National Bureau of Economic Research Working Paper No. 944. Cambridge, MA: NBER.

Le Grand, J. (1978), 'The distribution of public expenditure: The case of health care', *Economica*, **45**, pp. 125–42.

Le Grand, J. (1982), *The Strategy of Equality*, London: Allen and Unwin.

Le Grand, J. (1990), 'The State of Welfare' in Hills (ed.) (1990).

Lillard, L. (1977), 'Inequality: Earnings vs human wealth', *American Economic Review*, **67**, 2, pp. 42–53.

Longman, P. (1987), *Born to Pay: The new politics of aging in America*, Boston: Houghton Mills.

Lydall, H. F. (1959), 'The long term trend in the size distribution of income', *Journal of the Royal Statistical Society*, Series A, **122**, 1, pp. 1–37.

Macnicol, J. (1980), *The Movement for Family Allowances 1918–45: A study in social policy development*, London: Heinemann.

Marx, K. (1867), *Capital* Vol. 1, London: Penguin Edition.

Millar, J. (1994), 'Lone parents and social security policy in the UK', in Baldwin and Falkingham (eds.) (1994).

Miller, P. (1981), 'The rate of return to education – The evidence from the 1976 Census', Centre for Economic Policy Research Discussion Paper No. 25, Canberra: ANU.

Murphy, M. (1987), 'Measuring the family life cycle: Concepts, data and methods', in Bryman *et al.* (eds.) (1987).

Murray, C. (1984), *Losing Ground: American social policy, 1950–1980*, New York: Basic Books.

Nelissen, J. H. M. (1987), 'A microsimulation model for the Netherlands', Department of Sociology Working Paper Series no. 23, Tilburg: Tilburg University.

'No Turning Back' Group of Conservative MPs (1993), *Who Benefits? Reinventing social security*. London: Conservative Political Centre.

O'Donnell, O. and Propper, C. (1991), 'Equity and the distribution of UK National Health Service resources', *Journal of Health Economics*, **10**, 1, pp. 1–19.

O'Donnell, O., Propper, C. and Upward, R. (1993), 'Equity in the delivery and finance of health care in the UK', in Rutten *et al.* (eds.) (1993).

O'Higgins, M., Bradshaw, J. and Walker, R. (1988), 'Income distribution over the life cycle', in *Money Matters: Income, wealth and financial welfare*, Walker, R. and Parker, G. (eds.), London: Sage.

Office of Population Censuses and Surveys (OPCS) (1986a), *Birth Statistics*, Series FM1, No.15 1985, London: HMSO.

OPCS (1986b), *Mortality Statistics*, Series DH1, no.17 1985, London: HMSO.

OPCS (1988), *General Household Survey 1985*, London: HMSO.

OPCS (1993a), *Labour Force Survey 1992*, London: HMSO.

OPCS (1993b), *National Population Projections 1991-based*, Series PP", No. 18, London: HMSO.

OPCS (1993c), *General Household Survey 1991*, London: HMSO.

Orcutt, G. (1957), 'A new type of socio-economic system', *Review of Economics and Statistics*, **58**, pp. 773–97.

Orcutt, G., Glazer, A., Jamwill, H. and Nelson, P. (1976). 'Microanalytic Simulation', Institution for Social and Policy Studies Working Paper 9/21/76, New Haven: Yale University.

Orcutt, G., Greenberg, M., Korbel, J. and Rivlin, A. (1961), *Microanalysis of Socioeconomic Systems: A simulation study*, New York: Harper and Row.

Pahl, J. (1989), *Money and Marriage*, London: Macmillan.

Pahl, J. (1990), 'Household spending, personal spending and the control of money in marriage', *Sociology*, **24**, 1, pp. 119–138.

Paish, F. W. (1957), 'The real indicence of personal taxation', *Lloyds Bank Review*, **43**.

Parfit, D. (1984), *Reasons and Persons*, Oxford: Oxford University Press.

Parker, G. and Lawton, D. (1990), 'Further analysis of the 1985 GHS data on informal care, Report 1: A typology of carers', DH715, SPRU Working Paper, York: Social Policy Research Unit, University of York.

Parker, G. and Lawton, D. (1994), 'Different types of care, different types of carer: Evidence from the GHS', SPRU, London: HMSO.

Piachaud, D. (1987), 'The distribution of income and work', *Oxford Review of Economic Policy*, **13**, 3, pp. 41–61.

Propper, C. and Upward, R. (1992), 'The distribution of UK health care 1974–1987', *Fiscal Studies*, **12**, pp. 1–21.

Propper, C. and Upward, R. (1993), 'Modelling health and health care over the lifetime', STICERD Welfare State Programme Research Note WSP/RN/27, London: London School of Economics.

Rainwater, L., Rein. M. and Swartz, J. E. (1986), *Income Packaging in the Welfare State*, Oxford: Clarendon Press.

Rathbone, E. (1917), 'The remuneration of women's services', *Economic Journal*, **27**, March, pp. 55–68.

Rathbone, E. (1924), *The Disinherited Family*, London: Edward Arnold.

Rathbone, E. (1941), *The Case for Family Allowances*, London: Penguin Books.

Reischauer, R. (1989), 'HELP: A student loan program for the twenty-first century', in *Radical Reform or Incremental Change? Student loan policies for the federal government*, Gladieux, L. (ed.), New York: College Entrance Examinations Board.

Rivlin, A. and Weiner, J. (1988), *Caring for the Disabled Elderly: Who will pay?*, Washington, DC: The Brookings Institution.

Rowntree, B. S. (1902), *Poverty: A study of town life*, London: Nelson.

Rowntree, B. S. (1918), *The Human Needs of Labour*, London: Nelson.

Rowntree, B. S. (1941), *Poverty and Progress: A second social survey*, London: Longman Green.

Russell, C. (1993), *Academic Freedom*, London: Routledge.

Rutten, F., Doorslaer, E. van and Wagstaff, A. (1993) (eds.), *Equity in the Delivery and Finance of Health Care: International comparisons*. Oxford: Oxford University Press.

Samuelson, P. A. (1958), 'An exact consumption–loan model of interest with or without the contrivance of money', *Journal of Political Economy*, **66**, 6, pp. 467–482.

Schultz, T. W. (1963), *The Economic Value of Education*, New York: Columbia University Press.

Shirras, G. F. and Rostas, L. (1942), *The Burden of British Taxation*, Cambridge: Cambridge University Press.

Smeeding, T., O'Higgins, M. and Rainwater, L. (eds.) (1990), *Poverty, Inequality, and Income Distribution in Comparative Perspective*, Hemel Hempstead: Harvester Wheatsheaf.

Smith, A. (1776), *The Wealth of Nations*, London: Penguin Edition.

Sugden, R. (1984), 'Voluntary organisations and the welfare state', in *Privatisation and the Welfare State*, Le Grand, J. and Robinson, R. (eds.), London: George Allen and Unwin.

Summers, R. (1956), 'An econometric investigation of the life time size distribution of average annual income', Cowles Foundation Discussion Paper No. 9. Summary in *Econometrica*, July, pp. 346–347.

Thompson, F. M. L. (ed.) (1990), *The Cambridge Social History of Britain: 1750–1950*, Cambridge: Cambridge University Press.

Thomson, D. (1989), 'The welfare state and generational conflict: Winners and losers', in Johnson *et al.* (eds.) (1989).

Thomson, D. (1991), *Selfish Generations: The ageing of New Zealand's welfare state*, Wellington: Bridget Williams Books.

Titmuss, R. M. (1958), *Essays on 'the Welfare State'*, London: Allen and Unwin.

Titmuss, R. M. (1961), *Income Distribution and Social Change*, London: Allen and Unwin.

US Government (1992), *Economic Report of the President 1992*, Washington, DC: Government Printing Office.

van Doorslaer, E. and Wagstaff, A. (1993), 'Equity in the finance of health care: methods and findings of the COMAC-HSR project', in Rutten *et al.* (eds.) (1993).

van Vliet, R. and van de Ven, W. (1985), 'Differences in medical consumption between publicly and privately insured in the Netherlands: Standardisation by means of multiple regression', paper presented to the International Meeting of the Applied Econometrics Association, December 16–17, Rotterdam.

Vogler, C. (1989), 'Labour market change and patterns of financial allocation within households', ESRC Social Change and Economic Life Initiative Working Paper 12, Oxford: Nuffield College.

Waldfogel, J. (1993), 'Women working for less: A longitudinal analysis of the family gap', STICERD Welfare State Programme Discussion Paper WSP/93, London: London School of Economcs.

Whiteford, P. (1985), 'A family's needs: Equivalence scales, poverty and social security', Development Division Research Paper No.27, Canberra: Department of Social Security.

Winter, D. (1991), 'A cohort analysis of chronic morbidity and unemployment in the General Household Survey', STICERD Welfare State Programme Discussion Paper WSP/59, London: London School of Economics.

Winter, D. (forthcoming), 'Simulating lifetime earnings: The labour market module of LIFEMOD', STICERD Welfare State Programme Research Note, London: London School of Economics.

Wolfson, M. (1988), 'Homemaker pensions and lifetime redistribution', *Review of Income and Wealth*, **34**, 3, pp. 221–50.

Wolfson, M. (1990), 'Income tax/transfer Integration – policy implications and analytical challenges', in *Simulation Models in Tax and Transfer Policy*, Brunner, J. K. and Petersen, H. G. (eds.), Frankfurt: Campus.

Woodhall, M. (1989), *Financial Support for Students: Grants, loans or graduate tax*, London: Kegan Paul.

Wootton, B. (1954), *The Social Foundations of Wages Policy*, London: Allen and Unwin.

Wright, R. E. (1992), 'A feminisation of poverty in Great Britain?', *Review of Income and Wealth*, **38**, 1, pp. 17–25.

Young, M. and Wilmott, P. (1957), *Family and Kinship in East London*, London: Routledge and Kegan Paul.

Zedlewski, S. R. (1990), 'The development of the dynamic simulation of income model (DYNASIM)', in *Microsimulation Techniques for Tax and Transfer Analysis*, Lewis, G. H. and Michel, R. C. (eds.), Washington, DC: Urban Institute Press.

# Index